Uncertain citizenship

MANCHEStER
1824

Manchester University Press

Uncertain citizenship

Life in the waiting room

Anne-Marie Fortier

MANCHESTER UNIVERSITY PRESS

Published by Manchester University Press
Oxford Road, Manchester M13 9PL

www.manchesteruniversitypress.co.uk

British Library Cataloguing-in-Publication Data
A catalogue record for this book is available from the British Library

ISBN 978 1 5261 3908 5 hardback
ISBN 978 1 5261 6370 7 paperback

First published 2021
Paperback published 2022

Typeset
by New Best-set Typesetters Ltd
Printed in Great Britain
by TJ Books Ltd, Padstow

For migrant men and women living in precarious conditions, who wait and persist in the waiting room of uncertain citizenships. Their life in the waiting room is telling of the potentialities of a world of full inclusion.

And for Monique Salvas Fortier

Contents

Acknowledgements

It seems ages since I attended the citizenship ceremony where I became a British citizen in 2011. The process leading up to that piqued my curiosity and led me down the long journey to this monograph. So much has changed since then. Yet what remains unchanged is the generosity and kindness of strangers and the love and dependability of my family and friends.

In the course of researching for this book, I had the pleasure of meeting several migrants living in the North West and other parts of England, all of whom took the time to speak to me and tell me their stories. I am immensely grateful for their openness and willingness to meet with me and share their stories. They were not all in the same position, with some forced to persist and hope against hope in the face of perpetual uncertainty and precarity. They are a reminder of the uneven distribution of 'the good life', within and across national borders. But their *life* in the waiting room is also telling of what a world of full inclusion could look like.

I am also full of gratitude for the language teachers, registrars, dignitaries and other institutional actors I met for their time, for inviting me into their workspaces and into ceremony rooms, and for sharing their own stories. These individuals are variously conscripted in the dispersed governance of citizenisation. Their compassion and care at times defied the punitive state that they variously represented, mediated or served. They confirm the extent to which the state is not a unified entity that operates uniformly. Rather, they are the living proof that these intermediaries of the state have a fuller personhood and more agency than they are often granted when they are viewed solely as 'agents of the state'.

I only hope that this volume does justice to the accounts of these various inhabitants of the waiting room of citizenship.

In the intervening years between 2011 and now, my thinking was enriched by the proliferation of research on what I call citizenisation, as well as by the conversations, engagements with and support from colleagues and students across institutions. I am indebted to my students from my undergraduate modules at Lancaster University – especially *Nations and Migrations* – whose inquisitiveness and occasional scepticism challenged me in the most productive and engaging ways. I am also grateful to my colleagues Nicola Spurling and Francesca Coin who invited me to contribute lectures in the core module *Sociological Thought for our Time*. They and the students in that module helped me hone the argument developed in Chapter 4. My PhD students, for their part, have been and remain a constant source of learning and inspiration.

I have had the privilege of conversing with colleagues and students at Lancaster and beyond, some of whom read draft articles or other writings related to this project, and all of whose insights undoubtedly made this a better book: Les Back, Leah Bassell, Bridget Byrne, Katrien De Graeve, Sabine Gatt, Shona Hunter, Engin Isin, Danielle Juteau, Kamran Khan, Lidia Kuzemska, Gail Lewis, Katariina Mäkinen, Maureen McNeil, Kate Nash, Loredana Polezzi, Ben Rogaly, Riita Rossi, Sarah Scuzzarello, Tasneem Sharkawi, Divya Tolia-Kelly, Imogen Tyler, Neil Washbourne, Claire Waterton, Elke Winter, Joanne Wood. I shall forever cherish the 'salon-sessions' with Darcey Leigh, Melanie Richter-Montpetit and Cynthia Weber, where we'd write and talk in 'retreat conditions', and I look forward to repeat sessions if and when the world opens up again. Special thanks to my 'critical friends' who closely read draft chapters of the book: Bridget Anderson, Anne Cronin, Jonathan Darling, Breda Gray, Djordje Sredanovic, Ruth Wodak.

Anonymous reviewers of articles published in *Citizenship Studies*, *Collegium*, *Critical Social Policy* and *Sociology* were all very helpful in refining my arguments. While these articles are not reproduced here – except for some empirical material from the *Sociology* article in Chapter 4 – writing them helped me work out the framing of this monograph, which begins where I left off in those articles. This is especially the case for the *Collegium* piece, 'The social life of citizenisation and naturalisation: outlining an analytical framework'. This monograph is also an extension of my work on affective citizenship, which I explored in connection to citizenisation policies in 'What's the big deal? Naturalisation and the politics of desire' (*Citizenship Studies*) and in 'The psychic life of policy: desire, anxiety and "citizenisation" in Britain' (*Critical Social Policy*). I also thank anonymous reviewers of the book proposal and manuscript, whose supportive and critical comments provided useful guidance. A big thank you to Tom Dark from Manchester University Press for believing in this project from the start. His understanding of the broader disciplinary debates made him an astute editor, and his guidance and patience throughout were invaluable. I am also very grateful to Humairaa Dudhwala for her impeccable management of the final production process, which made it as painless and smooth as can be.

This book would not have materialised without the funding from the British Academy and the Leverhulme Trust, or without sabbatical leaves provided by the Sociology Department at Lancaster University. In the very early stages of this research, I had the great fortune of spending time as visiting fellow at the Gender Institute (GI) at the LSE, where I was so warmly welcomed by Clare Hemmings, then Head of the GI, and by Hazel Johnstone, the Department manager. I have fond memories of lively exchanges in seminars but also around coffee and tea in the GI offices. One highlight of my stay at the GI was enjoying gelato and conversations in equal measure with Wendy Sigle as we wandered the London streets on hot summer days.

I also had the great pleasure of being hosted as a visiting fellow by the Sussex Centre for Migration Research (SCMR), at the University of Sussex. Special thanks go to Paul Statham for his hospitality and for giving me the opportunity to present my work. The SCMR weekly seminars provided me with a welcome outing from my bolthole, and refuelled me with the pleasures of academic dialogue, questioning and exchange. I am also thankful for the invitations to present this research and to test ideas as I developed them. I was deeply touched by the warm welcome I received on all occasions and deeply appreciative of the conversations that ensued. Thank you to colleagues at the following universities: Birkbeck, Birmingham, Cambridge, Cardiff, City (London), Copenhagen, Durham, Edge Hill, Helsinki, Lancaster, Leeds, LSE, Manchester, Oslo, Ottawa, Salzburg, SOAS, Sorbonne, Vienna, Warwick.

Beyond academic circles, I am grateful to Autograph ABP, a London-based arts gallery, for inviting me to take part in their 'Exit series' of public lectures. I am also very grateful to the wonderful artist Laura Malacart and fellow academic Bridget Byrne for inviting me to collaborate with them on an exhibition about the citizenship test at the Manchester Central Library.

My friends and family have grounded me with their constant and steadfast support, and I am forever thankful for their patience as I hunkered down when a window of time opened up and 'disappeared' for a bit, or for their kindness in hearing me go on and on about the book. But more than anything, I am simply grateful for their friendship and love. My mother, Monique, 'the mamma', touched many people's lives with her kindness, compassion and care. She taught me a lot, not least ... the delights of freezing things. It was a shock to lose her so suddenly two months before completing this manuscript. I miss our regular phone calls, the singing of old French songs and her unparalleled sense of humour that had us in stitches – she still makes me laugh, even in her absence.

Other family members and dear friends, here and there, variously supported me with conversations, walks, coffee, food, wine, laughter, texts, deliveries, late nights and all that makes up the beautiful fabric of friendship: Lynne Boardman, Anne Cronin, Andrew Clement, Michel de Salaberry, Claude Fortier, Harry Josephine Giles, Breda Gray, Louise Hall, Peter Hall, Hilary Hopwood, Peter Hopwood, Beate Jahn, Anu Koivunen, Anna Marie Labelle, Mark Lacy, Liliane Landor, Darcy Leigh, Gail Lewis, Jane McElhone, Maureen McNeil, Nayanika Mookherjee, Kate Nash, Paul Newnham, Nicole Pagé, Ann Pollack, Justin Rosenberg, Andrew Sayer, Odile Sévigny, Martine Sigouin, Lucy Suchman, Divya Tolia-Kelly, Neil Washbourne, Ruth Wodak. A special thank you to Anne, Paul, Maureen and Odile for the everyday sustenance of kindness and care.

Finally, it is my partner, Cynthia Weber, who more than anyone else ensured that I see this book through. Cindy endured my ups and downs as I went through the travails of producing what at times appeared like an impossible project, supporting me when needed and teasing me as I turned around with a completed piece of work as quickly as I'd panicked about its hopelessness. Cindy's own visionary scholarship provided me with invaluable inspiration. But more than that, Cindy read through endless versions of articles, proposals and chapters, each time providing me with brilliant, acute, insightful commentaries that not only energised me, but that brought intellectual clarity and depth to some arguments. Words fail me to express my thankfulness for you Cindy; my love, my best friend, my certainty in these deeply unsettled and uncertain times.

Abbreviations

BNA	British Nationality Act
BN & SA	British Nationality and Status of Aliens Act
BNP	British National Party
BPP	British protected persons
BSA	British Social Attitudes
BSWC	British subjects without citizenship
CCA	Canadian Citizenship Act
CEFR	Common European Framework of Reference
CIA	Commonwealth Immigrant Act
CICC	Citizens of Independent Commonwealth Countries
CUKC	Citizens of the United Kingdom and Colonies
ELT	English Language Teaching
ESOL	English for Speakers of other Languages
IA	Immigration Act
ILR	Indefinite Leave to Remain
LUK	Life in the UK
NA	Naturalisation Act
NCS	Nationality Checking Service
NCW	New Commonwealth
NIA	Nationality, Immigration and Asylum Act
OCW	Old Commonwealth
SCS	Settlement Checking Service
SET(M)	Settlement on the basis of Marriage
UKVCAS	UK Visa and Citizenship Application Services
UKVI	UK Visas and Immigration

Introduction –
Uncertain citizenship

[C]itizenship is, through and through, precarious, recent, threatened, and more artificial than ever. (Derrida 1998: 15)

Citizenship is uncertain. It is volatile, its boundaries, limits and promises are forever revised, amended and deferred. Citizenship can be bought, taught, fragmented, multiple, probationary, precarious, stripped, disposable, impossible, gifted, strategic, disputed, relinquished, achieved, unprotected.[1] It has been deemed postnational, supranational, transnational, multicultural, cosmopolitan, flexible, nested, optional, colonial, postcolonial, as well as gendered, racial, sexual, intimate and affective.[2]

Despite its uncertainty and flexibility, citizenship is very high on national political agendas, as well as on research agendas, perhaps more in current times than it ever was (Dauvergne 2007; Shachar et al. 2017). At a time of the rising popularity of right and extreme right nationalism, patriotism, protectionism and anti-globalism, governments are tightening their citizenship regimes. Developments in EU member state policies that limit intra-EU freedom of movement and settlement testify to a larger tendency to erode 'denizenship' in many countries within and beyond the EU (Hagelund and Reegård 2011).[3] State powers to denaturalise and/or deport citizens or to strip individuals of their citizenship are increasing and access to settlement or citizenship for certain categories of immigrants are tightening, while at the same time fast-tracked (partial) citizenship is more readily accessible to migrant entrepreneurs with much capital to invest. As of June 2020, the scale of the impact of the COVID-19 pandemic on noncitizen residents in different countries remains unknown, but it will surely have raised anxieties and uncertainties about their access to health care and support systems. While uncertain or non-existent access to health care for people with precarious legal statuses long precedes this pandemic, the latter will undoubtedly shed more light on global and national inequalities in the distribution of 'full' citizenship and the concurrent growth of precarious statuses that render the racially minoritised poor more disposable. In turn, migrant workers losing their jobs, foreign students having to interrupt their studies, EU citizens living in the UK, and unknowable others who are unable to return 'home' live in fear of becoming 'illegal'.[4] In short, all this reveals the uncertainty, contingency and unequal distribution of citizenship. In many Western countries today, amendments to citizenship rules and the intensification of hostile environments make citizenship 'harder to get and easier to lose', as Elke Winter succinctly puts it (2016: 361; also Kapoor 2015). Such state practices are framed as responding to a perception of citizenship 'in crisis'; a crisis that governments claim results from a crisis of (too much) immigration, which in turn causes a crisis of national security and identity.

The language of crisis fuels conceptions of citizenship as 'uncertain' insofar as its boundaries have become blurred in global transnational migration regimes, where citizen-like rights and statuses are afforded to some migrants – EU citizens' rights within EU countries being a prime example. But rather than seeing state practices to restrict access to citizenship only as responses against a crisis of citizenship and its resulting 'uncertainty' in a global world, this book argues that uncertainty is and always has been central to the governance of citizenship. In other words, states are both responding to and using 'uncertain citizenship' in their national projects. This forces a reconsideration of how we understand citizenship politically and theoretically. Uncertain citizenship results not only from social and political struggles that contest its stability and certainty (Isin 2009; Clarke et al. 2014), but it results from its embeddedness in the very governmental practices that erase, even deny, the uncertainty of citizenship. Integration and naturalisation measures – the focus of this book – offer a unique vantage point from which to examine how uncertainty is integral to their design, while they also rely on narratives that set up citizenship as certain, stable and guarantor of universal rights and protection. To be sure, it may be argued that it is the prerogative of any state policy to use certainty and coherence as tools to manage the inevitable uncertainty and messiness of people's lives and of the national and international contexts in which they live (see Chapter 3). But I am less interested in state rationales for managing uncertainty than I am in exploring how both certainty and uncertainty are reproduced in state policies and practices of citizenship (e.g., playing down the uncertainty of acquiring citizenship against playing up the 'reward' of achieving it), how they have different effects on different subjects, and in turn, how different subjects navigate the process.

The uncertainty of citizenship is not new. While this book focuses on contemporary politics and practices of citizenship attribution, it takes the long view in acknowledging the role of imperial and anti-colonial histories in shaping what citizenship has become today. Jacques Derrida (1998) reminds us of how, under colonial rule, citizenship was always uncertain. In the epigraph above, he draws on his Franco-Maghrebian status and goes on to explain how he both lost and regained his citizenship in the course of his lifetime. For Derrida, the uncertainty of citizenship is not only about the deprivation of citizenship of targeted individuals; it is about how this can also happen to

> a 'community' group (a 'mass' assembling together tens or hundreds of thousands of persons), a supposedly 'ethnic' or 'religious' group that finds itself one day deprived, as a group, of its citizenship by a state that, with the brutality of a unilateral decision, withdraws it without asking for their opinion, and *without the said group gaining back any other citizenship. No other.* (1998: 15, emphasis original)

This bears disturbing resonance with the Windrush scandal in Britain in the spring of 2018.[5] It is worth pausing on this event, for it reveals a lot about contemporary practices and trends in citizenship regimes in the Anglo-European world (if not beyond).

In her review of the scandal, Wendy Williams (2020: 24) reports that the Home Office acknowledges that 164 individuals who had arrived in Britain before 1973 have been detained or deported since 2002. The Home Office admits that it most likely 'acted wrongfully in 18 of these cases by not recognising their right to be in the UK' (Williams 2020: 24). However, Williams adds that *all* of these 164 individuals 'were born in former British colonies in the Caribbean and had settled status. The majority (92) were from Jamaica, and most came to Britain in the 1950s and 1960s. Just over half (52%)

were male' (2020: 24). But the scandal affected hundreds, if not thousands of others, directly or indirectly – including individuals from other Commonwealth countries – with some losing their jobs, access to national health services and having their lives turned upside down.

As the 'hostile environment'[6] set up by Theresa May when she was Home Secretary (2010–2016) came crashing down on them, these citizens were pushed into what I call the precarious 'waiting room' of citizenship. This is a legal space (and social space; more in Chapter 2) where they suddenly became 'noncitizens' illegally residing in Britain until they could prove to the British state that they met all current requirements for citizenship: their legal entry into the country, their legal residency, their law-abiding lives, their right to work and so on. Having arrived on British soil at a time when they were Citizens of the United Kingdom and Colonies (CUKC) and held full citizenship rights under the British Nationality Act 1948 (see endnote 5 and more in Chapter 2), these long-standing legal resident-citizens who repeatedly declared how they *felt* British and nothing else now had to formally obtain British citizenship to 'regularise' their status. At the time of Williams's report, '8,124 people have been granted citizenship or had their settled status documented through the Windrush Taskforce' (2020: 24).[7]

It is noteworthy for our purposes here that the resolution came with 'regularising' the status of these residents and granting them British citizenship. While citizenship today privileges duties and obligations rather than rights, and it operates through sanctions rather than support (Wacquant 2010), citizenship remains widely regarded as an unqualified good and guarantor of protection, rights, safety. This is manifest in the offer from the then Home Secretary Amber Rudd to grant British citizenship to the affected Commonwealth residents and to waive the language and citizenship tests as well as the fees for naturalisation[8] (Crerar, Perkins and Gentleman 2018; Gentleman 2019a). In effect, Rudd was renaturalising those wrongly accused of residing illegally in Britain, in a form of 'defensive naturalisation' usually attributed to immigrants. Authors have written about 'defensive naturalisation', where migrants seek citizenship to protect their rights in an anti-immigration climate (Ong 2011/2012; Aptekar 2015). In the case of the Windrush scandal, the government was naturalising subjects to protect their rights against an anti-immigration climate *of its own making*. Citizens of the Windrush generation applied for citizenship out of necessity in response to being persecuted by the British government. British citizenship, here, is about seeking protection *from* Britain and the British state (El-Enany 2020: 224).

The Windrush story brings together two seemingly opposing forces within citizenship: it spotlights the fabricated, contingent nature of citizenship – its uncertainty – while it also shores up the certainty of citizenship as the only desirable outcome. Despite its increasingly notable fragility and the widely recognised gap between citizenship ideals and citizenship practices, the idea of citizenship as a stabilising status endures (Bosniak 2006: 1). The Windrush scandal was widely reported as an *extra-ordinary* situation that could not be conceived of within the traditional framework of citizenship; it was *inconceivable* that these citizens could become noncitizens overnight. Thus, while the scandal made it clear that states have the power to strip their subjects of citizenship, the gifting of citizenship reifies citizenship – particularly Anglo-European citizenships – as a valued *stable* object to 'own', therefore concealing its uncertainty.

Moreover, the Windrush scandal is also living evidence of racial citizenship and the legacies of imperial Britain and anti-colonial struggles; the expulsion (actual or virtual) of Windrush citizens was not merely the product of mistakes, mismanagement or abuse of power. Rather, it resulted from the very racist state structures and governing practices that brought them here in the first place and that today, cast them outside of state protection. I return to the long view of British citizenship in the next chapter. The point to emphasise here is that those racially minoritised (post)colonial citizens were subjected to firmly institutionalised structures of racial governmentality (Goldberg 2002) that enabled their citizenship to be questioned by Home Office officials seeking to reach their deportation targets (Goodfellow 2019; El-Enany 2020). What we learn from the Windrush scandal, then, is not only that citizenship is uncertain: that it changes, is unstable and subject to the conjuncture of political, economic and social events and interests. The Windrush scandal also gave us a glimpse of how uncertainty constitutes a mode of governing while being concealed within the reified promise of the security of citizenship. But more than that: it reveals how uncertainty disproportionately affects racially minoritised people, and that the racialised uncertainty of citizenship is *historically embedded*, rather than contingent on national institutional and political 'cultures' (path-dependency) or international trends (cross-national convergence). This is not to say that history repeats itself in an exact replica. Rather, it is to recognise the historical legacies of structures and imaginaries – such as the racial state and 'racial thinking' – and to ask how they manifest themselves in specific contexts and at specific times.

That said, what distinguishes the present conjuncture is the large-scale normalisation of uncertainty – that is, what was once lived, understood, experienced by colonial and minoritised subjects, as Derrida reminds us, is now established and widely understood as the normal state of things (Bhattacharyya 2015). *Uncertain citizenship* approaches regimes of citizenship integration and naturalisation – what I call 'citizenisation' measures (more in Chapter 1) – as exemplary of the ways in which precarisation and uncertainty constitute instruments of neoliberal governing, rather than being threats to the social order that past welfare states would protect its citizens from (Lorey 2015; also Anderson 2013; Bhattacharyya 2015; Jessop 2019). In a world where uncertainty is normalised, then, certainties like 'citizenship' are also normalised as uncertain.

This is not to deny that citizenship remains a highly significant and meaningful legal status that should secure rights for individuals. However, this security is not equally distributed in the global landscape (Shachar 2009), and citizenships from countries in the Global North acquire a value and currency that attracts citizens from the Global South. With this in mind, this book unpacks how the promise of the certainty of citizenship still operates even as it is normalised as uncertain. The book asks how uncertainty plays itself out, what forms it takes, and how it is smoothed over (or not) in practices of assessing, granting, learning about and applying for citizenship. Put simply, the study explores the complex dynamics and experiences that arise in a process where achieving citizenship makes all the uncertainties and anxieties to obtain it appear to be worthwhile.

In this respect, the Windrush scandal speaks volumes to and about contemporary citizenship beyond the UK context. Indeed, those who were adversely affected by the Windrush scandal are living evidence of contemporary policies of 'managed migration', integration and naturalisation. A striking feature of the treatment of the citizens from the Windrush generation is how the waiver for language and citizenship tests erases their history and positions them as 'immigrants' and 'foreigners' who would normally be obliged to take these tests. Amber Rudd *would not conceive* of a solution outside of the terms of what I call contemporary 'citizenisation' policies: twenty-first-century integration and naturalisation measures aimed at a range of presumed 'noncitizen' populations. She stated in the House of Commons that 'it is abundantly clear that everyone considers people who came in the Windrush generation to be British, but *under the current rules* this is not the case' (*Hansard*, House of Commons Debate, 23 April 2018: Volume 639, Column 619–620, cited in Giblin 2018, emphasis added). Rudd resorted to the current legislation to *decitizenise* them in order to citizenise them again. This gesture says a lot about the shifting grounds of citizenship in Europe and elsewhere. It testifies to a historical amnesia within legal and policy frameworks that disregard the historical legal contexts in which migrants arrive and settle in a country. Furthermore, Rudd's decision shows how citizenship is based on short-term policy and processes, rather than any enduring rights-based foundation. As a result, what counts as citizenship is continuously reshaped and redefined, while at the same time, there remain some constants such as the colonial impetus of European imperialism that repeatedly questions the rightful presence of racially minoritised citizens and residents (Tudor 2018; Goodfellow 2019; El-Enany 2020).

A further aspect of citizenship is its intimate connection to migration – both as 'reality' and as a legislative terrain. What we can observe from Amber Rudd's resolution is that she not only decitizenised Windrush citizens, but she also *migratised* them (Tudor 2018). Following the scandal, the Home Office guide to naturalisation was updated to include the 'Windrush Scheme' designed for those affected by the mismanagement of their status. It is noteworthy that the introduction explains that '[t]he Windrush Scheme is for people who arrived in the UK many years ago and do not have documentation confirming *their immigration status*' (Home Office 2019a: 3; emphasis added). By stating that the aim is to redress their immigration status rather than their citizenship status, this language is telling of how racially minoritised subjects – for the assumption is that those affected are predominantly black – are perpetually migratised as noncitizens, which in turn racialises British citizenship as white. Extending this lens further, we can also ask how and to what extent citizenship itself is migratised (Anderson 2013, 2019). Insofar as citizenisation processes are intimately connected to and operate as migration regulations, the idea of citizenship as a fixed and stable 'identity' and status needs to be questioned through the autonomy of a migration lens (Papadopoulos, Stephenson and Tsianos 2008; de Genova 2010). The Windrush scandal therefore forces three related questions about citizenship: how are migrants citizenised and decitizenised? How are citizens and citizenship migratised? But also, the endurance of ideas of citizenship as a stable status begs the question as to how citizens and migrants are made, unmade and naturalised as necessarily distinct categories and statuses.

As explained in Chapter 1, current integration and naturalisation policies grew in late twentieth- and early twenty-first-century Europe as means to (further) formalise immigrant integration and access to citizenship or permanent residency. In this context, integration and naturalisation are widely treated as separate moments in the achievement of citizenship, a conception that I challenge by proposing that both are deeply intertwined within what I call 'citizenisation'. The point I wish to emphasise here is that citizenisation is the institutional and discursive formalisation of two significant moves in how citizenship today is understood in the policy and political spheres. First, at a time when 'postnational' forms of citizenship are more commonplace (such as migrant campaigns for the right to vote, refugee activists' struggle for democracy in the countries they fled, or EU citizenship), there has been a re-animation of 'the national question' in European countries and others from the Global North since the early 2000s, which seeks to reassert the bond between citizenship and national identity. The links between citizenship and national identity and culture are renewed in contemporary integration and naturalisation measures as a way to counter the perceived 'thinning' of citizenship in a globalising world. Second, this resurgence of ideas of 'nation-ness' is framed in a discourse where citizenship signifies membership not to an 'ethno-cultural' community, but rather to a 'community of values', in Bridget Anderson's terms, that is 'composed of people who share common ideals and (exemplary) patterns of behaviour' which remain, however, 'expressed through ethnicity, religion, culture, or language' (2013: 2), as well as class, gender, sexuality, ability, nativism. In other words, discourses of values are inflected by 'culturalist' definitions broadly speaking, that reground 'values' in a decidedly national (cultural and territorial) setting.[9]

Such citizenship agendas imply ideal models of citizenship and distinguish between 'good' and 'bad' citizens.

In this regard, and though aimed at presumed 'noncitizens', citizenisation policies are very telling of the ways in which the state represents and imagines 'good citizenship' (Weber 2015) and its relationship to citizens. A secondary element of the analysis, then, concerns how state–citizen relations are enacted and by extension, how the state itself is made or remade. Scholarship in critical policy studies conceive of policy as performative, relational and as producing multiple effects, rather than as a set of fixed documents used in a unilateral way (Shore and Wright 1997; Shore et al. 2011; Newman 2013; Clarke et al. 2015; Hunter 2015; Dobson 2020). For the purposes of this book, this means examining how citizenship, the state and the state–citizen relationship come to be through enactments of policy (Clarke et al. 2014). In the vein of other literatures on the 'performative state' (Weber 1998; Sharma and Gupta 2006), literature on policy enactment sheds light on how the state is not a pregiven, disembodied and unified decision-maker. Rather, the theory of policy enactment insists on rethinking how the state is 'made up', in Davina Cooper's words (2015), both in the sense of how it is imagined and in the sense of how it is actualised in everyday practice (also Abrams 1977). Furthermore, like much of the policy world today, citizenisation (including naturalisation) is a dispersed form of governance that involves multiple actors across multiple sites – public, semi-public, private and voluntary. Consequently, as Clarke et al. suggest (2015: 52), it is hard to contain it within the linear narratives of 'path-dependence' (Bloemraad 2006; Janoski 2010; Goodman 2014) or cross-national convergence (Joppke 2010; Koopmans, Michalowski and Waibel 2012). Rather, *Uncertain citizenship* starts from the premise that there are international trends and what some might call 'converging outcomes' – such as the neoliberalisation and skillification of citizenship explained in Chapter 1 – that need to be understood *in context* in order to better capture the specific histories and social and political climates that shape and impact on definitions of, and inequalities within, citizenship regimes.

This book examines the integration and naturalisation process as it occurs in different meso-level sites of governance, both in the spatial sense – in locations such as local government offices, locally run language classes – and in the theoretical sense of understanding

individuals' experiences as both personal and collective. I approach
these sites as locations of 'relational politics', following Shona Hunter's
(2015) term: sites that are populated by a range of people and other
material and symbolic objects that enable state practices such as
the bestowment of citizenship. The book is about how individuals,
objects and symbols are brought together in what I refer to as the
waiting room of citizenship (more in Chapter 2), how the individuals
experience that world, how they variously enact 'citizenship' and,
last but not least, the different lives, subjects and 'realities' (including
citizenship) that are brought forth in the process. My focus is twofold:
first, the process in which citizenship is both controlled and produced
– how it is configured, idealised, attributed (or withheld), materialised,
spatialised, temporalised and felt. Second, how the complex landscape
of citizenship acquisition and attribution is enacted and experienced,
navigated, digressed, or disputed by the different actors whose lives
are variously touched by it in practical, material and emotional
terms. Therefore, rather than focusing on top-down institutional
processes dictated by the abstract – and abstracted – state of many
theories of citizenship and migration, *Uncertain citizenship* turns
to the unpredictable and manifold agencies, enactments and relations
that arise from the various encounters resulting from citizenisation
policies. Nor is this a bottom-up approach either: the very locales
of the study take us quite literally to the *meso*-level of governance,
in between the state on the one hand and civil society and the general
population on the other, where representatives of the state must
also navigate the perpetually changing legal pathways to citizenship,
like the migrants seeking to regularise their citizenship status, though
with very different consequences at stake.

Engin Isin and Greg Nielsen's (2008) theory of 'acts of citizenship'
has drawn much attention to the acts of those without legal status
and whose articulation of their right to claim rights ruptures the
dominant script. *Uncertain citizenship* extends this theory and includes
policy, the law, as well as the various enactments throughout the
process to probe citizenisation as a constellation of *acts of citizenship*
insofar as 'they *produce* subjects as citizens' (Isin 2009: 371; emphasis
added) or not, as well as producing specific social, economic and
political relations (Ruhs and Anderson 2013: 2). These policies
require a broad set of actors and operate in different sites and on
different overlapping scales (Isin 2009). The actors populating this

study are: applicants for citizenship or Indefinite Leave to Remain (ILR; permanent residency), language teachers, registrars and citizenship ceremony officials. As they meet in the waiting room of citizenship, these actors are all variously produced as citizens or noncitizens, directly or indirectly, by virtue of the position, role and relations they are cast in. Moreover, within citizenisation, the sites for claims to and struggles over belonging and identification are not primarily about voting, social security, education, health care, or military service. Rather, they revolve around language, migration stories, marital status, residence, property, mobility. Finally, the sites of citizenisation operate on overlapping scales that extend within as well as across national borders.

This book sheds light on the kinds of hierarchies of belonging and entitlement, old and new, that are produced in the process. It is worth noting that *Uncertain citizenship* centres on the processes available to those that the state has already identified as *potential* future citizens (as opposed to those that the state has already deemed 'unfit' for citizenship, such as unskilled migrants). Which is not to say that all participants followed the same routes to British citizenship – some came to this country as asylum seekers, others as spouses, others came to the UK for work, others initially arrived as students several years ago (see Scene 1). As will be explained in subsequent chapters, these different routes – which intersect with gender, race and class positions – shape individuals' experiences of citizenisation. At the same time, many share aspirations, hopes and ideas about 'good citizenship' and its promises. For however uncertain citizenship is, it continues to attract emotional, material, financial and political investment. Appreciating how citizenisation functions both institutionally (as a process, as conditional, etc.) and socially (as experienced, enacted, lived) is important if we are to gain a fuller grasp of the array of inequalities – old, new and emerging – that citizenisation produces and reproduces.

Outline of the book

The book includes stand-alone 'scenes'[10] as well as chapters. The purpose of each 'scene' is to provide factual information and/or to 'set the scene' for the chapter that follows, some of which include other scenes integrated in the text. Scene 1, which follows this introductory chapter, presents the current British citizenisation regime in a nutshell, for ease of reference for readers. It also details the fieldwork conducted for this study. Scene 1 therefore provides information about the institutional context and processes that are at the centre of this study while it also gives more details about the methods used and the general profile of participants.

Chapter 1, 'The world of citizenisation: life in the waiting room', has two aims. First, to situate integration and naturalisation policies (citizenisation) within the broader contemporary conjuncture that enables them to have become 'common sense' in Europe, and second, to introduce theoretical underpinnings and heuristic devices supporting this book. After situating 'citizenisation' in contemporary 'civic integration' policies, the chapter mines citizenisation as a productive analytical lens for examining changing citizenship regimes in the twenty-first century. Chapter 1 argues for studying the 'social life' of citizenisation, which forces a reconsideration of the relationship between integration and naturalisation by asking a deceptively simple question: what is naturalised in citizenisation? The chapter then presents a conjunctural analysis of converging trends of neoliberal governance that retool citizenship through its skillification, securitisation and renewed domestication. I argue that citizenisation – and by extension migratisation – is a 'social intervention' that reaches far beyond those that it targets – migrants – and reaches into the fabric of society as a whole.

Finally, Chapter 1 introduces 'the waiting room' as a useful heuristic device that foregrounds three axes of citizenisation: temporality – how citizenship *takes time*; spatiality – how citizenship *takes place*; and affect – how citizenship *takes hold*. In sum, the device of the waiting room captures the interplay between, on the one hand, the structural and institutional conditions that bring people to the waiting room – as language teachers, registrars, ceremony officials, or migrants – and on the other hand, how people inhabit these governing practices. In other words, it captures the tensions between uncertain citizenship and the endurance of the idea of citizenship as a stable status. Each subsequent chapter concludes by drawing out what it reveals with respect to each axis of citizenisation.

Chapter 2, 'Citizenising Britain', emplaces the current British citizenship regime in its historical context. The chapter adopts a long view of contemporary British citizenship in order to understand the imperial and colonial legacies underpinning current laws and policies, including citizenisation policies. If the current tightening of citizenisation in Britain aligns itself with several European and other Western countries, British citizenship is also distinctive in several ways. This does not mean, however, that studying the 'case' of British citizenisation reveals processes that are unique to it. Quite the contrary: citizenship entered the political scene in recent years because political leaders wished to align Britain with other (neo)liberal states. The long view of British citizenship therefore reveals a lot about the imperial and racial impulses of Western European citizenships, while it takes seriously specific British historical developments.

Scene 2, 'Documents, stories, pictures', turns to a scene from my fieldwork: a training session organised by two UK Visas and Immigration (UKVI) case workers, for registrars tasked with checking applications for Settlement on the basis of Marriage (SET(M)). The scene emphasises how documents circulate, are interpreted, and must be 'curated' to produce an appropriate 'picture' for an application to be successful.

Chapter 3, 'The documented citizen', follows on from this scene to examine how documents function and circulate in the waiting room of citizenship. The chapter is concerned with the *generative capacities* of documents, that is, how individuals engage with, relate and respond to documents as they are produced, exchanged, negotiated, transformed and moved by and between individuals and within the waiting room. Following the paper traces and trails as they circulate in the waiting room of citizenship takes us to the broader 'relational politics of curation' that position applicants and registrars in different relations to each other and to the state. The chapter reveals the role of documents in making and unmaking citizens, migrants and citizenship itself, which means that citizenisation impacts on the lives of migrants and citizens alike, though with significantly different effects. The chapter concludes with a summary of how the 'documented citizen' is fragmentary, contingent, ephemeral and caught within a set of interpretive gaps about the law and its effects, while it is at the same time emplaced, temporal, embodied and affective.

Scene 3, 'Conversing with Anglophones', takes us to a language school in the North West of England, where I met several migrants interviewed in this study. It highlights the inequalities embedded in the postcolonial Anglophone world – exemplified here in my own interactions with these migrants – and sets up the complex ways in which regimes of seeing and regimes of hearing operate in current language requirements for citizenisation.

Language requirements for citizenship are the subject of Chapter 4, 'The speaking citizen'. Drawing on a raciolinguistic approach, the chapter argues that the disappearance of 'national language' as a constructed category allows for the disappearance of other categories, such as whiteness. The chapter is concerned with the current common-sense politics around language, integration and citizenship that pervades most Western European countries, and where language is deemed a civil right that enables individual and social cohesion – *jus linguarum*, in David Gramling's term (2016). The chapter situates British language requirements in the colonial history of British expansion and the rise of English as a 'world language'. It shows how a form of 'provincialised English' arises from the tensions between the inevitability of multilingualism in today's global world, the status of English as a 'world' language, and the insistence of English as the 'national' language. The chapter then examines the effects of provincialising English and ongoing linguistic inequities as they are lived on the ground because of inextricably linked histories of colonialism and nation formation.

The chapter draws on material from interviews with migrants and ESOL (English for Speakers of Other Languages) professionals, ESOL teaching and learning practices, as well as citizenship ceremonies. It traces the social dynamics of race, class and imperialism and their effects on migrants who express different (affective) relationships to the English language. In turn, the chapter exposes the ways in which *jus linguarum* is normalised and naturalised in citizenship ceremonies through practices of verbal hygiene (Cameron 2013) and audial hygiene. The chapter concludes with a discussion of how *jus linguarum* has become given in Britain, and the effects this has on both the normalisation of white English monolingualism and on the 'migratisation' or 'racialisation' of those who speak otherwise.

Scene 4, 'Becoming citizen', depicts a citizenship ceremony from the point of view of Aisha, a new citizen, and Harry, a registrar. It serves as a description of typical ceremonies in England, and raises a number of themes that are picked up in Chapter 5.

In contrast to previous chapters that centre on processes of citizenisation, Chapter 5, 'The becoming citizen', focuses on how certainties of citizenship are reproduced and naturalised in citizenisation, starting with two of citizenship's key principles: the wilful autonomous subject and birthright. It does so by unveiling how naturalisation presumes a subject who not only chooses citizenship but also has chosen migration. The chapter unravels how choice and obligation are variously entangled in 'birthright' citizenship that relies on the global unequal distribution of hereditary citizenship. Birthright citizenship is founded on racialised heteropatriarchal reproductive familial relations that decidedly emplace 'new citizens' within the national territory and thereby extracts them from their diasporic belongings. The chapter further unravels the 'value' of British citizenship by scrutinising how the good life, happiness and 'luck' function in the idealisation of British citizenship as the source of happiness. Such affective technologies attach themselves to local celebrations of diversity that render difference a remainder that is at once privatised, depoliticised, but also the source of solidarity. The chapter's final section turns to 'ordinary' and postcolonial citizens who force open the borders of citizenship by revealing how migrants become otherwise throughout the citizenisation process. It draws out how people engage in extra-legal as well as legal self-representations and claims of citizenship *before* it is conferred and *because* it is deferred. Therefore, if ceremonies simultaneously citizenise and migratise the 'new' becoming citizens, these 'new citizens' have already and continue to 'become' otherwise. The final scenes focus on Sala, a postcolonial citizen, and untangle the constitutive and necessary postcolonial presence within citizenship, Britishness, or the British state. Ultimately, the chapter goes to the heart of the split between becoming British and identifying as other. But this split is not irreparable. When turning the lens of migration more squarely on citizenship, migrant-citizens are actively reconfiguring what it means to become (British) citizens.

The book concludes with 'Lessons from the waiting room: citizenisation and migratisation', which revisits the waiting room of citizenship and the spatial, temporal, affective processes and practices that produce and reproduce old and new inequalities not only at the national level, but on the international stage. It argues for the importance of contextual research on the social life of citizenisation and migratisation for a better understanding of the ways in which citizenship and 'the migrant' are naturalised as mutually exclusive. In turn, examining life in the waiting room also reveals the various ways in which this dualism unravels. My hope is that forensic examinations of the perpetuation of nativist, sedentarist politics of belonging and entitlement will not only make it more difficult to turn away from the inequalities they foster and reinforce, but that these examinations will contribute tools to help unravel these injustices and find alternatives to citizenship that embrace migration and difference as constitutive creative forces of all social life.

Scene 1

Researching citizenisation

This scene sets the stage for subsequent chapters. It includes two parts: first, it introduces the basic elements of the current British citizenisation process. Second, it details the fieldwork conducted for this study. The latter provides not only information about the type of material gathered and a general profile of participants, but the contextualisation of the fieldwork also adds more information to the citizenisation process itself, and the people and spaces that populate the waiting room of citizenship.

British citizenisation in a nutshell

The current citizenisation process in Britain was designed in 2002, in a Home Office White Paper on nationality, immigration and asylum (Home Office 2002), enshrined in the Nationality, Immigration and Asylum Act 2012, and implemented in 2004. The process formalised what had hitherto consisted of a postal application for naturalisation: since 2004, the process requires a citizenship test, a language test and a citizenship ceremony. Several amendments altered the process since then: in 2007, the citizenship test and language test were moved forward in the citizenisation timeline to applications for Indefinite Leave to Remain (ILR) for all non-EU residents (EU residents take the test only when applying for citizenship). In 2010, English language tests used for skilled migrants were extended to all third country migrants seeking entry in the UK as a spouse, civil partner, or fiancé(e) to a British citizen.

Up until 2015, EU citizens automatically acquired settled status after five years of residency in the UK, under EU law. Since November

2015, EU residents are required to apply for a 'residence card' as evidence of their 'settled' status. Without the card, applications for citizenship are refused henceforth. In the post-Brexit context, the permanent residence status was replaced with an EU settlement scheme announced in 2017 and opened on 30 March 2019. While the scheme still does not require the citizenship test to be completed until one applies for British citizenship, the assumption is that it will gradually align EU residents with non-EU residents in terms of their rights, notably with regards to their rights to bring a spouse to live in Britain.[1] In short, the 'Brexit effect' on the citizenisation process for EU residents in the UK is to incrementally standardised it following the process for non-EU residents. In this regard, EU residents are directed to the same waiting room of citizenship as non-EU residents.

Language requirements changed in the course of this study. Until October 2013, applicants for settlement or citizenship undertook either a citizenship test or a language test, depending on their level of fluency in English. Prior to that, the language requirement separated applicants for settlement or citizenship along two routes: the ESOL route or the Life in the UK (citizenship test) route. What determined an applicant's route was whether or not they had an entry level 3 ESOL proficiency.[2] Those whose level of English was below entry level 3 were entitled to take an ESOL with citizenship-content class. If they progressed a level, evidenced by passing a speaking and listening test, they were eligible for settlement or citizenship without having to undertake the Life in the UK (LUK) test.

Since October 2013, however, all applicants, unless exempt, must prove their English fluency *and* complete the citizenship test. In addition, the bar for English speaking and listening rose to the same level as that of the LUK test, which is level B1 of the Common European Framework of Reference (CEFR) or above[3] (Home Office 2013a). This means that the English fluency requirement set the bar higher for all applicants, whose progression from one level to another was no longer sufficient. Those exempt from showing an English speaking and listening qualification are those who obtained a degree taught in English and nationals of majority English speaking countries (white settler societies and countries in the West Indies; Home Office 2013a: Appendix A).[4] Migrants from white settler societies or the educated elites from the New Commonwealth or other countries are advantaged in this system (more in Scene 3 and Chapter 4).

The citizenship test, for its part, is undertaken at one of 30 test centres around the country, at a cost of £50 (as of December 2019). The test is computer-based and consists of 24 questions to be answered in 45 minutes. The pass grade is 75 per cent (18 questions). As of December 2019, the test and study guide are in their third edition (Home Office 2017).

Once they obtain evidence of succeeding in the required tests, applicants can submit their settlement or citizenship application. At the time of the study and up to December 2018, local authorities offered two optional services for applicants: the Settlement Checking Service (SCS; for foreign spouses of British citizens) and Nationality Checking Service (NCS). These services operated in ways similar to the passport checking service offered by the Post Office. In short, registrars checked through one's application for SET(M) (Settlement on the basis of Marriage) or for British citizenship and confirmed that all the required evidence was present and ready to send. Their services also included producing certified copies of documents such as passports and sending the application to the UK Visas and Immigration (UKVI). These services cost up to £60 per appointment at the time and grew in popularity because they usually ensured a faster processing time and increased the chances of avoiding refusals because of missing information or mistakes (see Chapter 3 for more).

All successful applicants for citizenship aged 18 and over must attend a citizenship ceremony (with exemptions made for ill health or other exceptional circumstances). Ceremonies take place at local authorities and are organised by registrars. They are officiated by a registrar along with another ceremony official, usually a local 'dignitary' (mayor, Deputy-Lieutenant, or a local person of notoriety in the community; see Scene 4 and Chapter 5 for more).

The fieldwork

This book results from of a study about practices, processes and experiences of the British citizenisation measures. The study is based on multi-sited fieldwork conducted in England between March 2012 and June 2017, with the bulk of it between 2012 and 2014. A distinctive feature of this study is that it includes both applicants for citizenship, SET(M) or ILR, as well as institutional actors who are variously involved in providing services en route to citizenship – local registrars, ceremony official and language teachers. The details above situate my fieldwork in what I qualify as meso-levels of governance, that is, a space in-between civil society and the federal state government, where local government or private language school actors are enlisted as 'intermediaries of the state' (see Chapter 3).

The fieldwork included observations of six ESOL classes and 11 citizenship ceremonies, as well as shadowing a 'citizenship and nationality' team of registrars at a London borough council (which I christened Stadlow Council) where, among other things, I observed SCS and NCS meetings between registrars and applicants and followed registrars as they sorted various documents or planned citizenship ceremonies. I also conducted semi-structured interviews with 46 individuals in total (more than one interview in some cases; one joint interview): 24 migrants (16 women, 8 men) at different stages of citizenisation, including 8 new citizens; 3 'exceptions'; and 19 institutional actors (ESOL professionals, registrars, ceremony officials). The names of all locations and participants have been changed to preserve their anonymity.

The migrants I met had come to the UK through different routes: as spouses, for work, or as asylum seekers (one with and one without refugee status when I met them). Five were EU nationals. They had been living in the UK for periods ranging from 1.5 to 29 years. The migrants came from 16 countries[5] spanning all continents except Antarctica, and were aged between 24 and 53 years old. All interviews were conducted in English (see Scene 3), and all of the 24 migrants declared that they speak at least one language other than English: 14 spoke one other, and 11 spoke two or more.[6] Their educations levels went from three years of elementary school up to doctoral degree.

There were three exceptions in my sample of 'applicants': these individuals were not themselves applying for settlement or citizenship, but were directly affected by citizenship regimes: Paul, a British-born man married to a Thai woman who was arriving in the UK three days after we met, after a long battle to secure her spousal visa. Likewise, Robert was married to a Thai woman, and I interviewed them both together. The third 'exception' was Charlotte, an Australian permanent resident (with ILR) who adopted two British-born children and who found out, when applying for a British passport for one of them, that the child's British citizenship had been erased upon her adoption. Paul, Robert and Charlotte are 'exceptions' insofar as neither is seeking legal settled status or citizenship in the UK. However, their stories are telling of the close connections between citizenship and migration, and the blurred boundaries between what are understood as distinct legal categories. If this volume privileges the experiences of those who undertake the citizenisation process, which ultimately demigratises them, Charlotte, Robert and Paul's stories (which we return to in subsequent chapters) reveal how citizens can also be 'migratised' or cast as 'foreign'.[7]

Institutional actors, for their part, include 11 registrars, three ceremony officials known as 'dignitaries', and five ESOL teachers or providers. All registrars (seven women, three men) were born in the UK. They were aged between 27 and 64, and had completed GCSEs up to Bachelor's degrees. The three dignitaries, for their part (two men, one woman), were aged between 66 and 73 years old, were born in the UK, Malaysia and Pakistan respectively, and had obtained a BA or Master's level degree. Of the 14 registrars and ceremony officials interviewed, only five said that they spoke one or more languages other than English; the rest spoke English only.

ESOL teachers, in contrast, all had two or more languages (including English) in their repertoire. The three women and two men were born either in the UK, Pakistan, or Bulgaria, and were aged between 35 and 64 years old.

The interviews took place in interviewees' work places, homes, in my own home, or in public spaces such as language schools or cafes. I was recognised as a foreigner because of my foreign accent by all institutional actors and by the migrants most fluent in English. I told all participants that I obtained British citizenship in 2011 by way of establishing my familiarity with and understanding of the process.

While access to institutional actors proved to be relatively easy, recruiting applicants was more difficult, if only because they were not as easily locatable as were registrars, ceremony officials, or ESOL teachers and providers. I sought applicants through ESOL classes as well as local and personal networks. I hoped but failed to meet new citizens at citizenship ceremonies. 'New citizens' often appear nervous before ceremonies and having someone who they might associate with the local authority or the Home Office approach them for an 'interview' might understandably make them wary (also Byrne 2017). Furthermore, my fieldwork took place primarily in the North West of England where the majority of new citizens had gone through the ESOL route. Hence their English fluency was adequate but limited, which made it difficult for me to effectively introduce myself in the informal context of the ceremony waiting room, where new citizens are usually having tea and biscuits with relatives or friends.

It was through ESOL classes that most of the ESOL-route interviewees were found. Some I met in a local authority class I observed over several weeks, which allowed me to develop some kind of connection with them as I occasionally took part in conversation activities by way of assisting the teacher. Others I met in a private language school that I visited for a day, where some participants were extremely keen to speak to me, stating that they wanted to tell their story, that they wanted it to be heard (see Scene 3).

The focus of the field research was twofold: processes and encounters. As suggested in Chapter 1, this means moving beyond top-down or bottom-up approaches in favour of 'studying through' (Wright and Reinhold 2011) citizenisation and naturalisation processes, shedding light on how policies and their effects and outcomes are not fixed but variously enacted by various actors in different settings. Furthermore, the research aligns itself with what Matthew Desmond (2014) calls 'relational ethnography' because its main object is not a single site or group, but rather a set of measures and processes. It includes actors and agencies who occupy different positions in relation to citizenisation, and it reveals how individuals are variously and unequally implicated in enacting citizenisation in ways that both bring them together and pull them apart.

I shall return to details of the current process in subsequent chapters. The point to note here is that the current regime in Britain is grounded in the relatively recent enshrinement of British citizenship into law (1981). Chapter 1 contextualises this development and the concurrent emergence of 'the waiting room' of citizenisation.

1

The world of citizenisation: life in the waiting room

We meet the people who are being citizenised, if that's a word. (Lucy, registrar who conducts citizenship ceremonies)

In the wake of the March 2016 bombings in Brussels that killed 35 people (including three perpetrators), Flemish MEP Mark Demesmaeker championed the Flemish 'Decree of Citizenisation' (*Inburgeringsdecreet*; Foblets 2006) as a 'real integration policy', which Brussels lacks but 'now realises' it needs as it faces 'the problem with radicalised young Muslims'. Demesmaeker explained that all newcomers 'should learn our language, they should learn about our values, and they should learn to accept the way we live, accept our values and norms ... This is something we have been doing for ten years and it works!'[1]

Demesmaeker's comments typify how questions of shared 'national' language and values have become a matter of national security in contemporary migration and citizenship debates (Khan 2014; Charalambous et al. 2015). They also exemplify the new 'common sense' around citizenship and citizenisation that has crystallised since the turn of the century in Western Europe; that is to say that the expectation that migrants should learn and speak a national language and learn and know about national values is taken as a given, incontestable requirement that 'makes sense'.

In the policy world referred to here, 'citizenisation' is a shorthand for a range of pro-active 'integration' and 'naturalisation' measures designed by governments to ensure the eligibility of immigrants seeking permanent residency or citizenship status. These include 'official' channels such as language and citizenship education and tests as well as citizenship ceremonies, but they also include 'unofficial tests' of residency, loyalty, allegiance, 'good character', as well as language fluency assessed when migrants call for queries and the like, and so on. Such measures have existed in white settler countries such as Canada and the US for several decades, while they are more recent in Western Europe where they have proliferated since the turn of the twenty-first century.

Contemporary forerunners to civic integration policies in Western Europe are the Netherlands, where the Dutch term *inburgering* 'means to "citizenize" without connoting naturalization' (Goodman 2014: 163).[2] Hence from the outset, citizenisation is cast in policy as a separate phase in one's 'journey to citizenship', to use the phrase coined by the British Labour government in the subtitle to the original citizenship test study guide (Home Office 2007). In contrast, the approach presented here interrupts the linear narrative that dominates not only the policy field but also the multi-disciplinary scholarship of citizenship and migration studies; a narrative that casts 'integration' and 'naturalisation' as discrete events on a same continuum.

This chapter includes three sections. First, 'The social life of citizenisation' details the theoretical scaffolding of the book, explaining why and how the concepts of naturalisation and citizenisation and their relationship to one another need to be rethought. What do we assume about 'naturalisation' as a theoretical and practical concept as it functions in citizenship theory and in the practice of citizenship attribution today? And how do *social* analyses of 'citizenisation' lead us to contest, complicate and refine naturalisation and its relationships to citizenisation?

The second section, 'Citizenisation in neoliberal governance', elaborates a conjunctural analysis of citizenisation by situating it within converging trends of neoliberal governance that shape citizenship in ways that bear continuities and discontinuities with past ideas, discourses and regimes of citizenship. This section centres on two aspects of neoliberal governance that enabled present understandings of citizenship to become common sense: dispersed governance, instrumentalism and the citizenship industry, on the one hand, and the connection between household governance and securitisation on the other.

Finally, 'Life in the waiting room' is the third section which details how I use the 'waiting room' to understand citizenisation processes. The waiting room constitutes a useful heuristic device that foregrounds temporality (how citizenship takes time), spatiality (how citizenship takes place) and affect (how citizenship takes hold). I elaborate on how conceiving of citizenisation as an imaginary waiting room to citizenship allows me to address the unequal distribution and experiences of time, space and affect. In other words, the waiting room of citizenship sheds light on how the distribution of power and inequality through time, space and affect works to enact particular conceptions of citizenship or the state–citizen relationship. It is a space where migrants (understood as noncitizens), state and nonstate actors meet as they encounter, experience and enact citizenisation in ways that both conform to and exceed the policy guidelines, timelines and expected outcomes.

The social life of citizenisation

Legally speaking, naturalisation refers to the acquisition of citizenship and nationality by somebody who resides in a country where she or he is not a citizen or national. In his historical analysis of the body of legislation and court rulings that define US citizenship, Rogers Smith explains that the term 'naturalisation' originated in feudal regimes when:

> subjectship to the political order under whom one was born was believed to be natural – sanctioned by divine will and rationally discoverable natural law. Persons who acquired allegiance to a new ruler were therefore said to be 'naturalized'. (1997: 13)

This feudal definition suggests that 'it is natural to be subject to the ruler under whom one is born and that it is so natural that one is subject to that ruler for life' (Smith cited in Kostakopoulou 2006: 95, n. 108). Smith goes on to say that '[t]he puzzling survival of the term "naturalization" is, however, only one tip of a huge iceberg of anomalies and contradictions that lurk below the surface of American citizenship law' (1997: 13).

Smith's puzzlement derives from an opposition that is still found in much of the current imagination, laws and academic scholarship about citizenship attribution in the Anglo-European worlds: the opposition between ascription (birthright citizenship) and consent (naturalisation), which Smith attributes to illiberal and liberal traditions respectively.[3] This opposition fails to recognise the extent to which 'subjectship' remains an integral part of citizenship in three ways, as Eldon Eisenach argues (1999: 200): 'subject to the laws (and their protections); subject to the political sovereign or "state" (and its protections) …; and subject to God'.[4] Like in much of the scholarship on citizenship and migration, what Eisenach intimates but does not develop is not only the limits of the consent–ascription dualism, but the many other ways in which 'naturalisation' operates if we consider it outside of its strict legal definition.

Contrary to the accepted understanding of legal naturalisation as a voluntary act, 'naturalisation' 'denotes the opposite of choice', as Christian Joppke points out (2010: 16). For through 'naturalisation', something is 'made natural' – brought into conformity with nature – as in the case of aligning one's permanent place of residence with one's nationality. In this form, 'naturalisation' re-establishes the 'natural' order of things because citizenship takes as its baseline assumption that most of us reside in the country into which we are born. Furthermore, stating that something is 'natural' establishes a value judgement about what is socially acceptable and desirable. As Judith Williamson (1978) explains in her classic theory of decoding ideology and meaning in advertisements, ideas of what is 'natural' result from a transactional relationship between 'nature' and 'culture'. She writes:

> precisely because of this reference to Nature as the determinant of what is good, as though it were an independent arbiter, 'the natural' becomes the meaning given *to* culture, *by* nature – although it is culture that determines 'the natural' anyway. (Williamson 1978: 123, emphasis original)

In contrast to Rogers Smith's puzzlement then, an understanding of 'naturalisation' as a social and cultural *process* and *product* resulting from transactions between culture and nature rather than solely as a legal process, allows us to examine how it continues to 'make sense' within the realm of citizenisation and citizenship attribution. This is more than a matter of semiotics. It is about how, *in practice*, integration and naturalisation are variously enacted, the different realities that they bring forth, and the 'ontological politics' (Mol 2002) surrounding the choice of some realities over others

(Law 2004: 13). Engin Isin (2009: 369) argues that the question is no longer:

> 'what is citizenship?'. Rather, the challenge is to ask 'what is *called* citizenship?' that evokes all the interests and forces that are invested in making and interpreting it in one way or another. (emphasis original)

Pushing this further, the question that this book asks is: what *counts* as citizenship. As explained below and in subsequent chapters, citizenisation regimes shore up the citizen–noncitizen and citizen–migrant distinctions, discounting migrants' citizenship as irrelevant – decitizenising them – as few migrants seeking to naturalise are without any other citizenship. At the same time, citizenisation also disregards the extent to which migration encroaches in the lives of citizens and therefore how citizenship is migratised (Anderson 2013, 2019).

The scholarly field on citizenship and migration constitutes a fertile ground for important debates concerning institutional changes in citizenship in the context of a globalised and mobile world. Indeed, the 'institutional life' of naturalisation and citizenisation is very well documented within this scholarship, where we learn how they have historically been subject to continuous reconfigurations within laws, rules and policies. More specifically, the large tranche of scholarship devoted to 'civic integration' and naturalisation reveals how practices of 'citizenisation' have extended beyond the conferment of nationality strictly speaking.[5] The scope of *integration* has altered insofar as individuals' integration potential is tested at different stages, from immigrants seeking entry, to individuals seeking permanent residence or citizenship. In turn, the legal and institutional parameters of *naturalisation* have shrunk insofar as, according to the integration and naturalisation narrative, citizenship is an end-point (not available to all) that marks integration as complete. For Sarah Goodman (2014), citizenisation and naturalisation are formally different, and that difference reflects a wider shift in state policies that promote 'state identity' rather than national identity. As a result of these policy developments, the scope of citizenisation has expanded while the remit and scope of naturalisation have narrowed.[6]

The differentiation between citizenisation and naturalisation highlights how 'citizen-like' statuses can be acquired outside of nationality, namely in the context of the strengthening of the rights of foreigners and the rise of minority rights (Soysal 1995; Bosniak 2006; Joppke 2010). But 'citizen*isation*' also opens up the possibility for thinking of citizenship as an ongoing process, not a finite 'status' or something that one simply has (or has not). While established uses, policies and theories of citizenisation assume citizenship (particularly Western citizenships) to be the best form of full political and legal (if not social) membership that subjects aspire to, I examine what the foundations of this assumption are, how they are produced, reproduced and naturalised at the meso level of governance. That is to say that in spite of the widely acknowledged uncertainty of citizenship, how is its promise of stability and security reproduced?

I argue for, and demonstrate, the need to bridge understandings of naturalisation as legal and political processes with understandings of naturalisation as a *social* process. Where the scholarship on citizenship in the policy fields of integration privileges the *institutional life* of citizenisation – where naturalisation is conceived as a discrete event at the end of the same continuum – I focus on the *social life* of citizenisation – which *includes* naturalisation as a *social ontological process*, and therefore is not reducible to integration measures and practices only. Concurrently, concepts of naturalisation and citizenisation and their relationship to one another need to be rethought. Therefore, the term 'citizenisation' used hereafter encompasses both integration and naturalisation and how they work together institutionally and socially.

This approach to citizenisation constitutes a threefold methodological, empirical and theoretical move. Methodologically, this means moving beyond top-down or bottom-up approaches in favour of what Wright and Reinhold (2011) call a 'studying through' of citizenisation, which sheds light on how policies and their effects and outcomes are not fixed but variously enacted by various actors in different settings; these actors include both migrants seeking citizenship or 'citizen-like' status, as well as institutional actors charged with implementing citizenisation processes. It also means scrutinising both how the promise of citizenship is framed and produced within citizenisation policy and processes, on the one hand, and on the other hand, how the promise is met by those who encounter the policy as applicants, advisors or enforcers.

Empirically, this approach contributes to research on 'citizenisation' in two ways: first, attending to the ways in which different actors representing different interests interpret and enact the citizenisation policies, in ways that foreground the complex relationship between uncertainty (e.g. unexpected outcomes of the process) and the presumed certainty of citizenship. This is about how institutional structures and processes are not enacted as coherently as they appear, where both the presumed 'agents of the state' and migrants seeking settlement or citizenship, enter the process with their respective responsibilities, hopes, expectations, pressures, confusions, desires and anxieties. Second, focusing on the social life of citizenisation attends to the citizenisation process as a whole, rather than fragmenting it into isolated 'moments' such as citizenship ceremonies,[7] or citizenship or language tests and education.[8] The little empirical research that explores the integration and naturalisation process as a whole does so either from the perspective of applicants or from the perspective of politicians or state bureaucrats.[9] What is missing, is the scrutiny of the relational politics of citizenisation as it is enacted and experienced by both applicants and other actors drafted by the state to assess or deliver services to applicants.

Theoretically, extending a social understanding of naturalisation into formal citizenisation measures is to scrutinise how citizenisation is framed, enacted and experienced, and to unpack the different and multiple 'realities' assumed under 'citizenship'. To be sure, the 'unnatural' character of citizenship is widely accepted in current scholarship on citizenship and migration. At the same time, the unquestioned distinction between chosen and ascribed citizenship still dominates the policy and theoretical worlds of 'integration and naturalisation', which suggests the endurance of some baseline assumptions about the 'reality' of how one acquires citizenship and its benefits. My sociological curiosity prompts me to question how this 'reality' is sustained as the state of 'how things are', what its effects are, and if it could be seen differently. To echo Isin's question: What *is* called citizenship? Taking the artifice and uncertainty of citizenship as starting points, understanding naturalisation as social ontological process invites an analysis of the ways in which the artifice and uncertainty of citizenship are *concealed or rendered irrelevant* in citizenisation. Put differently, we need to understand naturalisation as part of wider processes that produce understandings of the inevitability of citizenship as the 'gold standard', as one registrar I met in the course of my study called it. Thinking about the social life of citizenisation requires an analysis of how different categories or locales of existence (citizen/ship, society, culture, the state, the nation, [imperial] histories, geographies) are called forth and 'naturalised' in citizenisation practices, and how they combine to produce understandings of what citizenship 'really is'.

This takes us to a deceptively simple question: what is naturalised in citizenisation? Put differently, what *are* the assumptions of citizenship (cf. Clarke et al. 2014)? How do these assumptions circulate as a 'reality'? How, by whom and under what circumstances is one kind of reality enacted rather than another? What are the effects of privileging some realities over others on social relations? To address these questions, the task is to decipher the ways in which certain bases of citizenship differentiation (here/there, authentic/bogus, committed/uncommitted, safe/unsafe) are foregrounded and recrafted while others are minimised to make those who enter the citizenisation process come out at the end as insiders rather than outsiders.[10] How do individuals (migrants or institutional actors) learn and enact the modes of conduct that are required to make migrants into presumed 'insiders'? And what transactions do they undertake in doing so? What is discarded or backgrounded?

Studying the *social life* of citizen*isation*, then, forces the question of *how* and *which* identities, ideas, knowledges, affects, relations are (re)produced in the name of redressing the citizenship deficit of immigrants. Furthermore, it rejects the contention that citizenisation only concerns immigrants. Rather, citizenisation processes address the nation as a whole and embed the conditionality of citizenship into popular consciousness (Honig 2001; Bhattacharyya 2015), while at the same time reasserting the distinction between 'citizen-nationals' and 'foreigners'.

A social analysis of *naturalisation*, for its part, leads us into the diverse ways in which the natural and the artificial, the abstract and the 'material', the political and the social, are variously entangled, negotiated, exchanged or stabilised. The purpose of asking 'what is naturalised in citizenisation?' is to shed more light on the foundations of citizenship. It is to go beyond understandings of citizenship as inclusion/exclusion, us/them, inside/outside, thick/thin. While citizenship is undoubtedly a form of border control, it is also a site that rests on and reproduces a host of other assumptions about geographies, personhood, temporalities and histories, desires and anxieties, which should not be ignored.

Approaching citizenship through the lens of citizenisation contrasts with the established opposition, in both policy and scholarship, between adopting the requirements of being an insider or challenging them (Isin 2009; also Isin and Nielsen 2008, Clarke et al. 2014). Instead, it shows that even if citizenisation policies claim that those eligible for citizenship or citizenship-like statuses are potential 'subjects' rather than 'abjects', the enactments of the policies bring forth both affirmation and abjection simultaneously and in multiple concurrent forms than can be occupied by any actor. In this sense, citizenisation is *social intervention* that reaches into 'the fabric and depth' of society as a whole (Foucault 2008: 145), as I explain below.

Citizenisation in neoliberal governance

What I have argued so far is that we must attend to the social life of citizenisation in order to fully unpack the meanings, forms and uses of citizenship today. The next section explains how I do so by going into the waiting room of citizenship, where seemingly competing forces are brought together in making/unmaking citizenship, citizens and migrants, and investing them with a variety of meanings and uses. In the previous section, I situate my approach within the broad scholarship on the institutional life of citizenisation (integration and naturalisation), which either centres on state structures and processes, or on one discrete element of naturalisation (citizenship ceremonies, citizenship and language tests and education). This section explains how citizenisation must be understood as a feature of neoliberal governance characterised by the decline of the welfare state, the rise of politics of securitisation, and the growing influence of market forces (corporation, financial capitalism and deregulation) in shaping a global mobile labour force. My aim here is not to examine the workings of 'neoliberalism' *per se* and how it has colonised citizenship and other spheres of social life in such a way that its economic principles (such as competitiveness, freedom, quality, innovation, flexibility, internationality) have become naturalised (as in 'there is no real alternative'; Rojo and del Percio 2019). Rather, my aim is to understand the conjuncture that enabled current understandings of citizenisation to become common sense. Two specific aspects of contemporary forms of governance have shaped the rise of citizenisation policies as they broadly exist today: first, dispersed governance and the citizenship industry, and second the connection between household governance and securitisation. In what follows, I briefly outline the effects of these features in understandings and uses of citizenship. I then proceed to argue that citizenisation is a form of social intervention that reaches into the fabric of society as a whole.

Citizenship Inc., instrumentalism and the uses of citizenship

Citizenisation is a form of dispersed governing that outsources the design, development and use of new governing technologies to public, private and third-sector organisations: local, regional or national governments, private language schools, community organisations, legal services. Also involved are supranational institutions such as the EU, border forces and employers. Then on the periphery are migrant or other aid organisations in immigration and emigration countries, the media, illegal profiteers (e.g. bogus language schools), public and private print and online publishers, and a range of small businesses. The dispersed governance of citizenisation means that it is not singular, unidirectional or uniform, and that it cannot be removed from the relational, discursive, affective and material practices that sustain it, question it or undermine it.

What this form of governing citizenisation also reveals is the extent to which citizenship has become an industry: 'Citizenship Inc.' Scholars have variously examined the links between consumer culture and the commodification of citizenship (Evans 1993; Ong 1999; Abrahamian 2015; Bloom 2015; Mavelli 2018). For the purposes that interest me here, 'Citizenship Inc.' is about the *uses* of citizenship and how they reflect a mood shift about citizenship in contemporary Europe – where citizenship is 'in crisis' as a result of the perceived combined migration and national security 'crises' – and this has given rise to the proliferation of rules, regulations and assessments that have increasingly confined citizenship by reducing its accessibility while increasing in measurability. Once a promise of equality and democracy, citizenship has become instrumentalised[11]

(Vink and de Groot 2010), 'skillified' (Millar 2014) and securitised (Nyers 2009), as part of integration policies aimed at immigrants.

To some extent, the citizenship industry depoliticises citizenship by making it a technocratic exercise (Rygiel 2010): citizenship is dissected into discrete skills-sets and potential, where the entrepreneurial neoliberal *homo oeconomicus* has to self-invest to improve their value (Brown 2015: 32–33; also Ong 2006). Citizenship, under this regime, shuts out those deemed unproductive or undeserving (Raghuram 2008; Somers 2008). However, neoliberal citizenship cannot solely be understood in market economic terms; the skilling of citizenship is also about social and cultural '(re)productivity' of applicants, and not only their economic potential. The skilling of citizenship, then, cannot be understood outside of the intensely politicised context that has given rise to renewed emphases on citizenship that surround the citizenisation agenda.

The proliferation of citizenisation in Western Europe since the late twentieth–early twenty-first century is tied to major shifts in migration policy from a model based on rights – in theory if not in practice – to a model based on market principles and interests (Kofman 2005; Kundnani 2007; Fassin 2013; Mezzadra and Neilson 2013). This form of 'managed migration' is a feature of global capitalism that pushed post-industrial countries to depend increasingly on migrant workers and generated the conditions of large-scale emigration from many regions of the world, creating the migrant 'surplus population' that post-industrial economies need.

This market-led managed migration is part of what Sandro Mezzadra and Brett Neilson call 'cognitive capitalism' (drawing on Moulier Boutang and Vercellone among others), where point-system migration schemes control for many qualities and attributes other than educational qualifications or labour skills, and

> that promise to facilitate the migrant's productive integration into the social fabric: linguistic ability, family connections, health, age, religion, monetary wealth, and even (by means of recently introduced citizenship tests in some countries) familiarity with national culture and values. (Mezzadra and Neilson 2013: 139)

Such regimes differentiate between migrants in terms of their desirability, which is measured by their economic value and their integratability or assimilability value (Kundnani 2007: 144; Gerken

2013). But as Susan Ossman (2007: 1) points out, while the 'global economy facilitates mobility and logically works to produce more adaptable, moveable people', that very adaptability and flexibility challenges established understandings of integration, and by extension citizenship, as a form of belonging to a singular, territorialised national 'community'. The late twentieth century was a period where globalisation was simultaneously deracinating and bolstering racial and national conceptions of identity and difference. Citizenisation develops in this context as a means to stabilise and fix – in both senses of repair and fasten – migrant flexibility into a stabilised loyalty, attachment and belonging to the assumed chosen country of residence. A distinctive effect of managed migration is that it ossifies the figure of the un-integratable immigrant as a subject to be avoided through pre-emptive sifting, monitoring and redressing mechanisms, as suggested by Demesmaeker above. 'Integration' is embedded within the points-based system and is a function of, in the words of Gargi Bhattacharyya (2015: 132), 'the pre-emptive establishment of differential entitlement' that distinguishes between those deemed integratable and 'those deemed lesser at the outset'. In other words, skills and criteria for establishing one's human capital become pre-emptive measurements of their *integration potential*, as well as, where applicable, their longer-term *citizenship* potential.

An overlooked feature of contemporary forms of citizenship in scholarship on integration and naturalisation is the 'skilling' of citizenship (Millar 2014) where point systems extend into citizenisation, marking an important shift in integration practices and policies: the replacement of normative judgement with scales, scores and rankings, where tests and other evaluations are seen to 'objectively' assess the integration skills of immigrant workers and foreigners seeking entry, permanent residency or citizenship. In Britain, the skilling of citizenship was tied to the 'active citizenship' agenda introduced in the late 1980s[12] and was led primarily if not exclusively by a market-led ethos rather than any connection to a body of rights, as might have historically been the case in other Western European contexts.[13]

Testing regimes befit the neoliberal fondness for 'numerical hierarchies of relative worth', as Will Davies (2014: 30) explains. These numerical systems 'produce a vision of society in which all differences are represented as comparative inequalities. But this also means that *inequalities in power* are also merely empirical and quantitative, meaning that they cannot possess any legitimacy' (Davies 2014: 30; emphasis original). In other words, '[b]oth moral and empirical claims regarding the "worth" of humans and things depends on being *tested*' (Davies 2014: 16; emphasis original). Underpinning such claims about the higher reliability of techniques of measurement as opposed to normative judgement is the dependence of these techniques on broader social and political claims about '*what* ought to be measured, and how it is legitimate to represent this objectively' (Davies 2014: 16; emphasis original). In the world of citizenisation policies such as those praised by Demesmaeker, the reduction of individual achievement and (trust)worthiness to results in tests or on a point-system score sheet simultaneously erases both the unequal conditions under which individuals are assessed in the first place, and the role of the state in creating and reproducing inequalities between the more or less 'integratable' or 'able' (e.g. see Chapter 4).

Household governance and securitising citizenship

In his first speech as Home Secretary at the 2018 Conservative Party Conference, Sajid Javid mused on the title of the government department he was leading:

> There is something profound about that word 'home'. Most of my counterparts around the world run 'Ministries of the Interior'. Interior ministry – it has a cold, brittle feel to it. Home – is where you feel safe, comfortable and in control. It reflects your identity and your values. And it is your base for going out into the wider world. That's exactly the kind of place we want the UK to be.[14]

He went on to emphasise integration, home safety and security. Upholding 'our rules and values' is how 'we keep our home safe', he stated, and 'security underpins our liberty and our prosperity'. In a thinly veiled racist coding of 'national values', he cast these against 'medieval practices affecting women like forced marriage, female genital mutilation, and so-called honour-based violence', and promised to extend his powers to strip dual-nationals of British citizenship not only from those accused of terrorist offences, but from those guilty of gang-based child sexual exploitation.[15]

Javid's view is not new or unique. These are politics that celebrate the glue of values as the primary foundation of national cohesion;

politics that come with new forms of citizenship that turn social deficiencies – such as failures in social cohesion – into individual rather than collective responsibilities; and politics that turn those deficiencies into threats to national security. Finally, these are Janus-faced politics that have an eye on global market forces through an introspective looking glass that emphasises national culture, unity and security.

Javid understood his role as a form of 'household governance' where the state is conceived as a social domestic space. Some might argue, following William Walters, that Javid's words exemplify contemporary 'domopolitics', characterised by 'the government of the state ... as a *home*. At its heart is a fateful conjunction of home, land and security. It rationalizes a series of security measures in the name of a particular conception of home' (Walters 2004: 241), where issues of safety, cohesion and identity take priority. For Walters, this constitutes a shift away from household governance where the state is conceived as an economic unit to be managed (a household), towards a more social and familial conception of the state (as home). In contrast to the welfare state where security was equated with national social and economic processes – social security – within domopolitics, national and international security are brought into the same frame of governance – *societal* security (Waever 1995, 1996) – where the space of interstate relations positions states as homes, societies and cultures to be protected against the multi-level flows and forces of globalisation. However, what Walters and others omit is that *both* forms of governance – household governance or domopolitics – legitimate *domestication* as a governing tool to regulate the conduct of the citizenry (Owens 2015).[16]

Modern states have always governed themselves and their empire through domesticating power. Indeed, within imperial regimes, the 'national home' reached out into the colonies that were to be 'domesticated' and that, in turn, enabled a very particular domesticated, racialised, gendered and sexualised idea of the 'national home/metropolis' to be consolidated (McClintock 1995; Stoler 1995; Grewal 1996). The state–citizen relation, for its part, is designed around a relationship of mutual protection based on the state-violence-citizen nexus (Weber 2008). This is as evident in Hobbes's *Leviathan* (1651; see Weber 2008: 130) as it is in the George W. Bush administration's homeland security policy (Glass 2018). The embeddedness of security in matters of citizenship, and their intensification as a result of the war on terror, enabled the instrumentalisation of citizenship to become a marker of identity (Guillaume and Huysmans 2013: 5). Kim Rygiel (2006: 146) argues that 'the war on terror is being fought to a large extent through citizenship policies and practices aimed at securing identity and it is being fought on two fronts: protecting and proving identity. Protecting identity refers to the need ... to secure a white, western, male identity'. Proving identity, for its part, refers to 'how the war stories about the need to secure identity are used to implement a host of citizenship policies but in ways that camouflage the very racialized, gendered, and classed nature of these policies'.

However, the securitising of citizenship is not reducible to the war on terror; indeed, decolonisation (more in Chapter 2) and, more recently, discourses of globalisation, long preceded the war on terror and provided the context surrounding the emergence of a territorial imaginary of 'horizontally arranged, *interlocking*, and culturally homogenous states' (Feldman 2005: 876; emphasis added). The 'interlocked' arrangement of the 'globalising world' of the late twentieth century brought on fears of the dissolution of national borders along with heightened concerns about national sovereignty and the future of *national* identities and cultures (see Fortier 2008). In this context, modern conceptions of the nation as 'territory + culture + a people' are heightened by the putative incursion of external threats. Within this globalised international space, states are authorised – indeed deemed increasingly responsible for – protecting the security of the *national culture* (Feldman 2005). In this context, household, home or homeland governance comes with an introspective gaze that prioritises national culture, national identity and national security, where citizenship becomes framed primarily as concerned with securing the national culture. With its focus on 'insecure societies', contemporary forms of household, home or homeland governance converge towards one dominant figure of risk and unease: the migrant, as Didier Bigo argues (2002). As a result:

> Citizens are then conceived as nationals, understood by opposition to foreigners, and, migrants are framed through various cultural discourses as foreigners, or as citizens of a different national origin, who do not fit the 'national standard' of norms and values. (Bigo 2002: 67)

What is at stake in the skillification of citizenship as a marker of integration, then, is not only ensuring the 'productive integration of immigrants' (Mezzadra and Neilson 2013: 139), primarily conceived of as workers with potential economic utility. What is also at stake is the *reproductive* integration of immigrants to ensure the *reproduction* of the national culture (see Chapter 5 on the becoming citizen). What this means, then, is that security is not only the cornerstone of contemporary forms of household, home or homeland governance; security combines the *skillification* of citizenship as a marker of integration with the *domestication* of citizenship as a marker of national and cultural identity. In that respect, citizenisation is not only aimed at immigrants and other 'noncitizens'. Citizenisation is a nationwide social intervention.

Citizenisation as a social intervention

Citizenisation as a social intervention includes three features that follow on from the skilling and securitising of citizenship: the privatisation of citizenship as (social) obligation; the normalisation of conditional citizenship; and the blurring and reification of the citizen/ noncitizen distinction.

First, a central principle of citizenisation politics and policies is a renewed emphasis on citizenship as a personal responsibility and achievement. Citizenising immigrants becomes the responsibility of individuals who 'choose' citizenship and who are 'committed' to it (Löwenheim and Gazit 2009: 159). As indicated earlier in this chapter, the distinction between those who choose citizenship (through legal naturalisation) and those who don't (through birth) will be interrogated in this volume (particularly Chapter 5). The point to consider for now is that the new forms of governance underpinned by competitiveness come with new forms of citizenship that turn social deficiencies – such as failures in social cohesion – into individual rather than collective responsibilities.

The responsibilisation of the migrant subject to citizenise fits with former European leaders' Angela Merkel, Nicolas Sarkozy and David Cameron's dismissal of multiculturalism as a failed project in favour of what David Cameron called 'muscular liberalism' (2011a) in a speech he gave, it is worth noting, at a European conference on security. The notion of 'muscular liberalism' marked a step away from the multicultural ethos of cultural recognition towards the principle of integration not only as an individual obligation, but also as a *citizenship* obligation. Cameron's phrase resonates with Loic Wacquant's description of the shift to neoliberal governance as a period of the 'remasculinization of the state', 'the transition from the kindly "nanny state" of the Fordist-Keynesian era to the strict "daddy state" of neoliberalism' with '[t]he new priority given to duties over rights, sanctions over support, the stern rhetoric of the "obligations of citizenship"' (Wacquant, cited in Tyler 2013: 52–53). While tools like citizenship tests are designed as measures of 'inclusion through achievement' (Goodman 2014: 30), they are part of a larger set of conditions that are read as measures of one's commitment to staying and belonging to the country of immigration. The list includes residency requirements, language fluency, civic knowledge, oaths, integration agreements, bans on dual citizenship, or option models forcing children of immigrants to choose between the citizenship of their country of birth or that of their parent(s).[17] However, the emphasis on state practices and their promotion of individual responsibility overlooks the ways individuals respond to it, which might take the form of voluntary, strategic and desired participation as well as opposition, critique and alternative imaginaries and vocabularies.

Second, citizenisation foregrounds a bureaucratic regime to assess people's entitlement or disentitlement to citizenship in ways that embed the conditionality of citizenship in popular consciousness (Bhattacharyya 2015: 3). If we were all to be tested, 'failed citizenship' could apply to those deemed insiders as much as it can apply to those deemed outsiders, such as benefits testing that filters the 'deserving' from the 'underserving' poor (cf. Anderson 2013). In this sense, citizenisation is exemplary of the 'government of society', as Michel Foucault describes neoliberal governance (2008: 146); a *social intervention* into the 'fabric and depth' of society (2008: 145) insofar as the world is regulated by 'an ethic of competitiveness' (Davies 2014: 30) that naturalises not only the inequalities that have always been integral to citizenship, but also the uncertainty of citizenship. Put crudely, if citizenship is something to be tested, then its certainty cannot be guaranteed.

Third and relatedly, citizenisation is a performative border-marking process that distinguishes citizens from noncitizens/migrants, but where noncitizenship is largely 'no more than a hypothetical category that *enables* the terms of citizenship to be articulated' (Bhattacharyya 2015: 29; emphasis added). In contemporary domesticating governance, citizenship has become a key site where fears of insecurity for nations, nationals and national cultures are played out. The chapters that follow examine *how* the boundary between citizens and noncitizens/migrants is constituted, enacted, broken down and sustained in everyday practices of meso-level governance. They also show how anxieties about the conditionality of citizenship are smoothed over through the reassurance that 'we' ('citizens') do not have to be tested.

Furthermore, the citizen–noncitizen/migrant division maps onto the separation between political versus non-political subjectivity. Citizenisation policies operate from the broad assumption that noncitizens/migrants are not only non-members of the state in which they reside, but that they are also non-political subjects, even though some migrants might have some voting rights in their countries of residence such as Commonwealth citizens in the UK or EU citizens residing in other EU countries. The point here is that underpinning citizenisation processes is the idea that there is an outside, 'a space of non-citizenship where [citizenship] rights and entitlements do not apply' (Bhattacharyya 2015: 28; Bhambra 2015). Indeed, a question underpinning this volume is how citizenship *takes place*, following John Clarke et al.'s (2014) use of the phrase, and which I return to in the next section. Interrogating the spatial settings, scales and imaginings of citizenising practices sheds lights on the extent to which citizenship and noncitizenship are entangled. If citizenising subjects is integral to citizenisation, so too is their *de*citizenisation. That is, by reifying the citizen–noncitizen/migrant boundary, citizenisation strips migrants of their other citizenships – symbolically if not legally – by making them irrelevant and in some instances undesirable to 'naturalised' citizenship. Consequently, migrants entering the process of citizenisation are cast as 'irregular citizens', in Peter Nyers's phrase, insofar as their rights, duties and obligations are undercut and their *other* citizenship 'is unmade by being made unworkable' (Nyers 2013: 38).

Moreover, the citizen–noncitizen/migrant opposition is intertwined with another distinction: the migratisation–demigratisation of those who become naturalised citizens. The figuration of the migrant flagged by Bigo above points to a complex and nuanced process theorised by Alyosxa Tudor (2018) as the analytical distinction between migratisation and migratism, on the one hand, and racialisation and racism, on the other. The narrative arc of the citizenisation process is to conclude with the inclusion of 'new' citizens as insiders who belong – therefore demigratising them by substituting their migrant status with their citizenship status. However, the Windrush scandal reminds us that one does not have to be a foreigner to be seen as a migrant and reveals the ways in which racist ideologies of national belonging and entitlement framed the way that the anti-migrant (migratist) 'hostile environment' policy was enacted.

Tudor's intervention on migratism is useful to understand the connections and nuanced distinction between different forms of exclusions from the nation-state that are not only based on long-standing understandings of race and racialised differences. But what if we turned the lens of migratisation onto citizenship itself? Bridget Anderson (2013) suggests as much in her book *Us and Them?*, which examines the various ways in which immigration controls impact on 'citizens' as well as on foreigners (also de Genova 2010). For example, Chapter 3 shows how immigration regimes encroach in the lives of British citizens such as local authority registrars or individuals in a relationship with a foreign spouse.

Such processes are scrutinised in the following chapters. In studying how citizenisation is enacted, experienced and processed, this volume unpacks the concomitant (re)making and un-making of citizenship and 'migranthood' (Fortier 2003), of 'citizens' and 'migrants', and their entanglements with regimes of differentiation and inequality based on race, gender, sexuality or class.

Life in the waiting room

> Meanwhile Lily stays with her elderly mum [in Thailand] and just waits and waits and waits … And I sit at home, with my dog, and I just wait and wait and wait. (Paul, British, waiting for his Thai spouse to obtain her two-year spousal visa allowing her to enter Britain)

In his critique of European historicism, Dipesh Chakrabarty writes about how the colonised were consigned to the 'imaginary waiting room of history' as 'not-yet civilized enough to rule themselves'.

> We were all headed for the same destination, [John Stuart] Mill averred, but some people were to arrive earlier than others. That was what historicist consciousness was: a recommendation to the colonized to wait. Acquiring a historical consciousness, acquiring the public spirit that Mill thought absolutely necessary for the art of self-government, was also to learn this art of waiting. This waiting was the realization of the 'not yet' of historicism. (Chakrabarty 2007: 8)[18]

There is a similar historicist consciousness that informs the citizenship acquisition process whereby the deficient applicant has to be educated into becoming a 'becoming citizen'. But in contrast to the 'democratic citizen' aspired to by Mill in colonial times, today citizenisation regimes favour the neoliberal citizen who enhances their human capital and integration potential, in order to ensure the reproduction of a productive labour force and the securitisation of the domesticated national culture. Still, a historicist rationale underpins the citizenisation process insofar as the idea is to redress the citizenship deficit of migrants. They are 'citizens-inwaiting' (or *citizands*, as Bridget Byrne [2014] aptly puts it) where waiting is a key feature of all citizenisation processes.

This section explains how the waiting room allows me to approach it as a *social space* where variously enlisted 'agents of the state' and applicants meet. More specifically, the waiting room of citizenship includes a set of smaller anterooms, real or virtual: the language testing room, the ESOL (English for Speakers of other Languages) class, the citizenship testing room, the two-year spousal visa, the ceremony room, the solicitor's office and more. Depending on their circumstances and on where they fit in the migrant visa system, applicants will move through various combinations of these rooms, following the appropriate route. I imagine this waiting room with trails that are differently colour coded, as at the Liverpool UKBA (now UK Visas and Immigration – UKVI) offices I visited in 2011, where differently coloured footprints stencilled on the floor took us to different waiting areas: the metaphorical orange, blue, red or yellow brick roads to visas, settlement or citizenship. Along these roads, government agents, private or public service providers, or other policy practitioners are there to meet or guide the applicants.[19]

Waiting is an inescapable feature of human life, yet only recently has it attracted scholarly attention as an object of inquiry (Schweizer

2005; Bissell 2007; Hage 2009a; Conlon 2011; Janeja and Bandak 2018). This scholarship unpacks different modalities of waiting, approaching it as an object of inquiry in its own right: cultural, political, economic, technological. In turn, waiting is a perspective from which to see the world, revealing things that would otherwise not be seen (Hage 2009a), 'a trigger for various forms of social energies' (Janeja and Bandak 2018: 1). In short, waiting here is both object and method of inquiry.

Similarly, the temporalities of migration have drawn relatively little scholarly interest (Cwerner 2001; Conlon 2011; Griffiths, Rogers and Anderson 2013; Andersson 2014b; Robertson 2014, 2015; Baas and Yeoh 2019; Anderson 2020). Building on what is deemed the 'mobilities turn' in migration studies, much of this scholarship attends to the intimate relationship between mobility and immobility (Bissel 2007; Bissell and Fuller 2009) – a relationship that Avtar Brah (1996) captured in her concept of diaspora space, where genealogies of migration and genealogies of 'staying put' meet. Another theme of this body of work centres on waiting as an undeniable aspect of the experience of migration, particularly (though not exclusively) for asylum seekers and refugees (Mountz et al. 2002; Ahmad 2008; Gill 2009; Griffiths 2014; Allsopp, Chase and Mitchell 2015; Elliot 2016). Broadly, research on migration and temporalities highlights the various states of 'enforced temporariness and uncertainty' resulting from visa regimes that 'keep migrants in an extended state of arrival, or waiting' (Anderson 2013: 89), where plans for the future are suspended, as if waiting for their lives to begin.

This monograph is not an ethnography of waiting (Janeja and Bandak 2018). Rather, it uses the waiting room as a heuristic device that foregrounds temporality (citizenship *takes time*), spatiality (citizenship *takes place*), and affect (citizenship *takes hold*). I return to each of these constitutive parts of the waiting room below.

Moreover, *life* in the waiting room draws attention away from any conception of the waiting room – and waiting more broadly – as a space (or time) of passivity, stillness and suspension, but rather as a productive and active space (and time) (Cresswell 2010; Baas and Yeoh 2019). The waiting room is brim full of activity: citizenisation involves the (re)production and circulation of regulations, objects, documents, information, people, ideas between and within the anterooms, and it is punctuated by stops and starts, things and people moving forward or standing still, which together constitute what many experience as protracted waiting. Paul, cited above, described the year it took before he and Lily could be reunited as 'being in limbo'. But he also spoke animatedly about the energy that was fuelled by his frustration, by the uncertainty, by the constantly changing regulations. He might have felt that he was in limbo, but he was not standing still. He became an expert on matters of immigration, particularly spousal immigration, and spent most of that year writing to MPs and other government officials, contributing to blogs and Facebook groups for other British spouses facing similar hurdles and periods of 'limbo', and generally being very actively engaged in the whole process even while 'nothing moved'. If waiting can at times make us feel powerless and lacking agency, Paul's active waiting shows how in contrast 'agency oozes out of waiting' as Ghassan Hage puts it (2009b: 2).

Finally, life in the waiting room debunks ideas that noncitizens are passive (Tonkiss and Bloom 2015), or that 'migrants' and institutional actors respectively act in a unitary way, as if they were part of different (usually opposing) 'cultures'. Rather, the object is to draw out how *all* actors are variously affected by a state policy – how they variously experience, interpret, enact and feel those policies (e.g. de Wilde and Duyvendak 2016). Put simply, citizenisation measures inscribe different parties into different relationships: to each other, to the state, to nation(s), to space and place (here and there), to time (past [his]stories, aspirations, waiting times), or to affective states. Applying for settlement or citizenship puts in motion a range of social relations and interactions that are lived, embodied, felt, reasoned, processed and documented by those involved, in ways that exceed the kind of coherence that policy, as an instrument of the state, is expected to confer onto its subjects. In this sense, policies themselves will be differently enacted. As critical policy scholars have noted, tracking how policy moves through the waiting room, and how it moves (through) subjects, captures not only 'something of the livedness' (Lewis 2010: 214) of the policy's social life (how it is lived), but captures something of its *live*-ness as well (how it is 'living' (Hunter 2008: 507)). In sum, the device of the waiting room captures the interplay between, on the one hand, the structural and institutional conditions that bring people to the waiting room – as language teachers, registrars, ceremony officials or migrants – and on the other hand, how people inhabit these governing practices.

Citizenship takes time

Citizenship takes time in the sense that individuals – be they applicants or institutional actors – will be channelled through different waiting times and will have different experiences of waiting. The waiting room of citizenship is intimately connected to migration and visa regimes that control people's movements and determine the time it takes to become a resident or citizen. Furthermore, the historicist, developmental rationale of citizenisation brackets individuals as 'not-yet' citizens – indeed as 'noncitizens' – located somewhere between past lives and biographies and the promise of the future. From the state's point of view, becoming a British citizen is a privilege that is worth waiting and working for. Government citizenisation policy, and several registrars I spoke to, picture applicants as in between two legal statuses: that of their current nationality and that of their future new one, where the former is often cast against the promises that the latter will deliver, such as democracy, protection and freedom.

Critical citizenship studies reject the linear temporalities and spatialities of citizenship, which cast migrants and citizens as respectively outside or inside (political) membership of a nation-state (Nyers 2013; Isin and Nyers 2014; Ní Mhurchú 2014). As discussed above, the institutional view of citizenisation sees it as a linear process with an ultimate end point; indeed, that is how citizenisation policy is designed, with the promise of citizenship as that which will end the waiting. It befits the chronological, 'homogeneous, empty time' of historical progress (Benjamin, cited in Mezzadra and Neilson 2013: 134) that is also the nation's favoured temporal narrative (Anderson 1991; Gilroy 1993). Similarly, Chapter 2 points out how many historians of British citizenship wonder about its late birth. However, asking 'why did it take so long?' (Karatani 2003; also Hansen 2000; Heater 2006) suggests that there is or was a 'good time(frame)' where nations gave birth to their own citizenship, and these histories insinuate that Britain missed the cues to set up its own national bounded citizenship.

In contrast, turning the lens of *migration* (Papadopoulos, Stephenson and Tsianos 2008) onto the waiting room of citizenship reveals its 'heterogeneous temporalities' (Mezzadra and Neilson 2013: 134) and how migrants live in and with different temporalities. Saolo Cwerner (2001) writes of the 'heteronomous times' of migration that result from migration and visa regimes, where 'the politics of who is to wait' (Hage 2009b: 2) and for how long vary and are shaped by the human as well as financial capital that migrants bring. For those who took part in this study, there is also a heterogeneity of temporalities depending on the route and stage of the process. In addition, time moves at different paces, as things accelerate and require immediate action, or slow down and require waiting. And people will 'wait' in different ways, for different things; waiting *for* a letter, waiting *to* apply for citizenship, waiting *out* the court hearing – with each waiting mode having different qualities. Thus, different requirements, different circumstances, different ways of using or experiencing the heterogenous temporalities of citizenisation all come to bear in the waiting room. And they will be variously experienced and shaped by those who wait, those who make others wait, as well as that which makes people wait (the law, policy, technology, bureaucracy).

Citizenship takes place

John Clarke et al. (2014) write about how citizenship variously takes place, where 'taking place' is understood:

> not only as a metaphor (denoting an event happening), but also as consequential in spatial terms. Citizenship happens in places; citizens act in places; citizenship is practised (or not) in particular places. We begin from an interest in why some places (sites, scales, settings) are deemed (by states, social movements, citizens, etc.) to be 'proper' ones for citizenship, while others are not. (2014: 131)

The main interest for Clarke and his co-authors is 'citizenship from below'. Still, their definition of taking place resonates with my own concerns. Different citizenships 'happen', are 'practised', affirmed or erased in citizenisation's waiting room. The question is, how do geographical imaginaries of 'good' or 'bad' citizenship feed into, and in turn are reproduced or questioned in, citizenising practices?

Citizenship is not only a national system of inclusion/exclusion, it is also a global system of unequal distribution of the world's riches, as Ayelet Shachar (2009) and Shachar and Ran Hirschl (2007) pointedly argue. We live in a world where principles of birthright entitlements and kinship dominate not only our imagination but also our laws in the allotment of political membership (over 95 per cent of the world's population are citizens by birth; Shachar 2009). These laws renaturalise 'the "wealth-preserving" aspect of hereditary citizenship' (Shachar and Hirschl 2007: 274) and preserve the unequal global distribution of the world's riches. While where we are born may be 'accidental', the unequal distribution of our ensuing life-chances is not.

To be sure, such global inequalities share origins in imperial histories. In the case of Britain, the history sketched out in Chapter 2 shows how the empire's geography became more fragmented in terms of the political and economic connections between Dominions, colonies and Britain. Along with that came differentiated citizenships or subjecthoods, with different rights of travel, entry, settlement and naturalisation across the empire. This history therefore reveals a *heterogeneous geography* of citizenship that set the grounds, as it were, for imaginative geographies of citizenship that shape citizenisation practices today. That is, a practice that spatially distributes the 'worth' of citizenships along a sliding scale that generally places countries from the Global South at the bottom and those of the Global North at the top. Like with the remainders of racism and difference (see Chapter 2), the remainders of imperial imaginative geographies are not simply replicated in the contemporary global system of citizenship. Rather, the issue is to pay attention to the enduring logics and techniques of imperialism that (re)naturalise inequalities in a seemingly post-imperial world.

Citizenship also takes place in the confirmation of stability. First, residence requirements expect the transnational, diasporic individuals to make Britain their primary and permanent home, and, as we shall see, to stay put as much as possible, especially during the application process. Second, the narrative arc of citizenisation concludes with the celebration of (British) citizenship as a stable certainty. In this narrative, citizenisation is a performative border-marking process that distinguishes citizens from noncitizens, where noncitizens belong to a bounded exclusionary 'migrant' space that is outside of the political – the neoliberal governing of migration casts noncitizens/migrants as variously skilled but always as non-political (Ong 2006) or as not themselves politically constituted through relations of power. Citizens, for their part, are cast as belonging to an inclusionary space that is not precarious but safe and full of promise (Ní Mhurchú 2014; Bhattacharyya 2015).

Citizenship takes hold

Like the taking place of citizenship, the taking hold of citizenship refers not only to a metaphor – as something having an effect or becoming strong and established – but also to being consequential in affective terms. In this sense, citizenship takes hold in two ways: through the political economy of affect, and through various forms of 'grasping' bodies and subjects.

First, as I explain elsewhere (Fortier 2013, 2017a), citizenship takes hold insofar as all citizenisation processes are framed through politics of desire: the desire *for* and desirability *of* citizenship and national membership as well as the desire *for* and desirability *of* desirable citizens. What is more, citizenisation's frames of desire also take the form of anxieties and enact the ambivalent relationship between desire and anxiety that mediates the state–citizen relationship (Honig 2001). Subsequent chapters in this volume will extend this analysis of the psychosocial dynamics of citizenship to draw out the various ways in which the distribution of power and inequality operate through affect – desire, anxiety, but also hope, uncertainty, doubt, enervation, optimism or other feeling states (Fortier 2017a).

Citizenship takes hold in a political economy of affective citizenship that dictates how some feelings attach themselves to citizenship – feelings of belonging or rightful presence – and how citizenship itself can bring up certain feelings – such as the feeling of safety that the state is presumed to have the responsibility of ensuring for all its citizens (Weber 2008). Furthermore, the 'feeling rules' (Hochschild, cited in de Wilde and Duyvendak 2016: 977) of citizenship are organised around an economy of feelings: the production, circulation and distribution of legitimate feelings for and within the nation, where the burden of that labour largely falls upon those in minoritised positions – the working class, women, the racially minoritised, younger generations

– who are often required to make the majoritised subject feel better (Fortier 2008). The currency of feelings and their differential value within the wider economic structure of feelings delineates the codes of conduct of good citizenry. And their exchange value is political: different feelings are attributed different values – or rather, they are differentially located within the 'national values' against which the 'value' of citizens is assessed.

Second, the desire–anxiety nexus also takes hold *on bodies*, which have historically been racialised, gendered, sexualised, disabled and otherwise differentially marked as more or less desirable 'migrants' or future citizens. Central to citizenisation is the ideal of integration that figures different racialised subjects along a spectrum of their potential integratability. The historical account that comes in the next chapter ties in with developmental narratives that were central to the various civilising missions of imperial projects past and present (see Huntington 1996), which distinguish between the 'underdeveloped' and the 'un-developable' (Weber 2016; also Chakrabarty 2007). Likewise, current citizenisation processes separate the integratable and un-integratable subjects in ways that will reproduce hierarchies of belonging. Where such dynamics of 'taking hold' have most purchase is perhaps in the speaking citizen of Chapter 4, where racialising regimes of seeing work in tandem with regimes of hearing in what Rey Chow refers to as 'languaging', where migrants are 'racialized by language, and languaged by race' (Chow 2014: 9; also Fortier 2018).

Finally, citizenisation takes hold through the documentary capture of individuals through identification papers, forms and documents which 'grasp' their stories to be processed and identities to be confirmed (Torpey 2000; Caplan and Torpey 2001). It bears reminding readers that the migrants in this monograph are already documented subjects who are deemed eligible for permanent residency status or citizenship. Still, citizenisation requires them to enter 'in a network of writing; it engages them in a whole mass of documents that capture and fix them' (Foucault 1979: 189).

The waiting room, then, sheds light on how the distribution of power and inequality through time, space and affect/bodies works to enact particular conceptions of citizenship or the state–citizen relationship. It is a space where migrants (understood as noncitizens), state and nonstate actors meet as they encounter, experience and enact citizenisation in ways that both conform to and exceed the policy guidelines, timelines and expected outcomes.

Conclusion

This study starts from the premise that the uncertainty of citizenship is normalised in the contemporary world. This normalisation, however, is in tension with the endurance of the ideal of citizenship as a stable guarantor of rights and belonging – 'the gold standard' that is associated with citizenships of the Western world. Understanding citizenship today, then, requires different concepts, methods and data (Isin 2015). The analytical framework detailed above contributes to filling this gap with a theory and method for researching the social life of citizenisation that will offer a better understanding of how citizenship, citizens, *as well as* migranthood and migrants are variously 'made', conceived, enacted, connected and experienced. In other words, the theory of citizenisation prizes 'citizenisation' from the policy world in which it originated, and seizes the processual and social lives of citizenship as it is made, unmade and (dis)connected to 'migrants' and migranthood. Citizenisation is a concept that captures both 'integration' and 'naturalisation' measures, which remain widely understood – in theory and in policy – as separate moments in a subject's journey to citizenship. This chapter also outlines the current conjuncture that normalises the uncertainty of citizenship, focusing on two features of neoliberal governance: the skillification of citizenship under the combined regimes of managed migration and citizenship testing, and the securitisation of citizenship that inflects practices of domesticating governance in specific ways.

In sum, the chapter introduces the analytical framing that guides this book, and situates the world of citizenisation within converging trends. However, such converging trends must be understood and scrutinised *in context*.[20] This is what the remainder of this volume attends to, starting with an exposition of the history of British citizenship that traces the imperial and colonial legacies of contemporary citizenisation in Britain.

2

Citizenising Britain

Citizenisation processes are designed to redress the 'citizenship deficit' of migrants. However, an overlooked feature of theoretical and policy understandings of citizenisation is how they not only operate as a social intervention, as argued in the previous chapter. It is also how they shape definitions of the nation-state itself. This chapter turns to the history of British citizenship and to how the perceived 'citizenship deficit' of *Britain* has long since been the subject of political and scholarly discourse. Cast in this way, histories of British citizenship are about how Britain *itself* was citizenised. The aim of this chapter is twofold: the first is to explain why Britain is an interesting site for exploring wider issues concerning the uncertainty of citizenship today. Like many neoliberal Western states today, Britain adopted a market-led system of 'managed migration' in the late 1990s to recruit a transnational migrant workforce. The British citizenisation policy cannot be decoupled from the points-based migration regime described in Chapter 1, both in its spirit and in its practice: e.g. the measuring of 'soft' skills like knowledge of life in the UK and language competence, which were cast against a climate of urgency around external threats to national culture and security. Thus, like many Western countries since the turn of the twenty-first century, Britain tightened its naturalisation laws and expanded integration requirements in the face of what is cast as a national and international 'crisis of citizenship'. That said, the specificities in *how* citizenisation takes place are not universal – the sequencing of tests and encounters, the kinds of actors involved (public and private), and other features will vary – and this study details those specificities and their effects on citizenising and decitizenising subjects.

Britain is also distinctive because of its relatively recent history of national citizenship as a legal category and its history of imperial citizenship that does not follow the French Republican model. The current citizenisation regime is founded on a conception of *British* citizenship that was created in 1981, which is comparatively recent in relation to other Western democracies. Moreover, some authors argue that 'there is no such things as [British citizenship]' (Dummett 1994: 75) because of its vagueness and fluidity, and because Britain has no written constitution or comprehensive legal statement on citizens' rights (Yeo 2018). Contrary to such a conception, the long view of citizenship that this chapter takes shows how the presumed weakness of British citizenship is grounded in Britain as a 'global institution' (Karatani 2003). Furthermore, concerns about the vagueness of British citizenship are grounded in an idealised understanding of citizenship as the ultimate means of inclusion and political belonging. In contrast to this perspective, this chapter considers how the citizenisation of Britain resulted from its imperial project and its relations to colonies; a racialised citizenisation that both arose from and produced specific relations between subjects within and across territories.

A further distinctive feature of Britain is that, as a constitutional monarchy, the relationship between subjecthood and citizenship was the subject of several debates, iterations and changes through the centuries, but subjecthood is still regarded as compatible with citizenship in Britain (Goldsmith 2008) – indeed, allegiance to the Crown remains a feature of citizenship to this day.[1] The Home Office White Paper on nationality, immigration and asylum states that '[t]here is no contradiction in promoting citizenship so that people uphold common values and understand how they can play their part in our society while upholding our status as subjects of HM The Queen' (Home Office 2002: 29).

Relatedly, the history and legacy of imperial citizenship come to bear in the ways in which British citizenship as well the citizenisation process must be understood. Similarly, naturalisation laws in Britain followed a piecemeal path towards the contemporary version that, as elsewhere, establishes 'naturalised' status to be equivalent to 'natural-born' status, with equal rights and obligations. But this was not always the case. The first section of this chapter, then, gives a brief history of citizenship and naturalisation in Britain. It sheds light on how citizenship developed as a bounded status out of a logic of racialised differentiation, or what Partha Chatterjee calls 'the rule of colonial difference' (cited in Mongia 2018: 11); a history where marginalised subjects and marginalised territories are *central* to the continually shifting and reconfigured borders of the empire, the Commonwealth, the nation and the citizen. Colonial relations, decolonisation and national liberation movements have forced the articulation of different conceptions of citizenship – a neglected aspect of citizenship studies largely dominated by West European norms (*pace* Anderson 2013; Isin 2015; Sadiq 2017; Mongia 2018) – and Britain is a case in point.

Citizenship as remainder

Imperial and colonial naturalisation

Many of the contemporary developments in British citizenship are framed as filling the need to strengthen a 'weak' version of citizenship in British society; a conception that circulates in political, legal and scholarly discourses (e.g. Dummett 1994; Low 2000). However, as Rieko Karatani (2003) documents, the idea that British citizenship is 'weak' results from a long history of *power* tied to imperialism and colonialism. Indeed, it is impossible to understand contemporary conceptions of British citizenship without an understanding of how, as a 'global institution' (Karatani 2003), Britain developed citizenship laws in relation to its colonies that, in turn, played a key role in changing definitions of citizenship (Mongia 2018).

The history of colonial expansion and imperialism teaches us that British subjects have been distinguished from non-subjects in a range of different ways (Dummett and Nicol 1990; Anderson 2013). The feudal origins of subjecthood established an exchange between subjects' 'natural allegiance' to the ruler – 'birth within the king's ligeance'– in return for the ruler's protection (Karatani 2003: 17). The principle of indelible allegiance by birth extended to colonial territories as the English sovereign's empire expanded: all those born under the monarch's rule were English subjects. Originally there was no distinction between subjects and aliens, but the distinction developed with a body of rules regulating principles of inheritance and property ownership (Dummett and Nicol 1990; Anderson 2013; Karatani 2003; El-Enany 2020). By the mid-eighteenth century, subjecthood was granted 'to all men born within the king's dominions immediately upon their birth' (Karatani 2003: 41), and to children of natural-born subjects for up to two generations. 'Those who could not acquire subjecthood by birth were only admitted to it by a strict system of legislation, either naturalization or denization' (Karatani 2003: 42). Naturalisation and denisation were then used by the wealthy as a way to circumvent prohibitions on land ownership and inheritance. Naturalised or endenised subjects did not have the same rights as those conferred on the natural-born subjects; for example, naturalised subjects were prohibited from becoming members of parliament or accessing Crown land. Furthermore, naturalisation/denisation in England was a lengthy, burdensome and costly process – over £100 in 1843 (over £12,000 today) – which meant that it was pursued by very few (Karatani 2003: 51).[2]

Imperial expansion brought about two things: the separate development of imperial and colonial naturalisation systems, and the increased movement of persons within the empire. First, in the early nineteenth century, the British government began to 'place a stronger emphasis on overseas trade and economic expansion under the banner of free trade, so immigration came to be judged in the context of what would be to Britain's economic advantage' (Karatani 2003: 53–54). In that context, successive governments amended naturalisation policies to make them simpler, cheaper, and to grant naturalised subjects more rights than they had before and by the same token, bringing the status of naturalised subjects closer to that of the 'natural-born' British subject (Karatani 2003: 55), as enshrined in the Aliens Act 1844. In 1847, the Act for the Naturalization of Aliens ruled that the Aliens Act does not apply to the colonies and granted colonial governments the power 'to enact naturalization laws, statutes, or ordinances of their own' (Karatani 2003: 56). This recognised the legitimacy of a territorial limit to colonial naturalisation and the spatial anchoring of the legal difference between British subjects and aliens, where for example 'a Frenchman naturalized in New Zealand was a British subject there, but [was] a Frenchman in England' (Karatani 2003: 56).

However, as Karatani's example shows, within these laws the principle of subjecthood remained. Challenges to the principle of indelible allegiance in favour of the principle of voluntary naturalisa-tion came to a head with the loss of American colonies in the second half of the eighteenth century. Disputes between the United States and Great Britain led to the British Naturalisation Act (NA) of 1870, which abolished the doctrine of indelible allegiance, which was seen as incompatible with liberalism and individualism:

> [the doctrine of indelible allegiance] is at variance with those principles on which the rights and duties of a subject should be deemed to rest; it conflicts with that freedom of action which is now recognized as most conducive to the general good as well as to individual happiness and prosperity; and it is especially inconsistent with the practice of a State which allows to its subjects [*sic*] absolute freedom of emi-gration.[3] (*Report of the Royal Commissioners for Enquiring into the Laws of Naturalization and Allegiance*, 1869, cited in Karatani 2003: 49)

The self-determining subject was central to the 'transition narrative' of colonialism that is hinted at in Chakrabarty's words cited in Chapter 1. This is 'a story about the shift from the primitive to the civilised and from feudalism to capitalism' (Brace 2004: 210), where the colonised were expected to develop into being 'men of reason' that was foundational to modern ideas of citizenship. The NA 1870 therefore dug a further division within the empire – on one side of this divide, the incipient citizen (though not yet legally formed in the UK) who is no longer subject to the sovereign but who can make claims against the state and the sovereign based on their membership to a community of shared privileges that are no longer only granted to them at the sovereign's pleasure. On the other side of the divide, the colonised remain subjects and subjected to the coloniser's power to determine their status. This is a distinction that maps onto, since the mid-nineteenth century, the different relations between, on the one hand, Britain and its Dominions, which enjoyed greater autonomy and self-governance, and on the other, between Britain and the rest of the empire.

Like reason in Chakrabarty's account, private property was central to the notion of the self-determining subject (Brace 2004). It is no coincidence, then, that concerns regarding the impact of the NA 1870 on those who, having been originally British, now fall within the class of 'aliens' and lose property rights in the United Kingdom, led the Royal Commissioners to recommend the removal of such legal restrictions, thereby increasing the status of aliens in Great Britain (Karatani 2003: 50) and preserving the mobility of people between countries and into the United Kingdom. The Royal Commissioners considered that to deprive persons naturalised abroad of the right to hold or inherit land would be 'an impolitic restriction on the liberty of emigration' (Royal Commissioners for Inquiring into Laws of Naturalization and Allegiance 1869: vi).[4]

This ties in with the second point: imperial expansion came with the growing movement of persons between colonies – colonial administrators, slaves, indentured labourers, British subjects and aliens. Colonial naturalisation laws were simplified and cheaper in order to encourage settlement in the colonies, but colonies also had powers to refuse or expel undesirable incomers (Karatani 2003: 52). Similarly, naturalisation was not equally available to all. Pre-emancipation colonies restricted naturalisation to white men (such as in the US Naturalization Law of 1790; Anderson 2013: 32), and in the years following emancipation, the issue arose as to how to enable the movement of Europeans and indentured labourers, while controlling the movement of 'free' Indians (Mongia 2018). By the mid-nineteenth century, white dominions and settler colonies combined immigration control and naturalisation laws to exclude or refuse entry to some groups of people, particularly indentured labourers from Asia (primarily from China and India).[5] Thus, the territorialisation of naturalisation and immigration policies were shaping the basis for local racialised citizenships in self-governing colonies (later Dominions) alongside British subjecthood. Many of these ostensibly raceless policies in practice worked to 'cultivate whiteness', as David Theo Goldberg puts it (2002: 171), in settler colonies and Dominions. In turn, whiteness 'at home' was consolidated in opposition to 'blackness' abroad (Anderson 2013: 36; also McClintock 1995; Stoler 2002).

Meanwhile, the principle of British subjecthood parted into two groupings: those considered British subjects throughout the world and those regarded as British subjects only within a colony. Imperial subjecthood, in other words, was superimposed on localised formal memberships and was imperial in name, but not necessarily in practice. The imperial government therefore accepted an internal division among British subjects and differential controls of their movements between colonies. However, the movement of British subjects to the United Kingdom remained unregulated and it was numerically small, and the principle of free movement from all parts of the empire into the United Kingdom was repeatedly defended. As indicated above, it was the monitoring of *aliens* that was more of a concern. If early worries were about facilitating wealthy aliens to access rights of entry and property in the United Kingdom, they later turned to the exclusionary control of 'undesirables' with the 1905 Aliens Act. The Act was adopted at the time where large numbers of Jewish people were arriving in London, expelled from Russia and Eastern Europe. While it was aimed at the Jewish migrants, the act stipulated that undesirables were the poor, the sick or those with criminal convictions. Moreover, the Act did include a category that today would be recognised as refugees and allowed entry to a person fleeing persecution (Anderson 2013: 37; El-Enany 2020).

In sum, prior to the twentieth century and in spite of the weakening of the doctrine of indelible allegiance, the imperial concept of British subjecthood developed, as Karatani notes, 'in parallel with the expansion of the British empire into a global institution' (2003: 70); an expansion that came with the differential inclusion of mobile British subjects within the empire. The distinction between British subjects and aliens was constituted within the framework of common law, which safeguarded the privileges of property owners (Brace 2004). At the same time, and as the movements of people within the empire increased, concerns about the divergence of naturalisation laws led to the establishment of a common code standardising imperial naturalisation.

Commonwealth citizenship

In the early twentieth century, Dominions sought greater autonomy in controlling the movement of people within their territory, while retaining the principle of common status among British subjects. This tension was resolved in the creation of a common code in the British Nationality and Status of Aliens Act of 1914 (BN & SA 1914), which 'defined in statute [rather than in common law] who was to be considered a British subject' (Anderson 2013: 38): that is, anyone born within the Old Commonwealth and empire, or of the first-generation descendants of a father who is a British subject (Hansen 2000: 39–40).

While it ratified *jus soli* (status by territory of birth) as a statutory principle, the BN & SA Act 1914 also established basic requirements for imperial naturalisation: five-years residency within the empire, 'good character', being of 'sound mind' and an 'adequate' knowledge of the English language (Anderson 2013: 989; Karatani 2003: 80). However, the Act also maintained local naturalisation, that is, Dominions would retain the power to enact their own naturalisation laws and to treat differentiated classes of British subjects differently. As a result, subjects of Asian origin – namely Indians – continued to be treated differently (Mongia 2018): the 'common code' was not common to all. Meanwhile, efforts to define aliens and to design immigration laws to control their movement into Britain were further elaborated with the Aliens Restrictions Acts of 1914 and 1919 – extending war-time restrictions into peace time in dealing with 'enemy aliens'.

In the years prior to the Second World War, the distinction between British subjects and aliens was entrenched through the design of separate immigration laws for each category; a distinction that persisted until 1971 (Anderson 2013: 38; Karatani 2003: 83). At the same time, another feature of common membership also developed: the acquisition of British subjecthood by descent was extended to indefinite generational transmission in the BN & SA Act 1922. The birthright principles of *jus sanguinis* (status by descent) and *jus soli* (status by territory of birth) were thereupon combined in definitions of British status.[6] By adopting *jus sanguinis* as a principle of citizenship, the United Kingdom was falling into step with many European countries which, in the early nineteenth century, followed the trend set by the French Civil Code of 1804 and replaced *jus soli* with *jus sanguinis* (Weil 2001). *Jus sanguinis* consolidated the establishment of the citizenship as the basis of 'communities of birth instead of communities of faith' in European states (Mignolo 2006: 312). For Walter Mignolo (2006: 312), 'the figure of the "citizen" presupposed an idea of the "human" that had already been formed during the Renaissance and was one of the constitutive elements of the colonial matrix of power'. Furthermore, the legal principle of *jus sanguinis* emerged at a time when scientific racism was classifying humans into hierarchised racial categories that were mapped onto geographical locations. In other words, *jus sanguinis* emerged within an 'intellectual climate that favoured racial distinctions', thereby conferring 'a measure of scientific blessing on it' (Amunátegui Perelló 2018: 16; also Stepan 1998).

Dominions were not as keen as Britain in recognising blood lines in defining British belonging. Between 1907 and 1937, a series of Imperial Conferences[7] took place where Dominions and Britain debated over the tensions between sharing a common status and granting greater autonomy to Dominions over nationality laws and other affairs, such as trade. As Dominions became more assertive, the common code system was repeatedly questioned and reinterpreted. The common code, ratified with the BN & SA act 1914, allowed for Dominions to continue to control the movement of British subjects into their territory, as well as giving them power to decide to whom they would extend the right of British subjecthood. Dominions also acquired the power to design their own nationality laws and define who, among the holders of British subjecthood, would be entitled to becoming a 'national' of their country. In short, up to 1946, Dominions had a vested interest in preserving their autonomy *within* the common code system out of political and economic priorities. In this context, nation-based types of citizenship understood as founded on shared belonging and identity were growing and stood in contrast to British subjecthood, understood as a shared status – largely symbolic – that was 'granted from above' (Karatani 2003: 96).

The common code ultimately broke down in 1946 when Canada adopted the Canadian Citizenship Act 1946 (CCA), which gave precedence to Canadian citizenship based on national pride, common interest and shared consciousness *as Canadians* (cf. Parliamentary Debates, House of Commons, Dominion of Canada, 1945 and 1946, cited in Karatani 2003: 113, 119). The CCA 1946 ends the common code system set up in the BN & SA 1914 by separating national citizenship from Commonwealth citizenship, with the latter being appended to Canadian citizenship: one is a Commonwealth citizen only on the basis of being a Canadian citizen. Crucially, as Mongia argues, racialised mobility within the Commonwealth precipitated 'the emergence of nationality as a staunch territorial attachment' articulated in 'the idea and materiality of the "national frontier," premised on a notion of the nation as a territorially and demographically circumscribed entity' that blurs 'the vocabularies of nationality and race' (Mongia 2018: 113).

This paved the way to altering the definition and status of British subjecthood throughout the Commonwealth. The British response was not to follow suit and create a national citizenship of its own. The British government instead adopted the 1948 British Nationality Act (BNA), which introduced 'citizenship' for the first time in British law, but this was a multi-national, imperial Commonwealth citizenship. The BNA 1948 created four categories: two foundational categories of Citizen of the United Kingdom and Colonies (CUKC) and Citizens of Independent Commonwealth Countries (CICC), along with a further two categories that received less if any attention in Parliament: British subjects without citizenship (BSWC), and British protected persons (BPP). It is worth noting that the establishment of CICCs was a *pre-emptive move* to include individuals from countries whose independence was forthcoming (e.g. Ceylon, India, Pakistan; Hansen 2000: 46). The Act ensured that individuals fitting into any of its two main categories enjoyed 'broadly the same rights' as British subjects: freedom to enter the UK and secure employment, and in the case of citizens from Old Dominions, 'to register as British citizens after a year's residence' (Hansen 2000: 46).

The rationale was to prioritise the Commonwealth which, after the Second World War, expanded to include newly or potential independent countries that were part of the by now dismantling British empire. Economic, national and international political interests supported this approach that established, in theory at least, a distinction between the Commonwealth and the empire, but where the Commonwealth ensured Britain's strong position in the international arena. Thus, from the British policy-makers' perspective, the issue was to preserve a common ground shared by member countries, even while countries adopted national citizenship laws as their primary status.

The government of the time celebrated its expanded Commonwealth citizenship as multi-racial, multi-national, multilingual in nature (Karatani 2003: 112).[8] However, Commonwealth citizenship is not the same as common citizenship and Old Commonwealth countries such as Canada rejected the principle of reciprocity that the latter entails, refusing to open their borders and grant citizenship to people from New Commonwealth countries, namely India (Karatani 2003: 119; also El-Enany 2020: esp. Chapter 1). In contrast, India favoured common citizenship over Commonwealth citizenship because the latter is founded on subjecthood to the Crown and symbolises oppression (Karatani 2003: 123). As a result of these tensions between republican and monarchic conceptions, Commonwealth citizenship was not based on rights and obligations (Karatani 2003: 125). Member countries declared Commonwealth citizenship as nothing more than a name and evidence of their shared membership to the Commonwealth. In Britain, however, the common status was understood by many policy-makers as 'British subjecthood under a different name' (Karatani 2003: 119). In this sense, the BNA 1948 was 'a fundamentally backward-looking document reaffirming the status quo as it had existed for decades' (Hansen 2000: 35). Based on the distinction between citizens and aliens,[9] the BNA 1948 gave citizens full rights in the UK, 'while aliens possessed discretionary and alienable privileges' (Hansen 2000: 101) – although property ownership continued to protect some aliens against the loss of legal privileges or status.

Post-war Britain saw a shortage of labour in industries crucial to post-war recovery – coal mining, textiles and construction – and reconstruction relied heavily on foreign labour sources. In the years following the arrival of over 800 passengers from the Caribbean on the Empire Windrush in 1948,[10] the government sought to control the movement of Commonwealth immigrants ostensibly out of concern for the strains on the housing market and the dangers of racial tensions. Governments of the 1960s and early 1970s adopted a sequence of laws that created tighter immigration controls for Commonwealth citizens. The Commonwealth Immigrant Act 1962 (CIA) established the significance of the *issuing authority* of one's passport. In short, those born in the UK, those holding a passport issued in the UK or the Republic of Ireland, or their dependants, were not subject to immigration control and continued to enjoy the rights and privileges of CUKC's as enshrined in the 1948 BNA. This was a defining moment that preserved the idea of common ground among Commonwealth member countries and subjects, while using immigration control as a device that began to distinguish between Old Commonwealth (OCW), New Commonwealth (NCW) and aliens.

The distinction between OCW and NCW was further entrenched in the CIA 1968, in response to East African countries establishing their own 'national citizenship' after independence, to which only people of African descent were entitled. For example, Kenya established citizenship by descent after becoming independent in 1963, giving all 'non-Africans' – a great majority of whom were Asians – two years to apply for Kenyan citizenship, and dual citizenship was not allowed (Hansen 2000: 158). This further meant that CUKC passports issued by the colonial governor – and therefore subject to immigration control – were from independence issued by the High Commissioner '*under the direct authority* of the British government' (Hansen 2000: 171; emphasis original), and therefore *not* subject to immigration control (also Karatani 2003: 159). With pressure mounting on them, Kenyan Asians began travelling to the UK and by early 1967, approximately 1,000 were arriving each month (Hansen 2000: 159). The CIA 1968 was directly intended to curb the immigration of Asians from East Africa by adding the criteria of a 'qualifying connection' with the UK: 'only individuals, or their children or grandchildren, born, naturalized, or adopted in the United Kingdom could enter the country' (Hansen 2000: 163). In 1971, amid the crisis caused by Idi Amin's coup in Uganda and subsequent expulsion of tens of thousands of Asians,[11] the 'qualifying connection' was later thickened through the concept of *patriality* enshrined in the Immigration Act 1971 (IA), which limited the right of abode in the UK to individuals whose parents were born in the UK (this was extended to grandparents in 1973). This law was intended to secure access for CUKCs from the OCW, while denying it to those from other Commonwealth countries (Hansen 2000: 195; also Karatani 2003).

To be sure, colonial relations and anti-colonial struggles are integral to the development of citizenship in Britain in the post-war years. The reluctance of Britain to undertake a full constitutional change and to instead adjust its nationality laws in 1948 came from concerns about maintaining its status as an imperial power on the international stage. A noteworthy assumption of policy-makers of the period was that a 'British citizenship' would organically develop as the *remainder* of post-imperial Britain, that is, once colonies acquired independence and their residents would replace their CUKC with their respective national citizenship of an independent Commonwealth country

(Hansen 2000: 167). The assumption proved to be mistaken and came to a head when Asians fled East African countries to seek entry to the UK. In the post-war period leading up to 1981, a cumulative definition of *citizenship by racist exclusion* was sutured in law and ultimately became the foundation of British citizenship in 1981. Indeed, the 1971 Act was a key step in equating British citizenship with whiteness: in 1971, a person born in Britain was 98 per cent likely to be white (El-Enany 2020: 4).

Enter British citizenship

While the above sequence of legal acts was taking place, debates about British citizenship in the 1970s grew, along with concerns about the lack of clarity or 'positive content' (Karatani 2003: 179; also Hansen 2000) about what UK citizenship stands for, but more specifically, about who can enter the country. Repealing the BNA 1948 but building on the IA 1971, the BNA 1981 established British citizenship as a legal category and firmly connected the right of abode and citizenship to each other. It thereby significantly restricted *jus soli*[12] in favour of *jus sanguinis* by conferring British citizenship exclusively to those born in the UK whose 'mother or father is a British citizen or settled in the United Kingdom' (British Nationality Act 1981, para. 1(1): p. 1), in a gesture that ended the restriction on paternal descent and extended it to include maternal descent. However, this also comes with the restriction that the child be 'legitimate', that is that their parents must be married (section 47(1)(2)) and, in cases where the father has British citizenship, marriage is the only way for the relationship between a child and their father to be considered 'legitimate' (section 50(9)). The law changed on 1 July 2006, enabling children born *after* that date to acquire British citizenship 'through a British or settled man, whether or not he was married to the child's mother' (Home Office 2019b: 5), leaving those born before 1 July 2006 subject to the original BNA 1981 definition of legitimate fatherhood. Aside from the gendered and heteronormative ideas of legitimate human reproduction that the law entrenches and validates, it is noteworthy how some historical legal acts are allowed to endure in law, while others are disabled – such as the BNA 1948 that recognised those now known as 'the Windrush generation' as *citizens* of the UK and colonies (see Introduction). In both cases, a 'logic of facilitation', in the words of Rhadika Mongia, is superseded by a 'logic of constraint' (2018: 19) that segregates migration streams along racialised and heterosexist, patriarchal lines.

With regards to naturalisation, the 1981 Act maintains the requirements established in the BN & SA Act 1914: 'good character', being of 'sound mind' and an 'adequate' knowledge of the English language – to which Welsh or Scottish Gaelic were added. The Act also adds residency requirements that confirm that an applicant's principle home is in the UK. BNA 1981 also includes a section on the deprivation of citizenship on the basis of a fraudulent application, being sentenced for a criminal offence in any country in the five years prior to the application, disloyalty to the Crown, or acting as or engaging with an enemy alien (British Nationality Act 1981, section 40).

While the BNA 1981 formally separated naturalisation and immigration controls, in effect, it followed the strict immigration rules adopted in IA 1971 with regards to immigrants from the NCW, but under a different guise (Karatani 2003: 183): *British* citizenship is now bound to Britain, and the right to reside in Britain is bound to descent. Some entitlements associated with Commonwealth citizenship remain, such as the right to vote in local and national elections, but Commonwealth citizens with no 'real connection' with the UK – defined now through descent – are subject to immigration control. Moreover, and as Bridget Anderson (2013) reminds us, immigration and nationality remain closely connected through residential requirements which, in turn, will be restricted through immigration control: different visa statuses allow for different lengths of stay in the UK, which means that not all immigrants can accumulate the five-year residency required for naturalisation. As Anderson puts it, 'the residential requirement ... enables immigration control to do the dirty work of citizenship' (2013: 103).

This comparatively late arrival of British citizenship is understood by some scholars as the consequence of a combination of attachment to imperial (later Commonwealth) power and prestige and lack of foresight about the effects of decolonisation (Hansen 2000; Karatani 2003). Others focus on how the history of citizenship in Britain reveals the role of the law in hardening the connection between race and citizenship (Dummett and Nicol 1990; Anderson 2013). As argued above, in the years leading up to 1981, British citizenship developed by racist exclusion, and this laid the foundations for the BNA 1981.[13] But the BNA 1981 was also addressing a concern about the contradictions surrounding nationality law and its perceived misalignment from immigration legislation. By creating the status of British citizenship and separating it from the colonies for the first time (Hansen 2000: 213), the Act *citizenised Britain*: it redressed the country's 'citizenship deficit' and tooled it with a national citizenship tied to genealogical blood lines and ancestry which is firmly sutured to territory.

Enter citizenisation: the current integration and naturalisation legislation

With British citizenship established, the task became to citizenise *Britons* and 'migrants' seeking to naturalise – that is, to 'make' them good citizens through a range of education and integration measures. A unique feature of the British citizenisation[14] measures aimed at migrants is that they were inspired by the citizenship curriculum put in place in English schools in 2002, and both involved the same key architects.[15]

Guided by New Labour's 'active citizenship' agenda,[16] the citizenship curriculum in schools was part of a shift towards greater emphasis on the duties of citizenship in the context of a declining welfare state. Failing citizenship was at the basis of the curriculum, which grew out of concerns about political disengagement and anti-social behaviour and which emphasised individual 'social and moral responsibility, community involvement and political literacy' (Advisory Group on Citizenship 1998: 8, 11 *inter alia*). Indeed, the authors of the final report of the Advisory Group on Citizenship commissioned by David Blunkett MP, then Secretary of State for Education and Employment, recognised the importance of citizenship education 'at a time when government is attempting a shift of emphasis between, on the one hand, state welfare provision and responsibility and, on the other, community and individual responsibility' (Advisory Group on Citizenship 1998: 10). In this model, inequalities and the role of the state and market forces in facilitating political disengagement do not figure, and citizenship becomes a skill that prepares individuals to 'make themselves *effective* in public life' (Advisory Group on Citizenship 1998: 13; emphasis added). The Advisory Group stressed the notions of 'active' and 'participative' citizenship that separate the civic realm of citizenship from the individual realm of identity. For Bernard Crick who chaired the Advisory Group, the citizenship curriculum recommended by the group is deliberately *not* about national identity. Rather, citizenship here is about 'a skill, a knowledge, an attitude for citizenship' (cited in Kiwan 2013b: 33), in a move towards the 'skillification' of citizenship discussed in Chapter 1.

While citizenship and nationality were kept separate in the national curriculum, they were explicitly linked in the revised citizenship naturalisation process, which was laid out in the White Paper on nationality, immigration and asylum (Home Office 2002) and subsequently enshrined in the 2002 Nationality, Immigration and Asylum Act (NIA). But the notion of citizenship as a skill, a knowledge and an attitude was retained and fed into a shift in defining citizenship as something to *become* rather than as a status to *acquire* (Anderson 2013; Ní Mhurchú 2014).

Conceived in the aftermath of the civil disturbances in Northern England in the summer of 2001,[17] the new British naturalisation process was established out of concerns about integration, the 'weakness' of community cohesion and the need to 'rebuild a sense of common citizenship'.

> The reports into last summer's disturbances in Bradford, Oldham and Burnley painted a vivid picture of fractured and divided communities, lacking a sense of common values or shared civic identity to unite around. The reports signalled the need for us to foster and renew the social fabric of our communities, and rebuild a sense of common citizenship, which embraces the different and diverse experiences of today's Britain. (Home Office 2002: 10)

Cast as part of the solution to these issues, the more formalised naturalisation process was set up as an attempt to engage applicants more fully in the process which had hitherto been completed by postal application.

> The acquisition of British nationality is [up until 2001] a bureaucratic exercise, with almost no effort made to engage new members of the community with the fundamentals of our democracy and society. (Home Office 2002: 11)

Citizenship and/as integration entered the British political and policy scenes at the point of 'weakness' that many countries associate with the failures of multiculturalism (Löwenheim and Gazit 2009: 148–149). 'Community cohesion and commonality of citizenship is weak. Too many of our citizens are excluded from meaningful participation in society' (Home Office 2002: 10). But as the historical account above suggests, the idea that citizenship in Britain is weak was raised in various ways by past governments and policy-makers, with regards to concerns about a general lack of clarity about who belongs to the United Kingdom, who has a right of entry or, now, who has the skills and attitudes necessary for 'active' citizenship. However, I argue elsewhere (Fortier 2013) that the presumed weakness of citizenship in Britain distracts us from the state's own construction of certain migrants, as well as certain citizens, as 'strong' and others as 'weak' and thus as the subjects of the state's attention, monitoring and surveillance.

The NIA 2002 reformalises the link between immigration status and nationality by connecting nationality and settlement. Specifically, it does so by making naturalisation part and parcel of the integration agenda. In his foreword to the White Paper, David Blunkett made it clear that 'those coming into our country have duties that they need to understand and which facilitate their acceptance and integration' (Home Office 2002: n.p.). By 'preparing people for citizenship by promoting language training and education for citizenship' (Home Office 2002: 11), the new process effectively connects cultural dispositions, skills and knowledge with both a duty to integrate and access to citizenship, and the view is that new citizens will not only be better prepared, but that they will be more culturally and socially oriented towards British society and values. The government White Paper on nationality, immigration and asylum clearly stated its intent to develop an ESOL curriculum that would include some citizenship content because it deemed the curriculum at the time to be 'context-free' and in need of 'a specific citizenship context' (Home Office 2002: 33). Thus, the first study guide (Home Office 2007) and the citizenship materials for ESOL learners (NIACE and LLU 2010 [2006]) teach us about national and regional languages, religions, customs and habits, and ethnic make-up, in a bid for applicants to learn about the national culture. Subsequent revisions of the citizenship test under the Conservative-led coalition government 'put British history and culture at the heart of it' (Cameron 2011c) and were explicitly designed against the welfare state in favour of 'participative' citizenship embedded in a 'community of values' (Anderson 2013). Then Minister for Immigration Mark Harper said in 2013: 'The new book rightly focuses on values and principles at the heart of being British. Instead of telling people how to claim benefits it encourages participation in British life' (BBC 2013). Citizenship, here, is not an abstract legal status: it is clearly ethnicised and culturalised through a thickening of citizenship grounded in shared British values. As a technology of repair designed at enhancing cohesion, the White Paper and NIA 2002 emphasises becoming a citizen and the *becoming citizen* whose citizenship skills and attitudes are deemed fitting with the national community of value. Subsequent chapters in this book will detail the ways in which the attachment of British citizenship to a set of values becomes the benchmark against which the value of migrants and new citizens is assessed.

The point I wish to make at this stage is that the NIA 2002 and the White Paper shored up and solidified this idea of British values in the face of migration. The cohesion agenda casts migration – in the form of 'diversity' (see Kostakopoulou 2008; Fortier 2010; Anderson 2013) – as both a threat to and constitutive of British society. In this context, the assertion of citizenship in the form of tests and ceremonies serves to present it as stable and devoid of its historical and constitutive uncertainty and sketchiness. At the same time, citizenship is presented as under threat as a result of immigration which is the cause of poor cohesion and racism. Like policy-makers before him, David Blunkett defended immigration control as a means to reduce racism: 'Having a clear, workable and robust nationality and asylum system is the pre-requisite to building the security and trust that is needed. Without it, we cannot defeat those who would seek to stir up hate, intolerance and prejudice' (Home Office 2002: Foreword – n.p.).

Finally, the NIA 2002 extended the criteria for the deprivation of citizenship to include actions that are 'seriously prejudicial to the vital interests' of the United Kingdom or British Overseas Territories (NIA 2002, ch. 41, part 1, parag. 4: p. 3). Later amendments expanded the Secretary of State's power to deprive a person of their citizenship: first, the Immigration, Asylum and Nationality Act (IAN)

2006 gave the Secretary of State the power to deprive someone of their British citizenship if it was 'conducive to the public good', but not if this rendered the person stateless. Then the 2014 Immigration Act removed this restriction if the Secretary of State is satisfied that a person's 'conduct [is] seriously prejudicial to vital interests of the UK' (Immigration Act 2014, para. 66: p. 57).[18]

Thus, the citizenisation process examined in this volume is closely tied to *de*citizenisation: the sequence of amendments to British citizenship law often came with the extension of state powers to deprive someone of their citizenship. Likewise, citizenisation casts migrant applicants as 'noncitizens' as it is steeped in geographical imaginaries about where 'good citizenship' exists and 'takes place': 'here' but not 'there'.

Conclusion

The bounded 'national' British citizenship that exists today cannot be extricated from its imperial and colonial history. This is a citizenship that has always been and remains 'thin' in terms of any legally binding constitutional rights (cf. Low 2000; Heater 2006; Yeo 2018), but which was gradually 'thickened' in terms of genealogical, ethnoracial and cultural content. The history of British citizenship developed through a set of 'negative freedoms from [Crown or state] interference rather than positive rights to enjoy certain privileges' (Isin and Turner 2007: 6); for example, 'endenisation' was a means for aliens to avoid state interference in access to property or exempting imperial subjects from restrictions on their movements (Karatani 2003).

British citizenship historically grew through what we now call 'immigration policy'; indeed, one immigration lawyer describes British citizenship as 'essentially a form of immigration status' (Yeo 2018). Freedom of movement was for a long time a political principle of the empire, but as the empire grew, so did the movement of people and the racialised distinction between desirable and undesirable subjects. Marginalised subjects and marginalised territories are central to the historically shifting and reconfigured borders of the empire, the Commonwealth, the nation and the citizen. In addition, changing categorisations of persons exempt from or subject to restrictions of movement and, later, the right of abode – from subject to citizen, from aliens to migrants (cf. Anderson 2013; El-Enany 2020) – were shaped through emergent ideas of the liberal individual capable of reason and property that *took hold* of modern conceptions of citizenship. Furthermore, integral to the development of liberal ideas of the political individual and universal citizenship is the history of sciences of racial and gendered differences. The combination of these forces crystallised into geographical imaginaries that, as Chakrabarty suggests, gradually tethered citizenship to territory, in a *placing* of citizenship through racist exclusions that lie at the basis of the definition of British citizenship in 1981. Later developments that follow international trends in skillifying citizenship as knowledge and attitude, take hold of it as something, or rather *someone*, to become, rather than as something to acquire.

Citizenship *took place* in ways that could have refuted accepted understandings of citizenship as bounded to a single territory, but that instead precipitated national-territorial bounded citizenships. Imperial and Commonwealth citizenship were and remain transnational, and citizenship continues to *take place* within the global state system that regulates the mobility of people. The heterogenous geographies of citizenship set the grounds for imaginative geographies of citizenship that shape citizenisation practices today. For a large majority of the men and women I met in the course of my study, acquiring British citizenship means mobility as well as providing a sense of safety. The British passport facilitates visa-free access to a large number of countries and this appeals to many applicants from poorer countries whose passport does not open as many borders. The share of citizenships granted to EU nationals increased from 12 per cent in 2016 (Blinder 2018) to 30 per cent in 2018, in spite of the fact that they make up 60 per cent of non-UK citizens (Fernandez-Reino and Sumption 2020) – arguably as a result of Brexit. Migrants from poorer and less stable countries tend to naturalise more than those from EU or other richer countries. Additional reasons might include the high fees that non-EU migrants must pay to renew their visas and leave to remain.

In contrast to what policy-makers and politicians thought when adopting the BNA 1948, British citizenship did not organically grow as the remainder of decolonisation – that is, as the result of the disappearance of common citizenship once all former colonies acquired independence and established separate national citizenships. Rather, the development of British citizenship was hastened through a series of decisions, negotiations between Britain and its colonies, that combined logics of facilitation with logics of constraint precipitated by racialised migration and movement of subjects within the empire. Therefore, British citizenship *took time* not in the sense of taking too long to come to fruition. Rather, the history reveals the heterogenous temporalities of citizenship within the empire as Dominions and colonies acquired independence. But it also reveals its different iterations – the different forms it took – as historical, political and economic relations changed.

However, what *did* remain is 'difference' in *taking hold* of citizenship. If the current nationality act ensures that naturalised citizens have equal rights to 'natural-born' citizens, 'difference' is the remainder that is consigned to the personal and private realms. Susan Bibler Coutin (2003: 521) writes of the US naturalisation as a system that erases differences, which 'become remainders that lead the authenticity of naturalized identities to be questioned', but which in turn 'enable migrant groups to use ethnicity and nationality as a basis for political organizing'. In the UK what also ties into the remainders of difference are their racialised and imperial logics that endure – while imperial histories are forgotten (Williams 2020) – not in the form of replicas, but in the form of the logics and techniques of racism that (re)naturalise inequalities in seemingly raceless policies – for example through the migratisation of white-bodied Europeans who are racialised as 'other' by language (Chapter 4).

Furthermore, a widely neglected aspect of accounts of British citizenship is its embeddedness in, and reproduction of, heteronormative and heterosexist norms. It is noteworthy that it was until 2006 that children born of unmarried British or 'settled' fathers, or indeed recognised as a man's or 'second female parent's' child under the Human Fertilisation and Embryology Acts 1990 and 2008 (Home Office 2019b: 5), could acquire British citizenship. As the chapters that follow will show, life in the waiting room is a space where citizenship takes hold of such remainders of race, gender and sexuality (and class or status) in a variety of ways. However, the remainders of difference also open up ways of *rethinking* citizenship, 'migranthood' and their relationship as they meet in the waiting toom of citizenship.

One significant but neglected aspect of the waiting room of citizenship is how meetings between actors are often mediated by documents. The scene and chapter that follow consider the *generative capacities* of documents, that is, how individuals engage with, relate and respond to documents as they are produced, exchanged, negotiated, transformed and moved by and between individuals and within the waiting room.

Scene 2

Documents, stories, pictures

It's a crisp bright November morning, day three of my week with the nationality team at Stadlow Council. That day, the Council was hosting a training session about the new rules and requirements for Settlement on the basis of marriage (SET(M)). The training was led by two UK Visas and Immigration (UKVI) case workers, and it was open to registrars from other local authorities who offer Settlement Checking Services (SCS) for SET(M) applications. Twenty-four people attended from at least six councils. The training session lasted the better part of the day.

One of the trainers distributes a copy of the SET(M) version 10/2013: 'Application for indefinite leave to remain in the UK as the partner of a person present and settled in the UK and a biometric immigration document'. There are jokes and banter about the payment details being at the very front of the form. 'Do they get a refund if they fail?', someone asks. 'No they don't', is the answer.

The trainers go through the application form in detail, covering each question and sub-question, each item, each type of documentary evidence needed to prove that the relationship is genuine: from photos, to passports, correspondence, mortgage statements, ESOL certificates and so on. An extensive discussion takes place about how and when registrars can be satisfied with the documentary evidence that couples provide. Does this or that type of evidence count? What if the bills are only in one spouse's name? And what about certificates from 'bogus' language schools? As the UKVI trainers painstakingly go through the different types of ESOL certificates, a registrar exclaims: 'There are so many different types of paper, it's mental!' The trainer replies, 'Well that's where the ownership [i.e. 'onus'] is on the applicants, so the applicant needs to understand the requirements and that's where if they don't, the ownership is upon them to make sure that documents are right'.

The registrar's comment seems to capture a more general anxiety among the people in the room about documentary evidence and the burden they feel is on them to make a judgement, despite the trainer's repeated insistence that: (1) registrars can call them any time they are in doubt and (2) it is up to the UKVI case workers to make the decision, and registrars will not be blamed if they send a fraudulent or failing application. Still, registrars come back again and again: what about this scenario, what about that one? What if there is not enough evidence to cover each of the 24 months of the two-year period? How much of a gap do we allow? Three months? Six months? At one point, one registrar surmises: 'I appreciate when you arrive in the country it does take a little while to establish yourself and that you might not have evidence for the first months, but these people know that they are going to be applying for settlement two years down the line, so if that was me, my priority would be to get myself onto the system the moment I arrive into that country'. The UKVI trainer responded: 'You have to appreciate also that some people come from a country where they don't have that responsibility [to pay the bills]', and that it takes time to understand how things work in a new country. 'But that's the thing', another registrar says, 'what if for the first six months they have absolutely nothing at all and it's like 25 per cent of the [two-year] period?' To which the trainer says: 'Say, for example, a woman might not have documents in her name, she might not pay utility fees because everything is paid for by the man. In that situation we do go "ok" …'.

'And how many documents do you want?' Between 6 and 20 is the answer. However, the trainer adds: 'I wouldn't be too specific. It's got to be for me a kind of average across the board because you know in some situations, not everybody is going to have the documentation that you would like to see'.

Registrar: 'So just to re-cap what you said and I'm filling in 6 to 20 pieces of information, and whereas now I would prioritise looking for things in joint names, you're saying that "no, [evidence should include both] individual and joint names"'. Trainer: 'In the eyes of the case worker I have to build up a picture, "are these people actually together?" Like I said to you before I would be more inclined to think that there is something a little bit dodgy if everything is in joint names. I like to see a cross-reference to say that "yes you as an individual you've got your own thing going on as well". It may be a letter to say they have registered with a catalogue, even something as small as that, it's got their name on it, it's got their address on it, it's got a date on it. You've got to be fixed and all I'm saying to you is try to broaden that horizon a bit, so like build up a picture.'

3

The documented citizen

An image that has stuck in my mind from observing settlement or nationality checking appointments at local councils is that of applicants walking in with plastic bags, briefcases or large bulging manila folders full of documentary evidence in support of their application for Settlement on the basis of Marriage (SET(M)) or for naturalisation. A vast array of document types circulate in the waiting room of citizenship: application forms, Home Office letters, government certificates (birth, marriage/civil partnership, naturalisation), diplomas, language tests, language certificates, citizenship test certificates, checklists, policy documents, personal letters, certified letters, identity cards, photographs, passports, driving licenses, P60s, mortgage statements, personal correspondence, bank statements, council tax statements, TV licences, utility bills, proofs of subscriptions, membership cards and more. It is no surprise that a registrar at the SET(M) training session in Scene 2 exclaimed, 'There are so many different types of paper, it's mental!'

This chapter examines how documents function in the waiting room of citizenship. Documents are a good starting point to address the main question of this book: how are citizens and 'migrants' made and unmade? The chapter shows not only how migrants are (re)migratised or citizenised through documentation, but also how citizens can be citizenised or migratised as well. Existing research in migration charts the performative, formative and affective character of documents such as forms or letters (Navaro-Yashin 2007; Darling 2014; Gill 2014; Horton and Heyman 2020). Some draw on new materialism to highlight the intimate connection between material and discursive formations of phenomena – for example, understanding 'the migrant' or 'citizenship' outside of a strictly discursive frame of reference (Darling 2014: 485). Such a material-discursive approach (Barad 2003) clears a space for examining the effects of non-human matter in shaping relations, exclusionary boundaries and 'realities' such as 'British citizenship', 'the migrant', 'the spouse', but also 'the state' or 'the citizen' themselves.

My objective in this chapter is to take seriously the ways in which the numerous 'acts of citizenship' required of citizenisation policies must be understood as enacted by both humans and material artefacts such as documents (Hughes and Forman 2017). This is not to say, however, that documents are unmediated objects that have inherent power – 'thing power' in Jane Bennett's phrase (2010). Nor is my objective to examine how the material environment itself is shaped and reshaped through what Karen Barad calls 'intra-actions' (2003). Rather, my aim is to consider documents as objects that animate actions, subjects, feelings, but that are also animated in different ways as they circulate in the various antechambers of the waiting room of citizenship. Put simply, the chapter examines documents 'as in some sense "living"; ... as the product of relational practices, but also as productive of social relations' as Shona Hunter puts it (2008: 507).

How do requirements of documented intelligibility put different actors in different reading or writing positions, in different relationships to each other and in different relationships to the state? Registrars are asked to *check for* the state, applicants *narrate themselves into* the state and case workers *read for* the state – one of the two UK Visas and Immigration (UKVI) case workers running the training session described in Scene 2 said, 'I don't make the rules. I just enforce them'.[1] However, checking, narrating and reading are not specific to any given role, nor are they conducted in a monolithic manner: registrars must also read applications, assess their accuracy and interpret what counts as a 'legible' account. Applicants, for their part, read the law (or have someone do it for them) and check the accuracy of their 'picture'[2] as they collate relevant evidence. While UKVI case workers do not feature in this book, they are the imagined recipients in the minds of applicants and registrars, the ones who must be satisfied with the 'picture' sent to them. All in all, what registrars and applicants are doing is *curating* others or themselves as potential/desirable citizens. They gather, select, organise, present a range of documents and forms in order to produce the accurate picture of a spouse, resident or refugee.

The implementation of the current citizenship and settlement application process introduced new roles for local government registrars (see Scene 1). First, they conduct citizenship ceremonies (since 2004). Second, between 2005 and late 2018 local council registry offices offered Nationality Checking Services (NCS) and Settlement Checking Services (SCS) to applicants for citizenship or SET(M) respectively. In contrast to their statutory functions related to registering births, marriages, civil partnerships and deaths, and to officiating civil marriage/partnership ceremonies, NCS and SCS put registrars more squarely in the position of intermediaries[3] between the applicants and the state as their task was to check that applications were complete and accurate and advise applicants if not,[4] while they were empowered to produce certified photocopies of passports, marriage certificates or the like. Registrars conducting NCS or SCS did not have any decision-making power and could not provide legal advice, but they could provide guidance about completing an application.

When applications for settlement and citizenship were all digit-ised in 2018, NCS and SCS were made redundant, removed from local governments and replaced by the UK Visa and Citizenship Application Services (UKVCAS) managed by Sopra Steria, a government commercial partner. Guidance and support services were assigned to local libraries, sub-contracted by Sopra Steria. These services include telephone or face-to-face support (in a library or at home) for completing the online application form and submitting biometric information. Like registrars before them, librarians conducting UKVCAS do not have the authority to provide immigration advice. A noteworthy difference is that the UKVCAS added a layer to the dispersed governance of citizenisation: while registrars could contact the Home Office directly for advice when conducting an NCS or SCS, librarians contact the Sopra Steria helpline for any guidance. Sopra Steria also feeds libraries with any relevant legal updates.[5] It is worth adding that registrars continue to run citizenship ceremonies: in that role, they bestow citizenship *on behalf of* the state by handing the Certificate of Naturalisation to new citizens in the presence of the watchful eye of the monarch's photograph.

This chapter is not about the role of registrars *per se,* nor is it about bureaucratic processing systems. Rather, it is concerned with the *generative capacities* of documents, that is, how individuals engage with, relate to and respond to documents as they are produced, exchanged, negotiated, transformed and moved by and between individuals and within the waiting room of citizenship. Registrars' experiences are telling of broader matters arising when local government employees – registrars or librarians – are asked to act as intermediaries of the state. For example, Scene 2 intimates at the registrars' discomfort with the discretion, albeit limited, that they have in assessing the suitability of the evidence to submit in support of SET(M) applications. But the registrars' anxiety is also telling of their expectation that the state provide them with adequate tools that will allow them to make decisions about authentic or fraudulent documents, and indeed about authentic or fraudulent relationships (see Fortier 2017a).

Applicants also experience anxiety. I argue elsewhere (Fortier 2017a), drawing on Raymond Williams (1977), that anxiety is the dominant structure of feeling in the citizenisation process, where applicants are invariably anxious about the outcome but also about the continuously shifting grounds of citizenisation requirements. Applicants navigate the uncertainty through a combination of determination, resourcefulness and resources (Prabhat 2018: 216), sometimes at a very high financial or personal cost. The skills required to understand the requirements are a challenge to anyone, and those with poorer English fluency might seek assistance from acquaintances, friends or family, or from legal professionals. Beyond this, what all applicants experience is uncertainty and anxiety, albeit to different degrees and with different stakes. This is an anxiety that is constitutive of the state–citizen relationship (Honig 2001; Salter 2008; Weber 2008). In turn, the state is also anxious about separating the deserving from the underserving (Fortier 2017a). These anxious states combine with states of desire – the desirability of applicants is indexed by different measurements, while at the same time, the citizenisation process ultimately positions the applicant as desiring: as the one who desires 'us' (Honig 2001; Fortier 2017a). But what does it mean to 'desire'? How is that documented?

The introduction of the current citizenisation process means that applicants encounter 'the state' more directly and more often than they would have done prior to 2004, when the application was done by post. Put simply, applying for British citizenship (or settlement) puts in motion a range of social relations and interactions between intermediaries of the state and applicants; interactions that are lived, embodied, felt, reasoned, processed and documented by those involved, in ways that exceed the kind of coherence that policy, as an instrument of the state, is expected to confer onto its subjects. More than 'just' exploring how citizenship, citizens and migrants are made or unmade, this chapter also examines how they are 'made up' through documents, in the sense of how they are imagined, fictionalised or actualised *through the curation* as documents are handled and exchanged by state intermediaries or applicants. The citizenisation process requires a modicum of making up a story that fits with the imagined idea of a legitimate applicant and what it should look like on paper. That story can be in part a fiction, if only because it is only a selected fragment of one's life, and because curation requires certain forms of story-telling and disciplines stories into expected patterns. In turn, registrars or UKVI case workers might have suspicions that something is 'made up' in an application, or appears too good to be true, and so the default suspicion of the state always seems to be about how narratives are, or are not, 'made up' in a fictional sense.[6] At the same time, this chapter also touches on how the state itself, as well as state–citizen relations, are 'made up' (Cooper 2015; see Chapter 1), not only in the sense of how they are imagined, but also how they are enacted in ways that defeat the presumed coherence of the state and its alleged 'agents'.

What happens with the curation of documents, in those face-to-face encounters between state intermediaries and applicants where documents are processed, exchanged, handed over, filled out, read through and checked out? How does making a 'case', building a 'picture', come about in interactions that invariably abstract bodies, subjects and affect. How do the 'pictures' 'grasp' bodies, feelings, subjectivities?

The chapter addresses these questions in two sections. Section 1, 'Paper trails and traces', analyses how documents circulate in the waiting room of citizenship, and what they say and do about and to individuals. 'Paper trails and traces' first examines the relationship between documents and time: how documents are placed in the temporal sequence of bureaucratic time, while in turn, they punctuate and impact on the lives of applicants. The section then turns to documents as authoritative artefacts: for example, aesthetic features on government documents confer authority to documents. However, there are expectations of what state documents should look like and failures to live up to them can make some local officials feel let down. In turn, some documents leave traces and others do not. The way that the passport absorbs or erases traces of previous documents, for example, reveals more than may be initially thought about the contingency and fragility of birthright citizenship.

Section 2 examines the 'relational politics of curation'. It scrutinises the various encounters between registrars and applicants as they meet to curate applications for SET(M) or naturalisation, and it unpacks the power and status differentials that curatorial relations embed and are embedded in. The section covers three areas: first, curation means that documents exist in relation to other documents and acquire different meanings as they move in and out of different contexts. This 'inter-documentality' (Ahmed 2012) is integral to the governmentality of citizenship, where migrants are simultaneously obliged to 'give an account of themselves' (Butler 2005) and made responsible for understanding the law and responding to it as autonomous, entrepreneurial subjects. Second, along with documents, bodies can also become 'evidence', particularly when it comes to SET(M) applications and the fear of 'sham marriages'. In these cases, bodies are read for tell-tale signs of true or 'fake' love. Third, the multiple interpretations of legal requirements can create interpretive gaps. These interpretive gaps are not only about the terms of law. They can also be about different understandings, expectations and experiences of the (affective) relations that the curatorial relations engender.

The chapter concludes with considerations of how citizenship takes place, takes time and takes hold in the curation of documents, as 'pictures' are produced and moved around in the waiting room of citizenship.

Paper trails and traces

Scene A
Back at the training session, the UKVI trainers are giving the example of couples who spend much time of the five-year spousal visa period living abroad for legitimate reasons such as work.

Trainer 2: If they have been outside of the UK for more than six months they need to let us know on the application form but there is no requirement in the rules for absence [i.e. there are no restrictions on absence].

Trainer 1: Yeah they can come in for the NCS and get out the next day again.

At which point a participant expresses his bemusement at the fact that 'they are applying for indefinite leave to remain in the country ... but they go down the route of staying out of the country'.

Trainer 2: As long as they can show that they are in the relationship that's all were interested in for SET(M). When they want to become British *that's* when you have to show that you want to be here; that's why we give indefinite leave to enter.

The trainers are clear that they are only interested in a specific fragment of people's lives, in this case, the genuineness of the spousal relationship, regardless of where they live or plan to live. Aoileann Ní Mhurchú theorises citizenship as *trace* in order to capture 'the increasingly momentary fragments of self through which citizenship can operate beyond the idea of a sovereign presenting subject that is included or excluded from the state' (2014: 13). The documentary evidence of life fragments must produce the 'pictures' required by law – they 'add *to*' pictures that might or might not 'add *up*' (Ní Mhurchú 2014: 209; emphasis added) to the complete sovereign subject wilfully choosing to acquire citizenship. But prior to that, individuals are placed on different routes and within different legal categories that mark them as different types of immigrants who are always fragmentary: the migrant worker is primarily a worker, the spouse is nothing other than a spouse, the refugee needs protection. Put simply, legal categories and documents are mutually generative (Anderson 2020).[7]

This section follows paper trails and traces in the making and un-making of the 'realities' of citizenship. As Herman Gray and Macarena Gómez-Barris (2010: 5) state, a 'sociology of the trace' is about attenuating 'the distance between observable social worlds and those things that are not easily found through methodologies that attempt to empirically account for social realities'. Citizenisation processes privilege such evidence-based methodologies that ultimately determine someone's fate. By following traces that documents leave behind, erase or carry, this section attends to what is brought to the fore and what is left behind by documents. The section looks at: the temporality of documents and how they place individuals in time; their generative effects on people's lives and bureaucratic practices, and their capacity to exert authority (or not). But more than that, the section also reveals the capacity of documents to de-animate and re-animate personal histories and genealogies and, in doing so, they expose the utter ephemerality of citizenship itself.

Documents, bureaucratic time and timed lives

Documents relate to one another in the sequential temporality dictated by bureaucratic time. There is a sequence of steps leading up to the acquisition of citizenship, and few can skip any of these steps. Documents succeed each other in a person's 'citizenisation journey'. For example, non-EU migrants enter on a visa, then apply for Indefinite Leave to Remain (ILR), then for citizenship. Each application requires a new collection of documents to be curated (more on this below), and each application becomes evidence used for the next step, culminating, for the successful applicant, in the certificate of naturalisation used for the passport application. The time needed to go from entry to citizenship will vary according to one's visa status, or in the case of Tier 1 Investor visas, according to the amount of money the migrant invests.

During SCS or NCS appointments, registrars will use checklists to ensure the completion of an application. In the case of SCS, the checklist directs the registrars' attention and brackets applicants' lives into specific periods of time and specific types of documentary evidence. At Stadlow Council, the SET(M) checklist included a page formatted into boxes (one per year) that are divided into 12 rows (each row = a month) with 3 columns (main applicant, spouse/partner, joint/both names). The checklist enables a schematic visualisation of the 'evidence' of cohabitation. Once compete, the checklist itself becomes evidence as it is slipped into the envelope to be sent to the UKVI. The checklist is evidence of evidence: it evidences that the registrar did their job, and it evidences the evidence that is included in the application.

While the checklist aligns documents in a timeline, documents themselves 'place' individuals *in time* and *in place*. In the case of SCS, documents are 'placed' according to a grid showing continuous cohabitation – therefore aligning *place and time* of residence. When it comes to applications for naturalisation, the documented applicant must ensure that they were physically present in the UK five years prior to the application and *on the same date* as the application is received by the Home Office. Missing the date by only one day will lead to rejection and loss of fees. At Stadlow Council, registrars have a 'delayed send' paper filing system where packed applications for naturalisation are organised by the right dispatch date to ensure that they arrive on the right date. Here, envelopes themselves become 'documentary evidence' with the post office stamp acting as proof of sending at the right time (Anderson 2020).

In this sense, documents are not only aligned on a timeline. Their circulation between agencies is also 'timed'. For example, registry offices receive Home Office information about 'new' citizens approximately two days before the new citizens receive their letters confirming their successful application and instructing them to call their local council to book a ceremony. This well-choreographed timing allows registrars to enter each individual on their system in advance of the phone call. At Stadlow, this means that when individuals call to book a ceremony, the registrar taking the call will pull up their information but also open a 'ceremony form' that is used for organising and planning the event, and they will enter the caller's details. This work at Stadlow is but one instance where 'documents breed more documents' (Anderson 2020: 76), but also where documents breed more labour for processing, storing, saving and aligning official and other bureaucratic documents.

As documents are 'timed', they also punctuate, periodise and shape people's lives (Darling 2014; Anderson 2019). The complex and often changing legal, policy, but also financial terrain within which individuals make their decisions encourages them to think and calculate in certain ways. Individuals become acutely aware of crucial dates, timelines and visa expiry dates. Joy and Robert spoke to me at length about Joy's complicated journey to ILR. She came to Britain from Thailand as Robert's fiancée and had just recently obtained ILR. They told me how they needed two extensions for Joy because she failed to meet the language requirements as a result of bad advice. As Robert explained:

> I knew in my head that it would take up to six month for the visa to go so we still registered for the course ... just carried on as normal

while you're applying for your visa, everything's just normal anyway, erm, or you're applying for an extension and I thought well if it comes back I can appeal it [...] I'd already looked all this up, and I thought if I appeal I can always book her on a four-day [ESOL – English for Speakers of Other Languages] course into Manchester on one of these quick courses, get her that piece of paper that says she can do it. But we didn't want to do that because it wasn't of any help and we wanted Joy to learn some, to get something out of it. So, we applied for the visa extension which, erm, which in about December was refused. So I appealed against it cos if her leave to remain and her extension was refused she'd have to go back to Thailand. So I appealed against this, got a letter back, yes, your appeal's been accepted. At that point I'd already spoke to Marianne [ESOL teacher] as well and Richard [ESOL curriculum manager] and they were both of the same opinion: why doesn't she do the ESOL test now?

Robert and Joy made calculations about the best strategies to secure Joy's legal right to remain and to remediate the bad advice they were given about fulfilling the 'knowledge of life and language' requirement that existed at the time. Joy was advised to take the citizenship test route rather than the ESOL route.[8] Having failed the former, they had to take a different tack and seek extensions to her visa and appeal against a first refusal. This was 'very very hard and stressful' for them. Joy said she couldn't sleep.

Like Paul, cited in Chapter 1, Robert and Joy became highly knowledgeable of the law and how to use it – they were *both* citizenised through their engagement with the state as 'citizen' and 'migrant' respectively. What is more, the lives of British citizens with foreign partners or spouses, like Robert and Paul, are intimately affected by migration control – sometimes with potentially tragic consequences (see Taylor 2019). But migration control also encroaches on their everyday. For example, Paul spoke about other kinds of calculations: when we met, he had already calculated the days lost between his spouse's imminent arrival from Thailand and the visa issue date in Bangkok.

And already from Tuesday [the date his wife's two-year visa starts] to Monday [when she arrives], that's six days she wasn't here out of the 90 [days that she is allowed to be out of the country in a year], and already you're having to think: well that leaves us 84 days, that's 12 weeks we can have instead of 13 weeks.

As a mobile British citizen, Paul is now contending with a life of controlled mobility, where every day counts if you plan to visit friends or family in other countries:

> you know, say we have a week left, so we can have a week there [e.g. in France] but then we have to get back, and if we miss that ferry, you know and come back at five past midnight instead of five to midnight, you know, I could see us getting into all that.

As Paul envisions his immediate future, he also comes to the stark realisation of how in the next few years he will not be secure in his own citizenship; in other words, Paul's sense of citizenship is being migratised.

For others, the circulation of documents and their expected arrival is experienced as serial interruptions and states of suspension: 'I was sitting around ten days waiting for that piece of paper', Nabaz told me. That 'piece of paper' was Nabaz's five-year Leave to Remain that would regularise his status as a Kurdish refugee from Iraq. He tried to express how long those ten days felt: 'Very hard, it's causing me heart attack!'

Nabaz's account says a lot about the affective charge of documents, even when they have not yet materialised. That 'piece of paper' was invested with anxious hope and brought relief when it finally came: 'there's no heart attack. Nothing, anything. It should be all ok'. But this was a momentary relief, because Nabaz went on to tell me about his current anxiety about getting 'indefinite' (ILR):

> visa finish, now apply for indefinite. My time, my life, everything on hold. My wife says it's OK now everything now OK you have got piece of paper don't be, sometimes say don't be like children. I'm not being children because this very hard. I hope, inshallah it will be OK.

Documents have an affective as well as a 'phantasmatic quality' (Navaro-Yashin 2007: 83) insofar as they have a broad imaginative purchase that is not external to a 'reality', but rather part and parcel of the reality of people's lives (J. Rose 1996; Navaro-Yashin 2002). The day following the court case where she was granted ILR, Joy arrived a bit late at her ESOL class, breaking the silence as she walked in beaming and declaring 'I got visa!', which prompted us to erupt in heartfelt applause. For Joy, that document meant everything, and brought her and Robert immeasurable relief as they could plan for a future. Joy was 'very very happy' for the 'safety, more security' it brought her knowing that she can stay and work in the UK.

For Nabaz, in contrast, the experience of unbearable waiting exemplifies the 'asynchronicities' that Bridget Anderson (2020) writes about, that is, the difference between subjective experiences of time and the bureaucratic time and timing of documents. Moreover, once Nabaz becomes a 'documented' migrant whose status is 'regularised', he remains on a temporary visa that can be revoked at any time. He moves into a state of 'permanent temporariness' (Anderson 2020: 83) that limits his capacity to imagine a future.

For Nabaz documents conjure a nervousness and fear of being expelled again, for he had been detained some years back and was returned to Germany where he first arrived from Iraq. The 'piece of paper' was more than the confirmation or rejection of his right to remain and therefore that which allowed him to imagine a future in this country. That document was emblematic of his relationship with the British government. Letters from the Home Office transmit more than information: they transmit authority and conjure mixed feelings of anxiety and desire. Sala, an Egyptian woman with British citizenship since 2016, spoke of her nervousness each time a letter from the Home Office came through her letter box: 'any letter from the Home Office, when I saw, I knew the envelopes and when I saw the logo I had to you know breathe, make sure that I had enough oxygen in me before I read the letters. So yeah, it's a complicated relationship'.

However, waiting does not mean passivity, inaction or lack of agency, even though for some it can have paralysing effects. Joy and Robert, Paul and Lily, as well as Nabaz and many others I met, might have felt a feeling of 'being in limbo', as Paul put it (see Chapter 1), while waiting for a 'piece of paper', but they were not standing still. Elizabeth Povinelli writes of the 'bracketing' of people's lives in the waiting rooms of government procedures. However, she argues, the 'bracketed' subjects:

> are *living* within these waiting rooms ... They *persist*. But they do not persist in the abstract. From the perspective of the dominant worlds, the condition in which they endure has the temporal structure of limbo – an edge of life located somewhere between given and new social positions and roles, and between the conditions of the past and

the promise of the future ... But from the perspective of the bracketed, the problem is how to endure the material conditions that compose their limbo. (Povinelli 2011: 77–78; second emphasis added)

The material conditions constitutive of the 'limbo' include the governance of mobility, materialised in documents. Paul sums up the contradictions of migration management when he says: 'having not wanted Lily to come into the UK, now that she has a visa, now it's almost as if they don't want her to leave again'. The control of people's movement is an integral part of citizenisation and enters into people's intimate or everyday lives. For example, all applicants for citizenship, including children under 18, must enrol their biometric details in order for their application to be complete (Home Office 2019a: 27). They receive a letter from the Home Office requesting them to fulfil this requirement within two weeks of the date on the letter. Moreover, the post offices offering this service are not always near one's home. For Sala, finding the time was made more difficult because she was caring for a very ill family member whose bedside she could not leave for any period of time exceeding 30 minutes. 'We were in [a city where her relative was in hospital], not going to travel to [another city nearby] to do this and leave her, and I was thinking there are things that are more important in life. But also, you don't want ... I wanted to make sure that I can also stay legally if she needs me [in future]'. Sala had to juggle with her mixed feelings about her priorities, ultimately acknowledging the authority of the state to determine her ability to stay in the country for her loved one. Just as the two-week deadline was coming up, she found a post office near the hospital that provided the biometric enrolment service. Documents can fix subjects in place and time: failing to be in the right place at the right time can have dramatic consequences in one's life. Indeed, refusal rates for naturalisation applications due to delays in replying to enquiries from the UKVI have significantly risen in recent years – from 6 per cent in 2013 (Blinder 2018) to 11 per cent in 2018 (Fernandez-Reino 2020). While we can only surmise on the reasons for these delays, Sala's situation intimates at the challenges that tight response times might pose for some. Documents here not only 'inscribe the authority of the state' (Darling 2014: 487) by conveying demands and requirements, they become tools of governance when the failure to supply them in time becomes grounds for rejection.

Documents are part of the broader infrastructural and bureaucratic process with which states 'grasp' their subjects (Torpey 2000: 11–12, 121) by fixing them in time and place, while they also remind applicants of the presence of the state in their lives, up to the very end of the citizenisation process. The confirmation of citizenship attribution comes with a requirement that the recipient contact their local authority within 14 days to book their attendance at the citizenship ceremony. This led Sala to remark: 'So it makes you think, you know? They make it so tight that if anything happens, and even after you get your citizenship you also have, you know, a limited time to register for the ceremony'.

Documents circulate and operate within bureaucratic time, while they also punctuate, interrupt or suspend individuals' experience of time and govern their mobility. I now turn to the lifespan of documents themselves, as they make, animate or de-animate and erase various traces: of authority, of previous documents, of personal histories and genealogies.

Documents as authoritative artefacts: traces of the state, erasing traces

The waiting room of citizenship is full of official documents that materialise the 'spectral presence' of the state (Das cited in Hull 2012: 260). The state is materialised and rendered visible on documents in logos, coats-or-arms, symbols, ministerial photos and signatures. These 'badges of authority' (Hodder 2000: 114) confer power to documents and artefacts, and performatively attest the authority of their originator to instruct and probe applicants or to proclaim and welcome new citizens.

These aesthetic features confer 'a persuasiveness of form' and elicit 'a sense of appropriateness' (Strathern cited in Hull 2012: 255). Indeed, there are expectations of what official documents should look like. Registrars from one local authority expressed their dislike of the 'horrible' paper envelopes that replaced glossier and sturdier folders handed out to new citizens at citizenship ceremonies, enclosing certificates of naturalisation and other Home Office documents.

Described as an 'abomination' by one registrar, the envelopes did not live up to what local officials expect of government documents for momentous occasions such as citizenship ceremonies. Their dismay is telling of what local officials do in the name of the state, and their expectations about state propriety. Thomas Blom Hansen and Finn Stepputat suggest that: 'The state not only strives to be a state for its citizen-subjects, it also strives to be a state for itself and is expected by populations, politicians, and bureaucrats to employ "proper" languages of stateness in its practices and symbolic gestures' (cited in Fuglerud 2004: 26). In the eyes of this registrar and her colleagues, it is not the authority of the state that is diminished here, but its duty of care towards new citizens who 'pay a lot of money' for their naturalisation. In addition, these registrars themselves felt aggrieved, 'let down' by the government and consider that this sort of lapse in propriety reflects badly on them: 'We're the public facing ones, we're the ones that have to present new citizens with that [sub-standard envelope]'.

The significance of having an appropriate cover for the certificate of naturalisation also comes from the significance of the ceremony and the certificate itself as the symbolic arrival point in the narrative arc of citizenisation. An arrival point where the certificate of naturalisation, and the passport that usually follows, absorbs all the traces left by previous paper trails. If, as Freeman and Maybin put it, 'All documents exist in time' (cited in Anderson 2020: 75), that temporality is always contingent and, as a result, their lifespan will vary. For example, the Home Office guide for naturalisation states that: 'We expect you to arrange to attend a ceremony within 3 months of receiving your invitation otherwise it will expire and you will have to re-apply for registration and pay a further processing fee' (Home Office 2019a: 31).

Applying for naturalisation or settlement means navigating a world of constant change: new rules, new forms, new processes, new costs (Byrne 2014: 110); so much so that even immigration lawyers find it difficult to keep up, as a retired immigration lawyer told me in an informal conversation (also Brooks 2016: viii). For this reason, many individuals I met resorted to legal professionals for assistance, which added an extra high cost to the already expensive process. In this context, navigating the Home Office webpages is itself a difficult endeavour for anyone who is not fluent in the national legal and bureaucratic languages, regardless of their English proficiency. One woman from Jamaica appeared at an NCS appointment at Stadlow Council with a form that was no longer in use; she had downloaded it in September, and the rules changed the following October while she was collating all the required documents. The woman was also confused about the language requirements: she produced a language fluency certificate but not a citizenship test. As a Jamaican national, she was exempt from the former but expected to complete the latter (see Chapter 4). The registrar kindly did not charge the woman for this NCS appointment and gave her guidance about how to proceed from here. Navigating and making sense of the application process takes time and, in some cases, rules change in that time and people get caught out.

There is a linear progression of citizenisation that is manifest in the different documents that succeed each other in one's journey. But unlike the form that is made redundant, other documents seemingly dissolve into the certificate of naturalisation and the 'passport', the latter conceived as the ultimate authoritative state confirmation of citizenship. Throughout the citizenisation process, applicants relate to the state largely through application forms, documentary evidence and correspondence, and each stage of the process results in documents that communicate the authority of an agency to confirm one's eligibility for a given legal status (e.g. the citizenship test certificate produced by a private test centre) or the authority of the state to confer one's legal status and, by extension, to regulate one's mobility. These documents are aligned in a linear progression, each replacing the previous one, marking each step of the 'journey' towards full citizenship. For example, an individual can accumulate the following: the citizenship test certificate, a language fluency certificate, the Home Office letter confirming ILR, the ILR stamp in the passport, the Home Office letter confirming citizenship, the certificate of naturalisation and the passport. These documents come together as a specific material configuration of specific exclusionary practices. These artefacts of the state circulate beyond government departments. They authoritatively confirm one's status and one's right to travel, work, stay put, vote. This paper trail is part of the migrant's 'biographical footprint', which is based on information provided by the UKVI, employers, local councils and registry offices, landlords, banks and building societies, and other sources. It is constitutive of what

Matt Matsuda calls the 'memory of the state' (cited in Robertson 2010: 115), which consists of the innumerable records, data, algorithms that not only trace but also *organise* people's lives (Caplan and Torpey 2001; Amoore and de Goede 2008) as *migrants*, many of whom are also workers, tax-payers, drivers, mortgage-holders and so on.

Ultimately, the certificate of naturalisation bestowed at the citizenship ceremony may appear to confirm the (new) citizenship status of the individual, but it 'can only derive [its] authenticity from other state-issued documents' (Salter 2003: 2) such as visas, leave to remain, ILR, biometric card, residency card and the like. The lives of some of these documents are short, and some become redundant from one stage to another. The certificate of naturalisation absorbs all traces of previous documents, becoming in effect a birth certificate of sorts, which is submitted when applying for one's first British passport. The certificate of naturalisation materialises how Ayelet Shachar describes naturalisation: 'a postbirth admission to citizenship [which] is a symbolic and political rebirth into the new membership community. [A] postnatal path to membership' (2009: 128).

As discussed in Chapter 1, naturalisation suggests that something is 'made natural', brought into conformity with nature, as in aligning one's permanent place of residence with one's nationality, and thus re-establishing the 'natural' order of things insofar as citizenship takes as its baseline assumption that most of us reside in the country into which we are born. The certificate of naturalisation operates 'as if' it were a birth certificate, just like naturalisation offers the possibility to acquire an 'as if' status: 'to become established as if native', according to the Merriam-Webster dictionary.[9] What is more, both the certificate of naturalisation and the passport still state one's place of birth (always outside the UK), thereby undoing the birthright principle of *jus soli* (but also *jus sanguinis*). The documentary materialisation of naturalisation literally disrupts the birthright principle by migratising not only the passport holder, but also by migratising *citizenship* itself. These documents testify to the flexibility of citizenship and the constitutive character of migration in the very fabric of citizenship (see Chapter 2). That said, we should not reify such documents as radical manifestations of the debunking of birthright and nationalism; indeed, Chapter 5 returns to the question of birthright and how it endures as the privileged principle of citizenship naturalisation.

John Torpey (2000: 93), citing Zolberg, shows how the rise of identification papers such as the passport 'sharpened the line between national and alien and thereby contributed to what has aptly been called the "naturalization of nativism"'. And indeed, the 'as if' native status of the naturalised citizen reinforces nativism rather than inscribes migratism as a positive force of citizenship. But what happens when a presumed 'native born' is migratised? This had dramatic consequences for Charlotte, an Australian living in the UK with ILR status, who adopted two British-born siblings, Katie and Louis. A year after the adoption, she needed to apply for a passport for Katie (Louis' foster family had acquired one for him, prior to the adoption), only to find out that she was deemed Australian by virtue of her adoptive parents' nationality. Indeed, when Charlotte first enquired over the phone, the UKVI advisor, hearing her accent, asked why she was calling *them* about a passport for her daughter?

> So we ring up and say, 'We want to apply for a passport for our daughter. How do we go about it?' And they said, 'Well who are you?' Like, 'You're Australian – why are you calling us?' And they're like, 'Well your child isn't British because you're her parents, you adopted her, she belongs to you and you're Australian'.

The only way Charlotte could obtain a British passport for Katie was to prove that she is third-generation British, in effect re-animating the principle of patriality that existed in law between 1971 and 1981 (see Chapter 2). After some research, Charlotte eventually found the birth certificates of Katie's birth mother and grandmother, enabling her to apply for and obtain a British passport for her.

Charlotte and I reflected extensively on how adoption wipes out blood lines and here, the UKVI advisor was doing the same – legally, according to him, Katie is no longer British by birth. While adoption extinguishes blood ties, what the UKVI advisor suggested took Charlotte and her family 'back to biology' as she put it:

> on the one hand, the adoption wipes out blood, and it has to because then you're not, well it's not blood is it? It's citizenship, you're no longer British, because you have Australian parents. But then they were sensible enough to allow us to prove that, according to her original birth certificate, so it's almost like the birth certificate does still exist even though in a way it doesn't.

However, Katie's birth certificate was not enough – it had to be traced back two generations to make her *British* birthright 'real'.

The advisor assumed that Katie would be Australian based on hearing her parents' accent,[10] first establishing a biological bloodline between her and her adoptive parents, and then replacing that with a legal based kinship, and therefore discarding Katie's British blood line. Blood lines are elusive: they were erased for the purposes of adoption. Yet had Charlotte given birth to these children, they would have been deemed British by virtue of being born in the UK of at least one parent with 'settled' status. A mixed use of *jus soli* (status by territory of birth) and *jus sanguinis* (status by descent) operates in the UK, though the latter is privileged since the British Nationality Act of 1981, where the alignment between *where* you are born and *from whom* became salient. Furthermore, from Charlotte's point of view, Katie was in effect stripped of her British citizenship until Charlotte could prove otherwise – she was virtually decitizenised and migratised as Australian and then recitizenised again as British and decitizenised as Australian.[11]

What also emerges from Charlotte's story is the significance of the passport. She was puzzled about the relationship between the passport and nationality. She said, 'does it work backwards? That's the interesting thing isn't it? I mean will Katie actually be recognised as a citizen of this country just because she has a passport?' In contrast to Katie, Louis obtained the British passport because he was still legally his birth mother's child at the time of the application. Since the adoption, however, he would be understood as Australian in British legal terms where it not for his passport.

Katie's story uncovers the significance of the passport not simply as an entry pass into a country, but also as an *internal* pass insofar as it became her confirmation of citizenship while she was already (born) in the country. Passports are increasingly required by public services, notably health services, as proof of one's right to social citizenship. Passports do 'work backward' – both *inside* a territory and at its borders. And their acquisition is reliant on parentage, which is evidenced by birth certificates or the like. What puzzled Charlotte was the symbolic destruction of any trace of Katie's parental blood line, as if her birth certificate disappears without a trace. But she re-animated Katie's blood line by tracking it down and evidencing it in her mother's and grandmother's birth certificates. The certificates became the material traces of Katie's genealogical connection to the UK.

Charlotte's story is also telling how migration control enters into people's intimate lives. As she gathered and put together the necessary documents to evidence her daughter's British citizenship, Charlotte was citizenising Katie, while Charlotte herself remained migratised as Australian. Such co-constructions of legal categories are integral to the relational politics of curation, which I turn to now.

The relational politics of curation

'I ended up writing this thing that I called my memoirs'. (Ruby, dual Canadian and British citizen, the latter since 2013)

To curate means to collect, select, organise in view of presenting or exhibiting a collection, a biography, a story. It requires editorial work to ensure that the story, the picture, 'speaks' to the intended audience. The word 'curate' comes from the Latin root *cūrāre*, which means to cure or take care of. In Chapter 1, I point out how citizenisation is designed as cure to the presumed citizenship deficit of applicants, who are conceived as noncitizens even though the vast majority are citizens of other countries. Without neglecting that aspect, this chapter sheds light on the collaborative, transformative and at times caring aspect of curation. Curation is a collaborative process (Puwar and Sharma 2012) that involves several actors in creating something new from the ways that 'old' things are put together. The 'pictures' that the UKVI case workers read are the products of curatorial relations of exchange, transformation and collation of documentary evidence that acquire new meanings because of the relationships between them.

The fact that curation is collaborative does not mean that it is devoid of power relations. The relational politics of curation position registrars and applicants 'in a set of shared and divergent forces that bring [them] together and move [them] apart' (Povinelli 2011: 84). In this context, registrars act as professional curators who mediate – sometimes uncomfortably – between applicants and the state, while applicants become self-curators, ultimately responsible for curating the right constellation of evidence to satisfy the picture that fits the legal status they are claiming. This is another aspect of neoliberal uncertain citizenship: the expectation that subjects 'respond fluidly and opportunistically to changing political-economic conditions' (Ong 1999: 6) *as* 'good' neoliberal future citizens. Furthermore, as Jonathan Darling suggested to me, this process testifies to the extent to which it is *within* the uncertainty of citizenship that the hope of citizenisation is offered. The hope being that citizenship is not completely inaccessible, it is obtainable potentially with the right resources and, critically, with the right evidence presented in the right way, which means that all the labour needed to achieve it is worth it.

The relational politics of curation are about the differential positions that migrants or registrars occupy as they navigate the legal requirements of documentation. But they are also about how people variously inhabit those positions and what is expected of them.

'Inter-documentality' and accountability

Scene B

Okay, I'm going to go through the list of documents you will need to bring with you. Can I ask you to write this down please? [pause] Okay, so you need to bring a SET(M) form. October 2013 is the latest version. [pause] Set-M yeah, it must be completed. Your wife's passport, your passport … is the pass visa on the passport? Or does she have a biometric card? [pause] That's fine. Two passport sized photographs for your wife, and one for you; the names must be written on the back, in capital letters, in black ink. Life in the UK test certificate. We may not need your marriage certificate but bring that along just in case. And we need proof of your finance for the last three months. You can either use a pay slip, or you can produce bank statements, the original ones, that would obviously show your regular payments going in. We need to see that you have enough [...] they're interested in the last three months with some clarity of how much income is coming in so it's [pause]. Yeah, that's what they require, either one is fine, yeah. Okay, they need to see that you are cohabitating based on the spouse visa they've given to you; [they need to see that] you do have a relationship, you are living together. You need to bring obviously proof of that: we need to see things such as council tax bill with both your names on it, or individually, landline phone bills, utility bills such as water, gas, electricity [pause]. Yeah, yeah. And that's it really.

The registrar is speaking on the phone with someone who made an appointment for a SCS, informing them of the documents they should take with them for the meeting. As she itemises the list, she also connects some types of documents with specific aspects of what 'they' want to see: financial evidence that the British spouse can support the couple,[12] proof of marriage, proof of co-habitation, and the spouse's citizenship test certificate. In the conversation, 'they' is a reference to the invisible state, the invisible UKVI case workers.

At the end of the list, the registrar suggests a host of mundane bills and the like that will document their co-habitation. The list can be longer, less finite, as it requires the applicant to extract the documents from their mundane context and to put them in relation to each other to build a credible picture. The image conjured up at the opening of this chapter is that of individuals entering SCS or NCS appointments with more than enough material, presumably in response to the list given and the imprecise parameters of what counts as (enough) evidence. When describing her NCS meeting for her citizenship application, Agata told me how she brought a '*huge* amount of stuff', gesturing to a large pile with her hands, and then 'putting it all out in front' of the registrar, mimicking a spread, like fanning out the documents and papers on a table.

Similarly, Lucas recalled how he:

> went to the NCS interview last Tuesday. I took my documents in a folder, the ones that I was going to produce and to show. I took two bags, seriously this thick [puts his hands about one foot apart], supermarket bags of everything else that I could find that related to the last five years of my life including, you know, electricity bills and utility bills, council tax that was in the main folder. Anything you know, credit card bills or TV licence, I went through my entire records.

Lucas, who had come to the UK from Brazil several years before, described how uncertain and anxious he felt about the kind of evidence required: 'what sort of scale do they want?', as he put it. In response, he gathered everything he could: like Agata, any mundane thing became 'evidence' of his 'life in the UK'.

In the process, the material used acquires specific meaning only in relation to other material, and to the way that the material is organised and put together. The 'stuff' that people bring includes mundane documents which take on a different meaning within the currency system of legitimacy (Gill 2014). This is what Sara Ahmed, writing in a different context, refers to as 'inter-documentality' (2012: 89), where documents exist within a family of documents and make sense only by referring to each other. In the context of applying for SET(M) or citizenship, curating is about recontextualising documentary evidence in a narrative where the parameters are set by the state. Documents take on different meanings as they move in and out of shopping bags or folders, across the desk, in and out of virtual space, in and out of in-trays or filing cabinets. In the household context, the electricity bill materialises the abstract electric circuits into kw/hours and price per unit and materialises the contract between provider and customer. In the SCS meeting, the bill is not about how many kw/hours were used at what cost. It is about *who* uses those units, *where*, *when* and how it aligns itself with other bills and statements during the same period. As curators, registrars and applicants collate *older* content to produce *new* content (Bhatt 2014), creating a clear picture for the interpreter (the UKVI case worker) by giving a new life (or new 'reality') to an older document.

Inter-documentality is constituted by and constitutive of the governmentality of citizenship, where on the one hand the migrant subject is made responsible for curating their selves and providing the evidence. As the UKVI case worker in the training session described in Scene 2 stated, the onus is on the applicants 'to understand the requirements and that's where if they don't, the ownership [sic] is upon them to make sure that documents are right'. The expectation is that people should get themselves into the mentality of governing their lives and of being governed (N. Rose 1996, 1999), subjecting themselves to the scrutiny of the state in the hope of being accepted (Fortier 2013). As one of the registrars attending the training session stated, 'if that was me, my priority would be to get myself onto the system the moment I arrive into that country'.

On the other hand, migrants are required by the state to curate a collection of documents, photographs, memories that add to the 'picture' of themselves as spouses, residents, refugees. For some, the demand can extend into a protracted process of requests for more information. Ruby's 'memoirs' were the result of a convoluted to-ing and fro-ing between her and the UKVI, mediated by the lawyer provided at her workplace. Because her job with an international development agency required her to travel to several countries deemed 'suspect' by the UK government, such as Afghanistan and Pakistan, she was asked to provide more and more evidence about who she met, under what circumstances, for what purposes and the like. In the context of the securitisation of citizenship, the geography of the migrant's account of herself becomes highly relevant and triggers requests for fuller accountability. 'Inter-documentality', then, extends beyond connections between documents making up a migrant's story and feed into the associational logics of data mining and algorithms explored by Louise Amoore in the post 9/11 'war on terror' context. What were not suspicious, ordinary transactions – credit card purchases, booking a plane ticket – become suspicious when connected to other data, such as travel histories. Until she applied for citizenship, Ruby was what Amoore calls a 'trusted traveller' (2006: 343). But upon applying for citizenship, Ruby became an 'immigrant' and her travel patterns the object of closer scrutiny, which was heightened once the destinations became apparent. Ruby, a white Canadian working for an international organisation, was *suspect by association* with countries, and potentially individuals, deemed 'unsafe'. As the next section reveals, differently racialised bodies are read differently against the data that they are connected to. Such 'association rules' (Amoore and de Goede 2008; Amoore 2009) serve to identify potential citizens as more or less 'risky' and suspected of 'making up' their story until they can prove that they are 'safe'. Moreover, that proof is not easily accessible to all. Ruby had access to legal support and resources that are available to very few.

Ruby's metaphor of the memoir was apposite: applicants '"write" themselves into life and history'; they 'create themselves as "legible" subjects of their own lives' (Caplan and Torpey 2001: 6, 7) for the benefit of the state. And when considered in the context of associational logics and state suspicion, those subjected to citizenisation are seeking to curate themselves as *safe* potential citizens, as productive, trustworthy and legible.[13]

When the body becomes evidence

In NCS and SCS meetings, the creation of legible subjects is a collaborative labour of curation, but it is one in which registrars occupy the position of the authoritative state – a position that they do not all inhabit in the same way. Furthermore, when it comes to SET(M), the object of SCS meetings, registrars have a duty to report suspicious marriages (or civil partnerships), as dictated in the Immigration and Asylum Act 1999 (Section 24). Thus, for many registrars dealing with SET(M) applicants, the figure of the 'sham marriage' haunts every move they make.

Hilary, a registrar at a small local council, described the training she received from the UKVI as similar to that of border guards. She explained that she was trained 'to look for fraudulent documents', but also 'lots of different things. You know, kind of silly, you know ears don't change, the tops of your ears don't change, and certain pin point things, in the face that don't change, we can look for them'. When conducting the SET(M) checking service, Hilary added that she can instinctively detect a fraudulent marriage or civil partnership thanks to her long-standing experience as a registrar who regularly performs marriage or civil partnership ceremonies.

> I've done this job twenty-six years. You get a general feeling that people aren't interacting and you just, kind of, oooh, right, I'm going to watch out for this couple. I can simply know by something that they've actually said on the initial booking, the phone call, and I'll flag it up for the staff: this is one I want them to watch [...] We get an instinct about couples that aren't really functioning, [because of] their body language. We see people in love every single day of our working lives, that genuinely *want* to be together and in a partnership, and they're in love. They come in our office, so when you don't see that in a couple, those are the ones where you think, well, oh right, that's a bit off the wall here. This is when you're starting to have a little bit of a closer look at these couples.

Legibility requires not only that documents be checked, but also that bodies be read *against* identity documents such as the passport photograph, or that registrars read *off* bodies for tell-tale signs of true or fake love. The migrant's body becomes the evidence against which she must present herself, and against which she must prove her genuineness.

Hilary's approach is a reminder that migrants here are *both* subjects of communication and objects of information. Registrars meet them, engage with them, learn about them through immediate personal engagement (more on this below), but they also 'see' migrants through the mediated practice of following policy guidelines. In the case of SET(M), 'feelings' become part of the 'technologies of love' that 'are central to the governmentality of marriage migration', as Anne-Marie D'Aoust argues (2013). These technologies are grounded in normative understandings of 'true love' and its expressions, and they are mobilised in a political and moral economy of suspicion (D'Aoust 2018). Moreover, racially or culturally minoritised bodies must align themselves with what is understood as culturally appropriate expressions of true love (D'Aoust 2018); those who digress too much may become suspect – for example, if a Muslim couple touch each other too much.

While registrars are required to express their suspicions about 'fake' love, the UKVI case worker at the SET(M) training session explained that they are not asked to judge the strength of that love: 'it's not up to us to judge on how strong we deem that relationship'. The focus should be on whether the couple are in a 'substantive relationship', which UKVI case workers were at pains to define, eventually boiling it down to 'two people who spend the majority of their time together, and possibly share finances together and responsibilities that come with that'. Here, the strength of love is backgrounded in favour of pragmatic co-habiting arrangements, which remain, however, grounded in normative assumptions of coupledom and how 'couples' should share their lives. If, in theory, the SET(M) application makes allowances for couples who do not live together, when that is the case individuals must further explain *why* they live apart.

The governance of marriage migration uses the 'couple' model as a governing instrument in the attribution of legal status by applying different rules for migrants who are married or in a civil partnership, such as different settlement application routes for spouses of British nationals. Similarly, up until 2006, children born to non-Irish and non-EU/EEA migrant parents were deemed British not only if at least one parent had settled status in the UK, but if that parent is the father, he must have been legally wedded to the child's mother at the time of the birth.[14] In short, by distinguishing different routes to settlement or citizenship based on spousal or kinship relations, the governance of migration naturalises 'coupledom', monogamy, romantic love and heterosexual reproduction, and reproduces the 'sexual citizen' where intimate and familial relations are the basis of differential conceptions of citizenship (Berlant 1997; Bell and Binnie 2000; Johnson 2002; Plummer 2003; Mongia 2018; more in Chapter 5).

In turn, the division between 'migrant' and 'citizen' is further ossified by adding an extra layer of scrutiny for couples where one partner is 'migrant'. Indeed, any couple where at least one partner is subject to immigration control when giving notice of their intention to marry/enter into a civil partnership must 'get permission to marry', as Maya put it. This upset Maya, who had come to Britain from Lebanon on a student visa, and who had to change to a spousal visa when she married her British husband. She was dumbfounded by the extra interview that she and her then fiancé were obliged to sign up for at a local authority, which was some miles away from their residence. 'Why should we get permission to marry?', she kept asking. These extra layers of bureaucracy that search into individuals' intimate lives reveal something of what Susan Bin Hyatt calls, drawing on Dana-Ain Davis, the 'intimacies' of social policy, 'where "intimacies" are, in this context, those encounters among individuals and between citizens and the bureaucracies that monitor their everyday lives' (Hyatt 2011: 108). For Maya, the obligation to appeal to the state in order to receive the 'right' to marry was a level of control that she didn't anticipate or appreciate. To add insult to injury, she and her husband had to pay £600 to acquire her spousal visa.

For Sala, it was the intrusiveness of the NCS that got to her:

> It's like you have to go through your life story with strangers and some of these questions don't seem bureaucratic to me. They *are* bureaucratic, I understand, but they're also deeply personal, and they do overlap with difficult issues and stories in my life and that's why I hate these applications. It's because I feel that I'm going to be exposed. Not exposing something that I'm hiding but exposing things that are personal.

Sala's and Maya's accounts are telling of the interpretive gaps between subjective understandings of intimacy and the bureaucratic enactments of the intimacies of policy. But interpretive gaps can also take other forms.

Interpretive gaps, affective relations and geographical imaginaries

There is a fine line that registrars are asked to tread between detecting 'fake' relationship and ignoring 'weak' ones. In this context, registrars find themselves pressed by the law's impossible demand to distinguish between sincere and fraudulent applicants, worrying about the risks of misrecognition. Anxieties expressed by registrars at the training session result from their ambivalent position as agents of the state who are also alienated from the state. When faced with monitoring and evidencing people's intimate lives, some registrars also see limitations in the legal code, which comes up against the incommensurability between the kind of coherence stipulated by the law and the much less coherent ways that people live (see Fortier 2017a).

The UKVI case workers, for their part, were speaking from the positions of those who review 'cases', where the quality of a couple's feelings is made invisible in favour of evidence of a 'marital' relationship. 'Cases' are created at SCS and NCS meetings, where the multi-dimensional subject is turned into a two-dimensional policy object to be 'processed' (Feldman 2011: 44). The very nature of forms is to distil the 'facts' of people's lives into documentary evidence and abbreviated explanatory stories that fit in a small box on an A4 page. The resulting pictures will invariably obscure the complexity of each case and the varied ways in which people lead their (marital) lives. Indeed, one of the UKVI case workers at the Stadlow training session described in Scene 2 seemed to understand this. She suggested that being presented with too neat a picture raises rather than lowers her suspicions, for example, if all correspondence submitted as evidence of co-habitation is in both spouses' names: 'cos you can put anyone [on joint bills], you can do a favour by putting her name on your bill, that's doesn't mean that you live at that address', which led her to conclude: 'I would be more inclined to think that there is something a little bit dodgy' if all the correspondence is in joint names. The application forms and supporting evidence give a partial picture of applicants, obscuring the journeys that got them there, extracting emotions from the evidence in favour of material evidence of shared lives.

If the 'feelings' of registrars about a couple's feelings for each other can become indicators of a suspicious marriage, the feelings that an applicant for citizenship has for the 'nation' can also become an object of interrogation. Naturalisation policy is founded on the presumed lovability of the country granting citizenship and sets the terms of this imagined love (Somerville 2005) – for example, being 'committed' to Britain. In the extract from the training session cited in Scene A, one of the UKVI case workers says that it is at the point of applying for naturalisation that 'you have to show that you *want* to be here' (emphasis added). Indeed, the White Paper on nationality, immigration and asylum in which the new citizenisation measures were laid out distinguished between an instrumental desire and a more 'committed' desire:

> becoming a British citizen is a significant step which should mean more than simply obtaining the right to a British passport ... British citizenship should bring with it a heightened commitment to full participation in British society. (Home Office 2002: 30)

Yet how this desire is assessed is open to interpretation. This was a source of frustration for Agata, a 'resident'[15] German citizen, married to a 'resident' German man, with a child born in England (with British citizenship), who had been living and working in Britain for close to 20 years and was applying for British citizenship when I met her in 2013.

> I think what astonished both of us [her and her husband] was the level of questioning our intention to stay in this country ... it seemed so unnecessary and it seemed, I mean it was slightly offensive ... cos all the things she [the registrar conducting the NCS] was asking us, all this evidence. We've been working and living here and paying taxes for a very long time. So in a way we felt that all this was questioned in a way that was completely unnecessary and was in a way going deeper in the sense of questioning whether did we really want to become British, did we have a basis on which to ask for this, almost like did we have a *right* to ask for this. And that's what made it sort of, in a way emotionally quite difficult. And I know we came out after this and we were both very upset.

Agata came up against the interpretive gap between her belief in her legal and moral right to claim membership, on the one hand, and her not-yet legal full membership status. Agata's sense of entitlement to citizenship was based on the formal requirement of residency, and on her existing legal 'resident' status, while she understood the registrar's questions as putting this entitlement in doubt in favour of seeking confirmation of the genuineness of her desire to become British, which she could only express in abstract terms. To be sure, up until recently EU nationals who were long-term residents had greater access to legal rights and other advantages not available to non-EU nationals residing in the UK (Prabhat 2018: 68). And it may be because of this that Agata was upset. What distressed her was that her legal 'resident' status was not enough to evidence her long-standing presence and her desire to stay in the country. Within this interpretive gap, she was effectively (re)made into a 'migrant'. Agata was 'caught out in a distinction between "residence" and "presence"' (Anderson 2020: 79). As Sara Stendahl (2016: 235) pointedly asks, what, then, does it mean to 'reside'?

> Residing has to do with territory and with notions such as living, staying and belonging. It seems clear however that mere presence in a given territory is not enough to achieve the status of being resident[.]

It was also clear to Agata that formal 'resident' status in itself did not suffice to confer her commitment to stay. Although she had brought 'a huge amount of stuff', Agata and her husband were still asked for more: their son's birth certificate, a letter from their son's school, evidence of addresses in England in the past five years, letters from their respective employers explaining their numerous travels abroad. Why were these additional documents requested? 'I think she used the, I can't remember if that's the phrase that she used but she said something to show that you've kind of "built your life here" [motioning air quotes] and to show that you are clearly committed to living here'. This is another instance exemplifying how 'documents breed more documents' (Anderson 2020: 76) in an attempt to 'evidence' an abstract feeling.

Because 'commitment' opens itself to many interpretations, registrars might be overly cautious about how to prove that commitment. In the world of dispersed governance such as the citizenisation process, interpretive gaps between various state actors will invariably arise. One registrar, Lucy, spoke to me about her uncertainty about how decisions are made:

> we can't go and sit with the case worker and look at everything they do. You don't know exactly what they're looking for. With marriage or births or deaths I know exactly what I'm looking for. But with this [nationality and indefinite leave to remain] I'm just checking … And sometimes you feel a little bit as though the person who's applying thinks that you know everything but you don't.

As Annelise Riles might suggest, curation is about how 'moments of document creation [e.g. SCS] anticipate future moments in which documents will be received, circulated, instrumentalized, and taken apart again' (Riles 2006: 18). Lucy was conjuring the invisible state, an invisible case worker as the unknow decision-maker whose reasoning she cannot access. She was mirroring the applicants' uncertainty, as they also collate their application in anticipation of a 'reader' – though the risks for her are of course not the same as the risks for the applicants. Still, her relatively new role in everyday bordering made her nervous.

While she welcomed the UKVI helpline as a big 'benefit' that assisted her when she was in doubt, she remained uneasy about the law because her role was 'just checking'. Lucy was tapping into how uncertainty plays itself out and can proliferate rather than disappear in everyday bureaucratic practices of checking for the state. Moreover, her position as a 'knowing' agent of the state in the eyes of applicants added to her unease. Immigration control was encroaching on her life as a registrar, and this made Lucy very anxious. She told me how she worried about either sending off a fraudulent application and, by implication, supporting it, or making a mistake that will make the applicant *appear* to be fraudulent even if he or she is not.

> You get to know the people, you know? You can be sat here an hour and a half or an hour, depending on just what you're doing, and then there's families that come in with their children and you think, 'Oh I do hope they get it' you know? Cos you think if I've made a mistake and it's a lot of money! We don't know if people get it or not you know cos once they go they go. I go home sometimes at night and I'm thinking, 'Oh, I really hope…' [pauses]. All those sleepless nights I have.

Several registrars expressed a similar connection with those they met at NSC or SCS meetings, including Hilary who enjoyed seeing people through different stages of their lives – SET(M), registering the birth of a child, NCS, citizenship ceremony. Lucy and others care about and collaborate with the applicants in ensuring the 'case' is as complete as possible. During these encounters, relations oscillate between personalised, intimate, face-to-face relations, and the depersonalised crafting of the one-dimensional 'case'. As Riles suggests, the exchange of documents and the filling out of forms at SCS or NCS meetings 'effectuates a particular experience of the exchange taking place' (Riles 2006: 19). Documents mediate these encounters and have the ability to shape the mood of a meeting and of those present.

Scene C

I am sitting in a small meeting room in Stadlow Council. Caroline, the registrar, is meeting with an Egyptian man applying for SET(M), i.e. indefinite leave to remain on the basis of marriage (in this case to a British woman). Caroline is concerned because there's a gap in proof of cohabitation for early 2012, especially for his spouse. She makes a copy of her checklist for him to take home, as a guide for what he's looking for. He goes home and promises to return later that afternoon. When he leaves, she tells me that she is worried; worried that he might not have the necessary documents to get through. He may not be a genuine applicant, she muses.

He returns after about 1–1.5 hours, with the missing proof of cohabitation for early 2012. Caroline checks, selects and makes copies. After he's left, Caroline turns to me, smiling, and says 'I am happy now'.

Caroline's mood changed when the documents appeared. She was satisfied that the application was complete, even though she could not forecast the outcome. But because documents operate as mediators, they also disappear – 'there is a "tendency of media to disappear in the act of mediation ... to redirect attention to what is being mediated"' (Eisenlohr cited in Hull 2012: 253). Applicants and registrars are fully aware of that future moment when documents will not only be scrutinised and taken apart again, but where they will also 'disappear' and direct attention to a 'picture': a couple or a 'committed' resident will be conjured, imagined, and a body will come into a case worker's mind's eye.

To be sure, this is materially supported by the required passport-size photographs of a naturalisation applicant or of both spouses (and children) attached to the application. The evidence of co-habitation and the photographs combine to produce a 'picture' of how people share their lives, which is read against racially and culturally coded expectations of how couples 'usually' organise their domestic lives. When discussing the absence of bills in joint names, one of the UKVI case workers explained that 'You have to appreciate also that some people come from a country where they don't have that responsibility'. The second trainer then adds:

> Say, for example, a woman might not have documents in her name, she might not pay utility fees because everything is paid for by the man. In that situation we do go OK and there's things along the lines of that.

Here, a gendered 'picture' arises of how people live – a picture that connects to geographical imaginaries about 'others' who come from 'there'. Geographical imaginaries mediate a 'case' insofar as they are constitutive of the regulation of marriage migration. For instance, debates about 'bogus marriages' have been confused with public discussions about 'arranged' and 'forced' marriage with spouses from South Asia – where both are often conflated (D'Aoust 2018).[16] Likewise, in the course of my research, the government expressed concerns about marriages between EU citizens and non-EEA spouses occurring 'on an industrial scale' (in D'Aoust 2018: 47).

But as the discussion above suggests, geographical imaginaries will also shape the everyday curatorial relations between registrars and applicants, as well as how a case worker will read a SET(M) application. The 'picture' is constituted through curatorial relations that read off bodies for evidence of love, but that also locate these bodies in transnational geographies. One registrar from a large city council with several SCS appointments each week spoke about how:

> In the last couple of weeks, you'll see either Asian or African men and Eastern European women getting married cos obviously Europe, you can stay in the country if you're married to a European person. So we are seeing quite a lot of an increase. [...] I mean you can make a judgement and say, 'I bet he's only marrying her for a passport' but you just don't know. I mean it's a hard thing to call I mean especially as you only see someone for half an hour.[17]

Thus, the generic figure of the 'sham marriage' is embodied and suspicions are raised when registrars see particular bodies enter the room. This registrar's imaginary fits with the figuration of sham marriages that circulated at the time. At the same time, she reminds us that her curatorial role to check for the state puts her in the impossible position of identifying fraudulent relationships.

In sum, the relational politics of curation set the scene for the materialisation of the 'migrant' and the 'citizen'. To paraphrase

Butler (1997: 91), citizenship is materialised to the extent that it is invested with power; it is a site of power relations, as both vector and instrument of power. In the encounters described above, applicants are indubitably cast as 'migrants', and registrars indubitably as 'citizens' endowed with the authority to ask for and scrutinise evidence (Chalfin 2008). *Never* can one be both migrant and citizen. In these moments, registrars stand in for the state, or for a border to cross in order to reach the state. The applicants, for their part, become the wanting, waiting ones, who are both subjects of communication and objects of information.

Conclusion

The requirement of documented intelligibility puts local officials and migrants in different reading or writing positions, in different relationships to each other, and in different relationships to the state. Applicants and registrars must become fluent in the state's language, rites and processes in order to aptly curate documents and create accurate 'pictures' that fit the legal status claimed by migrants. In this sense, the application process is itself a process of *citizenisation* that impacts on the lives of both 'migrants' and 'citizens'.

There are many interpretive gaps that open up when individuals have different understandings of the law, and different affective experiences of the curatorial relations. But gaps also develop in the paper trails and traces: from life fragments that each 'picture' captures, to the waiting times that migrants endure, to the erasure of some documents that are absorbed in another (the passport), to the 'biographical footprint' left by documents, or erased when documents are made redundant, such as Katie's birth certificate. By examining the generative capacities of documents, their traces, and the relational politics of their curation, this chapter gives an account of how citizens and migrants are made, unmade and deeply entangled beyond the strict legal scripts of 'documented citizenship', and how, concurrently, citizens and migrants are variously migratised and citizenised.

The generative capacities of documents are numerous: they mobilise, immobilise, shape moods, conjure bodies, 'pictures', or the state itself, tell stories, trace and erase genealogies, connect or disconnect people, animate actions and reactions. Documents play a significant role in the waiting room of citizenship as they emplace migrants in place, time and specific affective relations to the state. Here, citizenship *takes time* as the circulation of documents is regulated by bureaucratic time. In turn, documents will punctuate individual lives, leaving some in a sense of 'chronic waiting' (Jeffrey 2010; Anderson 2020), while others learn to think and calculate in certain ways as they learn to navigate temporal constraints. Documents are timed – visas expire, documents are organised in a sequence or become redundant – and their timing structures people's lives and the labour of institutional actors.

Curation *takes time* and effort. The sheer weight and volume of documents that individuals gather testifies to the labour needed to build the right picture. In the process, some older documents animate memories, stories, relations that connect or disconnect subjects to their own histories, kin and other locations – as it was for Katie and her mother Charlotte. In Chapter 5, we return to Sala for whom the citizenisation process re-animated her relationship to her biography, identity, kin relations, to Britain and to Egypt. In this sense, the process of gathering documents potentially (re-)animates old or new relations for migrants, which exceed their relation to the state.[18]

Citizenship *takes place* through documentary practices that govern people's mobility. What is more, the extent of the account of themselves that migrants are required to produce will vary and is highly dependent on the geography of a person's mobility or trajectory that brought them to the UK. Citizenship takes place in geographical imaginaries as well, which mediate how 'cases' are put together, collated and taken apart again by the UKVI case worker charged to read and assess on behalf of the state. Such imaginaries *take hold* when bodies become evidence to be read *against* identity documents such as the passport photograph, or to be read *off* bodies for tell-tale signs of true or fake love that are themselves culturally or racially coded.

Citizenship *takes hold* through documents that have the capacity to 'grasp' individuals by fixing them in time and place. The curation of documents to produce the accurate 'picture' requires that everyday objects be aligned with official documents in the creation of a 'picture'. Curating, in that sense, is stopping time, stopping movement and grasping a snapshot of one's life.

If 'migrants' and 'citizens' are continuously made and unmade through curatorial practices of documentation, so too is the state. The interpretive gaps between local officials' understandings of the law or of state propriety, shows that 'the state' does not operate in a monolithic matter and that presumed 'agents of the state' do not act in a uniform way. In turn, the state is omnipresent in the lives of migrant applicants, in the form of letters, forms, webpages that generate different actions and reactions. Citizenship *takes hold* as the state–citizen/state–migrant relation is repeatedly materialised in the process. A relation that takes the form of 'anxious states' as individuals wait anxiously, are unsure about how to interpret documents, how to put them together, or how to evidence their love or commitment to the nation.

A feature highlighted in this chapter is how the circulation of hope works within the waiting room of citizenship. Hope is woven into the very fabric of uncertain citizenship and incites individuals to subject themselves to the scrutiny of the state. The uncertainty of citizenship feeds the hope that it can be achievable, albeit with the right 'evidence' curated into the right picture, which makes all the anxieties and labour to obtain it appear as worthwhile. What is more, as Jonathan Darling pointed out (personal communication), hope not only motivates the labour of curation, but it also shapes the *care* that curation entails, not just for oneself but also for others, such as the registrars who care enough to advise on the best means to curate a story beyond their functionary duties, or who care so much that they lose sleep. Part of the care here is in seeking and communicating ways to curate in a more effective manner, to make clear how it is possible to tell stories that will be legible to the state, even though that process of making legible may involve greater time and effort for all involved.

All migrants going through the citizenisation process are set on a legal course that renders them continuously accountable. Judith Butler argues that accountability 'takes a narrative form, which not only depends upon the ability to relay a set of sequential events with plausible transitions but also draws upon narrative voice and authority, being directed toward an audience with the aim of persuasion' (Butler 2005: 12). But what does this mean when accountability is also about speaking the 'national language'? And what happens to those less skilled to speak 'with authority'? What does it mean when one's 'voice' is marginalised, if not stigmatised, as outside of the acceptable repertoire of voices and languages? How are other languages and 'other Englishes' heard, but also 'seen'? The next scene introduces the inequalities and inequities constitutive of the transnational Anglophone world, leading to Chapter 4, which turns to how regimes of hearing and regimes of seeing combine in the language requirements that are integral to British citizenisation.

Scene 3

Conversing with Anglophones

I arrived early at the language school, and was warmly greeted by Alan, its founder and director. The school is one of many privately run schools established since early 2000, when ESOL became part of the citizenisation process. Private schools also proliferated as a result of government cuts on ESOL funding through the years. Alan was made redundant in the early 2000s from the further education college where he'd been teaching for several years. His school is accredited by the British Council and recognised by the UK Visas and Immigration (UKVI) as a testing centre to confirm any applicant for Indefinite Leave to Remain (ILR) or citizenship that they have achieved level B1. The school offers a range of courses for ESOL learners, including specially designed courses to prepare them for the Life in the UK (LUK) test.

Alan had invited me to meet and interview some of their students. He set me up in a small meeting room and went to one of the classrooms to ask for volunteers. I do not know how the invitation was issued or received, but Alan returned and informed me that six learners volunteered, some of them very keen to speak to me. This was certainly the case of two of them, who were very eager to speak to me, stating that they wanted to tell their story, that they wanted it to be heard. I was less sure about the others. Overall, these six individuals had the weakest English-speaking skills of all participants I had met thus far. Indeed, the school is located in one of the North West areas that records higher than average failure rates of the LUK test. In 2016, 44 per cent test takers in the North West failed, compared to 36 per cent of failures across England (Aru and Lubin 2017).

On several occasions, I felt that the stress of requiring them to 'tell me their story' in English was quite high. They volunteered to speak to me even though they knew that the interview would be conducted in English – one of the keener ones even saw it as an opportunity to practise his English. It seems that the expectation that we would all speak English was normalised by the fact that we met in an ESOL environment where the school director introduced me. I do not know how my interlocutors 'heard' my accent – which to first language British English speakers sounds like that of a 'native' North American English speaker. But in the ears of these ESOL learners, with weaker English language skills, I may have sounded British English.

What I do know is that these encounters were normalised by our respective positions in the power differentials constitutive of the 'Anglophone' worlds we inhabit, where my status as a presumed white 'English native speaker' meant that I stood in for the English-speaking majority – if not as the state, then at least as an immigration 'expert'. My status as 'expert' was borne out when some hoped to get information from me about how to get 'the passport', the shorthand many migrants use to refer to British citizenship. In contrast to the ostensibly harmless definition of 'Anglophone' offered by the Cambridge English Dictionary as 'a person who speaks English, especially in countries where other languages are spoken', the implied spatial location of Anglophone casts it outside of Britain. As Peter Hitchcock points out: '[a]s soon as one begins to specify this person, and this English …, the innocence of the word dissolves into a history of colonial and postcolonial import. Anglophone is always somebody else's English, just as Anglophone literature is somehow not American or English' (2001: 758).

My positionality in these meetings was more complex than that oscillating between 'Anglophone foreigner' and 'British'. As a white French-Canadian, my interlocutors and I share a modicum of histories of encounters with (the) English and an appreciation of how this language has been imposed from without, albeit unevenly and with radically different social and political effects. I am the daughter of two competing and intersecting white settler colonial regimes that continue to operate at the expense of indigenous populations and indigenous languages. I am the Francophone and Anglophone descendant of white settler colonialism where French and English appeared as the natural outgrowths of Canada's two 'founding people' and consequently of the 'massive leveling force of language continuously imposed by the West', in the words of Édouard Glissant (1989: 249).

For my interlocutors in that small language school in the North West of England, the story is significantly different. These multilingual Anglophones from Pakistan, Iran or Iraq, came to Britain bearing the aural/oral traces of linguistic imperialism, which seems to force a kind of self-estrangement, where English appears not some much as an 'inner thing' that is deeply embodied, but more like 'an artefact – a type of sound effect' (Chow 2014: 13). As I think back at how my interlocutors adapted their bodies to speak in English with me – contorting their lips and tongues to pronounce English words, or stretching their necks, intently watching my lips, turning their ears towards me, moving closer to me, hesitating, stammering (Gunew 2005) as they search for the English words – I cannot deny the symbolic and epistemic violence of these encounters where language is a form of injury. These Anglophone encounters were sites where language was itself a 'postcolonial experience', as Rey Chow puts it, which is imbricated in class and racial systems of differentiation through which we were 'racialized by language and languaged by race' (Chow, 2014: 9); a racialisation that was inherently unequal and that (re)produced new hierarchies of belonging and entitlement indexed by linguistic racism.

4

The speaking citizen

The previous chapter explores how migrants and citizens such as registrars must become fluent in the state's language and processes in order to curate documents and create accurate 'pictures' that fit within the currency system of legitimacy. It documents how applicants curate themselves as '"legible" subjects of their own lives' (Caplan and Torpey 2001: 7).

This chapter moves from the requirement of 'legibility' to the requirements of audibility. More precisely, it asks: What happens when 'legibility' intersects with 'audibility'? How do seeing and hearing intersect? The focus is on language requirements in the British citizenisation process, but it speaks to a broader international trend. Language requirements for citizenship, citizenship-like statuses or entry visas are prevalent in Western Europe and elsewhere (Van Avermaet and Gysen 2009; Krzyzanowski and Wodak 2010; Pulinx and Van Avermaet 2015; Wodak and Savski 2018). So much so that, as David Gramling argues, language has become the basis of a new model of citizenship:

> a model that conceives of prospective citizens no longer through their supposed blood-rights to citizenship (*ius sanguinis*) or territorial rights (*ius soli*), but through their demonstrated language competences (*ius linguarum*).[1] (2016: 25)

He goes on to argue that the 'right to language(s)' is framed as a legal right that protects migrants and new citizens from exclusions that result from not speaking a national language (2016: 205). *Jus linguarum* signals what Gramling refers to as 'post-ethnic lingua franca'; that is that the politics, policies and discourses surrounding language requirements untether language from ideas of what constitutes 'national culture' and instead present it as a public good that promises individual and social integration. Gramling further argues that *jus linguarum* is developing as a post-ethnic model of citizenship that is replaced by superdiversity and multilingualism 'as the organizing heuristic device[s] for the twenty-first century state' (2016: 26). For Gramling, this 'post-ethnic' model is rooted in the recognition by national governments that superdiversity and multilingualism are the norm in today's world (2016: 196), but a problematic norm that governments must 'manage' and respond to.

In short, *jus linguarum* has become the new common-sense politics of language, integration and citizenship. But *jus linguarum* as it exists today is enabled by a long history of putting value on language. Monica Heller and Bonnie McElhinny (2017) track how language became salient through the history of interlocked colonialism and capitalism. They show how language gets bound up in complex circuits of mobility and exchange, where it acts as a *resource* that is unequally distributed, but also that reproduces inequalities and boundaries through the unequal distribution of other kinds of resources needed to access it. In addition, language also acts as a *legitimation* that enables these inequities to 'make sense' (Heller and McElhinny 2017: 3). These two threads – language as resource and language as legitimation – run through the fabric of *jus linguarum*.

Jus linguarum, however, is a distinctively neoliberal product, positioning language fluency within broader governing strategies that emphasise 'added value' and skills as key organising and sifting mechanisms. Language fluency – along with other skills – indexes the integratability of migrants, and determines who enters, under what conditions and who is eligible to stay. The rationale surrounding language requirements purports that a shared national lingua franca is (1) an enabler of integration and civic participation for migrant populations; (2) an upskilling opportunity for migrants, who are responsible for taking it up; (3) an efficient way to ensure peaceful cohabitation between 'communities'; and (4) a necessary channel for developing and sharing interpersonal, social and cultural values. Language is instrumentalised as a neutral civic resource detached from its historical and contemporary connections with race, class, gender and sexuality.

This chapter centres on language, race and nation and asks: what gets marked and unmarked in enactments of *jus linguarum*? What eludes Gramling (2016) is the historical and contemporary dynamics through which language and race are mutually co-naturalised, and how this co-naturalisation is integral to, and has historically enabled, the development of *jus linguarum* policies and politics. Drawing on a raciolinguistic approach (Alim, Rickford and Ball 2016; Rosa and Flores 2017; also Chow 2014), the chapter argues that the disappearance of 'national language' as a *constructed* category allows for the disappearance of other categories, such as whiteness. As a result, *jus linguarum* in Western Europe reconstitutes 'national languages' and whiteness as unmarked and 'worldly'.[2]

Raciolinguistics emphasise the interplay between 'racing language' and 'languaging race' (Alim 2016), drawing attention to how 'the instability of race is negotiated through language' (Alim 2016: 7; Roth-Gordon 2016), on the one hand, and to how theories of race shed light on linguistic variation, on the other. In a similar vein but with a focus on subject formation, Rey Chow (2014), drawing on A. L. Becker, uses the term 'languaging' to refer to the ways in which subjects are 'racialized by language and languaged by race' (Chow 2014: 9). In short, raciolinguistics bring to the fore the intersections of regimes of visibility (or regimes of seeing) and regimes of audibility (regimes of hearing): what do we see when we hear someone speak a minoritised language? What do we hear when we see a minoritised subject speak? Expanding the theory of 'languaging' further, this chapter also examines how subjects can be *migratised by language* and *languaged by migratism* (anti-migration politics and discourses).

My focus is not on sociolinguistic variations *per se*, as is the case for the critical linguists. Rather, my focus is twofold: first, how language requirements that institute *jus linguarum* both conceal and reproduce racial inequalities between English speakers and speakers of other languages (including 'other Englishes'). And second, how such inequalities and inequities are enacted, experienced and lived by state intermediaries or migrants as they encounter the language requirements for citizenisation.

The chapter includes three sections: the language requirement policy itself, the speaking citizen part I, and the speaking citizen part II. The first section, '*Jus linguarum* in Britain: provincialising English and naturalising inequalities', situates the language requirements for migrants in the British historical and contemporary context.

A crucial and distinctive feature of English is its status as a 'world language'. This section details the rationale surrounding the inception of the current legislation while it also offers a brief account of the colonial history surrounding the simultaneous spread of English as a 'world' language and its standardisation as a 'national' language. Tensions arise between the effects of the historical spread of English in the empire *over there*, the inevitable multilingualism *over here* that ensues, and the insistence of English as a *national* language and indicator of *national* belonging. As a result of these tensions, I argue that the British version of *jus linguarum* amounts to 'provincialising English' both in the literal spatial sense and in the abstract sense introduced by Dipesh Chakrabarty (2007). This first section goes on to examine how these tensions are dealt with in government strategies aimed at resolving them and how they have led to the naturalisation of inequalities through language.

The next two sections examine the effects of languaging and provincialising English and ongoing linguistic inequities as they are lived on the ground because of inseparable histories of colonialism and nation formation. How do injunctions to learn, speak and teach English affect those who are variously tasked to do so? How do languages injure (Chow 2014)? 'The speaking citizen part I' (subtitled 'on (not) speaking English') begins with ESOL teaching and learning, and the experiences and work required of those tasked to teach or learn English. It highlights the different conditions under which individuals labour to learn English, particularly gender inequalities in the division of domestic labour that mean that some women take years to achieve the required fluency for citizenship. In turn, language requirements have changed how ESOL professionals teach and experience their teaching, as they are conscripted in practices of everyday bordering for the state. This first sub-section ends with a discussion of how language and race intersect in figures such as 'the Jamaican' or 'the Asian spouse' who both loom large in imaginaries of *jus linguarum*.

'The speaking citizen part I' then turns to migrants who bear the aural and audial traces of 'linguistic imperialism' (Phillipson 1992; 2010), and reveals how they are differently racialised by language and languaged by race. These postcolonial migrants testify to how *jus linguarum* perpetuates and exacerbates the racial hierarchies within the Anglophone world and to how they are perpetually *seen* as linguistically deficient, and *heard* as racial and migrant outsiders. These postcolonial migrants speak of their complex relationship with the English language; a relationship of desire and subjugation that takes the form of cruel optimism, enervation and anger.

'The speaking citizen part II' (subtitled 'the verbal and audial hygiene of *jus linguarum*') focuses on citizenship ceremonies as sites where *jus linguarum* is normalised and naturalised. It looks at practices of verbal and audial hygiene required of new citizens in the name of national cohesion and serenity. The section situates such practices in the broader political climate and moral panic about multilingualism leaking into the public domain and disturbing the audial serenity of English-Britishness. Consequently, speakers of other languages are stigmatised and expelled from the public space in a move that migratises them as perpetual outsiders, and racialises them as not (quite) white. The section extends understandings of languaging to the expulsion of presumed white European languages that are not only migratised as undesirable intruders; rather, the violent injunction to 'speak English' constitute acts of purifying whiteness – 'speak white' – that add foreignness to the layers of white hierarchy marked by class, gender, race and ethno-nationalism.

The chapter concludes with a discussion of how *jus linguarum* has become given in Britain, and the effects this has on the normalisation of (white) English monolingualism and on the 'migratisation' or 'racialisation' of those who speak otherwise. Provincialising English and languaging practices are inextricably linked to linguistic imperialism, past and present: other languages (and other Englishes) are spoken *here* because English was *there*. The conclusion returns to the waiting room of citizenship and unpacks how provincialising English and languaging *take time*, *take place* and *take hold* on aspiring citizens.

Jus linguarum in Britain: provincialising English and naturalising inequalities

The current citizenisation process and its language requirements were conceived in the aftermath of civil disturbances in Northern

England in the summer of 2001, as a means to ensure better integration and community cohesion and to 'rebuild a sense of common citizenship' (Home Office 2002: 10). Crucially, growing up in an 'English-free home', as David Cameron later put it in 2016,[3] was singled out in 2001 by Ann Cryer, then Labour MP for Keighley (a constituency in Bradford), as the main factor behind the perceived radicalisation of racially minoritised youth, particularly British Asians. In a speech she gave in the House of Commons in July 2001, and after criminalising and stigmatising Asian youths (particularly Pakistani and Bangladeshi) as under-achievers and trouble-makers, Cryer stated that:

> There is little point in blaming the situation simply on racism and Islamophobia.[4] We must instead consider in detail what causes the under-achievement that I have mentioned. The main cause is the lack of a good level of English, which stems directly from the established tradition of bringing wives and husbands from the sub-continent who have often had no education and have no English. (cited in Blackledge 2005: 103)

Other politicians subsequently followed suit,[5] reiterating the connection between language at home and radicalisation, and consequently stigmatising non-English speakers – particularly non-English speaking spouses from the Indian sub-continent – as failing or unwilling to participate in British public life and as potentially causing unrest and violence. By way of remedy, Cryer suggested (among other things), that language requirements be established as means of 'entry clearance' for spouses from non-European countries, as well as the requirement for them 'to take a full-time English course to reach a reasonable level' (cited in Blackledge 2005: 108).

Cultural political conflicts around language, race and class are not new in Britain (Hewitt 1986; Crowley [1989] 2003). But Cryer's speech sowed the seeds of what became the cornerstone of the new nationality bill adopted in 2002: language fluency is now legally and more formally tied to British *citizenship*. Cryer also set the stage for establishing correlations between monolingualism and social cohesion, on the one hand, and between multilingualism and social fragmentation, conflict and indeed terror, on the other (Cameron 2013: 69).

The White Paper on nationality, immigration and asylum laid
the grounds for current citizenisation measures and stated that:

> We need to develop a sense of civic identity and shared values, and
> knowledge of the English language (or Welsh language or Scottish
> Gaelic ...), can undoubtedly support this objective. (Home Office
> 2002: 32)

Thus tighter language requirements for immigrants seeking entry
(to work, study or marry) or seeking to settle in the UK were hailed
as key actions by the government aimed at creating 'common ground'
constitutive of a 'community of values' (Anderson 2013), that is:
'A clear sense of shared aspirations and values, which focuses on
what we have in common rather than our differences' (Department
for Communities and Local Government 2012: 10). The rationale
surrounding citizenisation measures purports that a shared *national*
language is a necessary channel for interpersonal, social and cultural
values, and an efficient way to ensure peaceful cohabitation between
'communities'. English proficiency is not only a vehicle towards
shared British values; it has become both a *British value* and the
standard upon which the *value of foreign citizens* and their will and
capacity to integrate are judged.

Implicit in the legislation is the idea of 'one-nation-one-language'
that is widely linked to the birth of the modern European nation
that required the standardisation of language as a means to
create the imagined national community (Haugen 1966; Anderson 1991; Balibar 1991). What is more, with the creation of the
nation came the creation of 'language' as a discrete object, in what
has been variously described as a 'linguistic ideology' (Bourdieu
and Boltanski 1975), 'lingualism' and 'linguistic invention' (Makoni
and Pennycook 2007); that is, the creation of languages as separate, discernible and locatable systems (also Heller and McElhinny
2017).

The construction and naturalisation of language developed
alongside the construction and naturalisation of race, both of which
were key components of European colonial formations. Languages
were ascribed to different racialised groups, and, '[a]s with race,
the creation of language hierarchies positioned European languages
as superior to non-European languages' (Rosa and Flores 2017:
623). It followed that colonial regimes 'stipulated mastery of European

languages as a requirement for the evolution of colonized populations' (Rosa and Flores 2017: 627).

However, the management of the languages of the colonised was not uniform across empires. In the case of Britain, Alastair Pennycook explains that the standardisation of English was 'a very particular construction of the nineteenth century, one that was held in place by the discipline of linguistics', which in turn, developed in part as a reaction to 'the rapid expansion of the empire' (1994: 109, 115). Pennycook observes that the spread of the English language around the world produced a need to discipline it in a way that 'held the language and its desired meanings firmly in the hands of the central colonial institutions' (1994: 104). Just like citizenship in Britain developed through a history of immigration control (see Chapter 2), British linguistics grew out of the desire to contain, delineate and fix the English language – in both senses of repair and suture into place – as it migrated outside England.

The spread of English in the empire was subject to careful management. Colonial policies limited education in English to the few because English was linked to limited higher status jobs in the colonial administration, and the fear was that 'natives' who acquire even a little English would consider manual labour – much needed by the colonial regime – to be beneath them, leading them to foment social unrest (Pennycook 1994: 85–87). Therefore, what gave the English language its power was not so much its widening use, but rather the more prestigious social, economic and political positions that it gave individuals access to. As a result, English Language Teaching (ELT) became the locus of tensions between those who sought access to improve their status and colonisers who were hesitant to provide that access (Pennycook 1998).

Postcolonial and decolonial scholarship on English as a 'world language' examines the role of colonial regimes in 'disciplining' the English language and its speakers (Phillipson 1992; Pennycook 1994, 1998; Phillipson 2010; Gunew 2017), or in genocidal practices against indigenous languages (Skutnabb-Kangas 2000). Other decolonial critics call for education and support of 'native languages' as a means of resisting the global spread of the English language (Ngũgĩ 1986). A connecting theme among this scholarship is that the spread of English paradoxically cleared a space for the rise of 'other Englishes' as well as other languages that challenged, and continue to challenge, global hegemonic English (Bhabha 1994; Derrida 1998; Hitchcock 2001; Brutt-Griffler 2002; Chow 2014; Gunew 2017). Colonial policies and practices around language resulted in a 'linguicism'[6] that established a hierarchical distinction between the 'anglicised' and the 'English', where the former were and continue to be *'emphatically* not English' (Bhabha, 1994: 125, emphasis original; also Rosa and Flores 2017).

Such histories feed into ongoing inequities between monolingual English and multilingual Anglophones. As Scene 3 suggests, the Anglophone world is a spatial concept that is inhabited by speakers of other Englishes and other languages located outside of Britain and of the US. It is a world woven from raciolinguistic ideologies that marginalise the English of racially minoritised subjects as inferior, inadequate and in need of redress. As for the multilingual skills of the racially minoritised, they are disregarded or expelled from citizenisation as threats to cohesion and as barriers to integration, which I return to below ('The speaking citizen part II').

Language requirements for citizenisation continue to be shaped by colonial raciolinguistic ideologies, and migrants from white settler societies or the educated elites from the New Commonwealth or other countries are advantaged by the requirements (see Scene 1 for details).[7] The logic around language requirements is further shored up by the presumed 'global' status of English. In the White Paper on nationality, immigration and asylum, the then Home Secretary David Blunkett stated that the reason that so many migrants seek to enter Britain is in part 'because the universality of the English language and global communication flows mean that millions of people hear about the UK and often aspire to come here' (Home Office 2002: Foreword, n.p.).

Assumptions about the 'universality' of English presume its status as natural and timeless rather than the product of colonisation and raciolinguistic ideologies. Former Communities Secretary Eric Pickles suggested as much in his praise of the power of the English language around the world, leading him to declare that speaking English at home is a measure of good parenting:

> From Mumbai through to Beijing, every aspirational parent is trying to get their kids to learn English ... Because anyone with ambition – anyone with aspiration – values our great language. English is a passport to prosperity. (Pickles 2013)

Assumptions about the value of English frame the language practices of racially minoritised subjects 'as inadequate for the complex thinking processes needed to navigate the global economy', as Jonathan Rosa and Nelson Flores pointedly argue (2017: 627). In addition, assumptions about the worldliness of English take it as natural, equal and to the benefit of all. The expansion of the use of English in the world is seen as natural because it is understood as resulting from external global forces, such as 'globalisation'. It is seen as equally distributed, rather than as operating as a gate-keeping mechanism within colonies as well as in international migration flows (past and present). Finally, as Pennycook states, 'it is considered beneficial because a rather blandly optimistic view of international communication assumes that this occurs on a cooperative and equitable footing' (1994: 9).

Naturalised understandings of English as a global language deter-ritorialise it and make it the property of the world. What is unmarked here is how 'powerful English-speaking nations are both the producers and beneficiaries of English as a global language, and they tend to be monolingual' (Ellis 2006: 189). In the case of Britain, while 'national languages' such as Welsh and Scottish Gaelic are recognised, taught and spoken by some sections of the population, English remains the dominant language of the United Kingdom and, impor-tantly, speakers of English as their first language tend to be mono-lingual.[8] The unmarked monolingual English is the norm against which bilingualism and multilingualism are cast, regardless of the fact that the majority of the world's population is bilingual or multilingual, particularly in the Global South (Ellis 2006; Coetzee-Van Rooy 2016).

Such denials constitute a form of *provincialising English* in two ways. First, in the literal spatial sense of grounding the English language decidedly in Britain and concurrently, expelling multilingual-ism as something which occurs elsewhere but which, when reter-ritorialised here, should not leak into public civic life for it threatens national cohesion (more on this below). In addition, if *jus linguarum* is rooted in the acknowledgement of multilingualism as an inevitable reality, tensions arise between insisting on the prevalence of English as the 'national language', the status of English as a 'world language', and the 'reality' of multilingualism among the majority of the world population. Following Dipesh Chakrabarty's (2007) definition of provincialising Europe, the second way in which provincialising

English operates is that it acknowledges the indispensability of multilingualism to representations of English as both a world and national language, 'and yet struggles with the problems ... that this indispensability invariably creates' (Chakrabarty 2007: 22).

From the government perspective, one way to resolve these tensions is to adopt 'segregative strategies', which 'minimize the effect of multilingualism on public life' (Gramling 2016: 196). For example, cutting translation services in public institutions: in the *Sun* article where he praises the worldliness of English, Eric Pickles announced a cut of millions of pounds from translation services in order to put in '£6 million to encourage people to improve their lot' (Pickles 2013). Wrapped in a pedagogical rationale, the attitude towards translation has shifted from being 'endorsed as a way of providing access to ... ethnic minority communities in settlement services and policy' (Millar, 2014: 199), to being discouraged because it is seen to 'prevent interaction between groups, prevent language skills being developed, and in extreme cases even cause suspicion across groups' (Commission for Integration and Cohesion, cited in Millar 2014: 199).

Another strategy adopted by the government is to promote English proficiency as a necessary common good. Since language testing for migrant spouses or citizenship applicants was first suggested in 2001, the British government produced countless documents on integration: consultations, reports, guidance papers, green papers, white papers and several policies, laws and amendments regarding integration and language. At the time of writing, the latest output was the *Integrated Communities Action Plan* published in February 2019 (Ministry of Housing, Communities and Local Government 2019), which includes a plan for 'boosting English language', which is directed primarily, if not exclusively, at immigrant populations and learners of 'English as a second language'. 'Speaking and understanding English means you are less vulnerable to isolation, improves your work prospects, increases your chance of friendships with people from different backgrounds and allows you to feel more confident when accessing local services' (Ministry of Housing, Communities and Local Government 2019: 13). Such rhetoric exemplifies *jus linguarum* by establishing fluency in the national lingua franca as a ticket to greater economic, social and personal integration.

Furthermore, when tracking the trajectory of British policy on language and integration, a noteworthy qualitative shift can be detected through the years: *language skills have become ossified as markers of inequality*. The 2019 government action plan follows up on a Green Paper on integration published in March 2018 (Ministry of Housing, Communities and Local Government 2018), which in turn was informed by recommendations issued by Louise Casey in her review on integration published in December 2016 (Casey 2016). These two texts repeatedly connect poor English language skills with poverty, unemployment and poor integration. For example, low English skills are correlated to the 'increased segregation among Pakistani and Bangladeshi ethnic households' (Casey 2016: 14) and the increased 'likelihood that a person lived in a more deprived area or in an area with a higher proportion of people who spoke the same (non-English) language' (Ministry of Housing, Communities and Local Government 2018: 36). Both documents recommend the promotion of English language for those 'too many people who don't speak English' (Ministry of Housing, Communities and Local Government 2018: 35): those 770,000 people aged 16 years and over who 'cannot speak English well or at all' according to the 2011 Census (Ministry of Housing, Communities and Local Government 2018: 35; also Casey 2016: 94). It is worth noting that 770,000 people represents about 1.8 per cent of the total population. More to the point, there is no sense of what 'speaking well' or 'low' English skills mean, nor is there any indication of what other languages these individuals might speak fluently and how much they use, indeed need, these other languages in their daily lives. Moreover, there is no consideration of how 'good' English speakers might also have limited prospects.

This is one way in which migratism works (Tudor 2018) – migrants are marginalised by virtue of being migrants, which here is signalled by their use of other languages. There is no account of how migrants might share the same precarious conditions with other, non-migrant 'good' English speakers (who have poor literacy skills, for example). Class and racial inequalities are erased in favour of linguistic inequalities. As a result, the repeated equation between poor integration on the one hand, and poor English language skills or the use of other languages on the other, *naturalises inequalities through language*. Framed in the discourse of opportunity rather than inequality – the Casey review is titled 'a review into opportunity and integration' – government policy on language and integration skirts the ways in which inequalities and inequities are reproduced through language.

The normalisation of inequalities through language is also about the erasures of the different material conditions of English acquisition. In the world of *jus linguarum*, the reduction of individual achievement to results on language tests erases both the unequal conditions under which individuals are assessed in the first place, and the role of the state in creating and reproducing inequalities between the more or less 'integratable' or 'able'. Fluency in the national lingua franca is framed in a neoliberal, post-ethnic vision of the 'freedoms and equalities' afforded by language, as one ceremony dignitary told me with reference to Asian wives,[9] which I return to below. The point I wish to make here is that what escapes Gramling's analysis is how superdiversity and multilingualism are normalised and incorporated into *national* framings and enduring colonising desires. In Britain, language grounds a renewed version of ethnic and racialised citizenship. As Deborah Cameron (2013: 69) argues, the re-emergence of language in political debates and its formalised connection to citizenship were motivated by the political need to define 'Britishness', which:

> often became bogged down in an unsatisfactory mixture of general principles with no distinctively British content (e.g. belief in democracy and the rule of law) and trivial minutiae (e.g. talking about the weather and forming orderly queues). Language offered a solution to this coding problem: monolingualism and multilingualism were pressed into service as the metaphorical correlates, respectively, of social cohesion and social fragmentation, while speaking English became one of the marks of Britishness.

Indeed, during the course of my fieldwork a British Social Attitudes (BSA) survey in 2014 found that 95 per cent of respondents agree that to be 'truly British' you must be able to speak English (compared to 86 per cent in 2003).[10]

Such is the discursive and policy context of the pedagogical monolingual state that 'provincialises English': it establishes English as a 'natural' foundation of the civic nation, as a 'natural' aspirational skill for everyone in the world, and it brackets multilingualism as elsewhere, secondary and privatised. This is the context in which aspiring settled residents or citizens are compelled to speak English.

The speaking citizen part I: on (not) speaking English

'They're making for us very hard … too much hard', said Malika, a 36-year-old Pakistani woman who came to the UK on a spousal visa one and a half years prior to our meeting in 2013. She was attending a one-week intensive ESOL class in the hope of achieving the English fluency credentials she needed to renew her spousal visa after two and a half years, and eventually to be granted Indefinite Leave to Remain (ILR) and perhaps citizenship.

Knowledge of traditions, values, laws, histories and language are the mainstay of integration requirements, and they are measured by tests. The acquisition of such knowledge is presented as an upskilling opportunity that is easily accessible to all. What is obscured in such representations is the labour needed to acquire the 'right' level of English fluency and to pass the citizenship test; a labour that is uneven among those seeking ILR or citizenship, and which impacts on the time it takes to be ready to submit their application for ILR or citizenship. This section includes two parts: first, it contemplates the labour (including emotional labour) required of those tasked to teach or learn English and prepare for the citizenship test. Second, it then examines different affective relationships to the English language that migrants have – particularly migrants who themselves carry the aural and audial traces of linguistic imperialism – shedding light on colonial legacies of languaging that emplace individuals in variously injurious speaking relations.

Labouring to learn

Scene D

The classroom has gone quiet as the learners are working through the exercise sheet they were given. The teacher walks around the room, stops to assist a student and perhaps correct their mistake. There is an assistant in today's class, because it includes learners of E1 and E2 level. This requires a lot of planning in order to ensure that all learners get through enough material in each session. E1 and

E2 learners are working on different exercises, each suitable for their level. The E2 exercise includes listening to a recording about shopping; I wonder how the other learners can concentrate. As the teacher is helping the E1 learners, the assistant is attending to the E2 learners. Then they swap when the teacher gets the discussion going for the E2 group.

Scene E

Teacher: The next word is popular. So if you are popular do people like you or do they not like you?

Pupils: Popular/ [Ana] 'particular'

Teacher: No. Po-pu-lar

Ana: Popular

Teacher: Ok, good. The next word is portable. If something is portable what can you do with it?

Learners: Portable

Teacher: Por-ta-ble. Portable

Learners: Portable.

Teacher: [lifting a laptop] This is portable, you can carry it, it is portable. The next word is radio.

The ESOL classroom is a place of work: learners concentrate and bend over their worksheets to listen to a recording and identify the items named in the recording. Some consult their neighbour for help. They shape their lips and tongues to repeat sounds, syllables, words as they echo the teacher, again and again. Only a minority of those enrolled in the classes I observed were seeking ILR or citizenship. The majority of others were either settled residents with ILR or EU migrants.

Initially and up to 2013, language requirements for citizenship separated the process into two routes: either the Life in the UK (LUK) test for those fluent enough in English, or an ESOL speaking and listening test showing progression from one level to the next for those will lower levels of fluency (see Scene 1). The differentiation between those on the citizenship route and those who are not is invisible in the classroom. If teachers know who is on a route for ILR, settlement or citizenship, legal statuses dissolve in the classroom under the principle axis of differentiation that is fluency level: two groups of different levels in the same class will be busy doing different exercises. While differentiation of legal status between learners is made invisible, differentiation of social status based on language is made apparent: the levels have the effect of reinstating fissures between individuals, reinstating their different positions, histories, cultural capitals and futures.

Language tests (as well as citizenship tests) are means of inclusion and exclusion which are framed as beneficial to integration and participation in ways that distract from the experience of the testing regime by those affected by it (Cooke 2009). One woman, Fatima, who came to Britain from Pakistan ten years before we met in 2014, did not understand what the fuss was about and found it very difficult to find time to study for the citizenship test.

> I don't know what the important thing because ... I've very keen, I'm a housewife, look after children and is really what I enjoy ... Because I haven't got time.

Fatima's life revolves around her family, and the demands that citizenship puts on her exceed its significance in her understanding of her everyday life. Aisha, introduced in Scene 4 that follows this chapter, also told me about the challenges of pursuing ESOL classes while working part-time and caring for two children on her own. Moreover, that these women had been in the country for several years before their naturalisation was indicative of the ways in which '[i] nequalities both "inside" and "outside" of the [citizenisation] process ... shape migrant women's experiences of naturalization' (Bassel, Monforte and Khan 2018: 232). Leah Bassel and her colleagues (2018: 233) argue that integration processes cannot be understood outside of the inequalities that shape people's lives, such as the enduring gender inequalities in the division of domestic labour as well as inequalities on the basis of race, class and gender in the labour market. Citizenship took a long time for Fatima and Aisha, and sometimes was put on hold, as they navigated domestic and paid labour responsibilities.

For ESOL professionals, in turn, the introduction of language requirements to the citizenisation process impacted on ESOL provision and teaching practices. One of the consequences of the ESOL route to ILR or citizenship was to increase enrolments to ESOL classes, which already had limited spaces. Fran, an ESOL professional, said that this cleared a space for 'an open market' and 'handed the [ESOL] business on a plate to private training providers'. Accreditation regulations were implemented to ensure that these new businesses had the appropriate credentials and to avoid 'bogus' language schools, which have drawn much media attention over the years. Successive governments cut funding for ESOL provision, which meant a drop in enrolment as well as a drop in provision. Still, private schools continue to attract learners, especially those that design courses specifically to prepare for the LUK test, which now all applicants for ILR or citizenship must undertake.

Another consequence of introducing language requirements in the citizenisation process was that ESOL provision, which had hitherto a relatively low status in the education landscape, became highly politicised (Han, Starkey and Green 2010). Several ESOL teachers expressed their unhappiness about the changes to their teaching that resulted from the introduction of language requirements for citizenship (and for ILR since 2007). Many struggled with the dilemma of teaching as a political practice (Kiwan 2013b) or even simply a caring practice, versus the expectation that they decide on someone's fate when assessing migrants' levels of English proficiency. Fran explained the initial ESOL requirements thus:

> [I]f you are examining [immigrants] for a language exam, they can talk about anything they like. I've had refugees talk about torture, … who can't use anything but the present tense, but, my God … you understand *exactly* what they're saying. But if you're examining them on their language, you know, then the national curriculum says that Entry 1 you do present tenses and Entry 2 you can do simple tasks and going to futures and Entry 3 you've learned your tenses … They've got the vocab, they've got an endless vocab, but not necessarily the grammar.

Fran was distinguishing between communication ability and grammatical skills, the latter being integral to the benchmarks for assessing progression between levels, which in turn was, prior to 2013, a necessary criterion for obtaining settlement or citizenship. She is favouring communicative ability rather than linguistic competence (Phipps 2013), the latter being the basis of *jus linguarum*. If language requirements were only about communicating, she argued, many applicants would be eligible for citizenship status.

Fran's distinction is akin to distinguishing between listening like an ally and hearing like a state (to paraphrase James Scott 1998). More specifically, what ESOL professionals are required to do is to hear *for* the state by *listening for* grammatical accuracy according to standardised English. For Fran and several other ESOL professionals I met, communication skills are trumped by the technologisation of standardised language as a measurable skill (cf. Millar 2014). What is more, institutional assessments and distinctions between levels (L1, L2 or 'beginner', 'intermediate', 'advanced') 'are often measures of the capacity to inhabit and enact idealized whiteness rather than empirical linguistic practices' (Rosa and Flores 2017: 633). Indeed, the institutionalisation of language competence as a citizenship requirement is not only about disciplining subjects into 'good' English speakers. It is also about disciplining them into an idealised white bodily comportment – a white habitus (more on this below). Listening for the state is also about seeing like a state (Scott 1998).

Fran's critique is shared by most ESOL professionals I met, and ESOL pressure groups persistently challenge government policies around ESOL and citizenship requirements, among other issues. But in practice, ESOL teachers and examiners find themselves in very difficult positions, as Alan explains:

> this is not just the standard course ... it's a life changing course for them ... it's getting that stamp on the passport, and so, ... you know, we charge three hundred and fifty pound for an eight week course and it's like seven hundred quid if they've had to come on two blocks and they've failed and it's a horrible, horrible thing to do. ... I've never experienced being put under that sort of pressure. ... So it's, it's all a bit, it's not as enjoyable and I know a lot of tutors are really stressed out in ESOL now.

On the one hand, Alan is profiting from the citizenisation measures, as are many private schools that have filled the space left open by successive cuts in ESOL government funding. On the other hand, Alan and many other ESOL professionals also recognise the stakes involved in assessing their students. But what interests me here is how Alan's and other ESOL professionals' critiques are underpinned by a sense of loss of the pleasure of ESOL teaching. Several teachers contrasted the past joy of teaching when it was 'only about language', and one teacher put it to me, which some see as a 'common ground' that both learners and teachers share. Citizenisation is understood as having created new inequalities and pressures for learners and teachers. It is worth noting, however, that ELT provision has and continues to be a global enterprise that is complicit in the unequal spread of English in the world, and the 'common ground' was never a level playing field; the current language requirements for citizenship are merely an extension of that history (Phillipson 1992, 2010; Pennycook 1994). That said, what becomes apparent to these ESOL professionals is that they are unwillingly conscripted in the transnational field of professionals charged with securitising the state and its national culture, as Didier Bigo put it (2002), by being expected to use language as a form of everyday border control.

Many teachers expressed their concerns about engaging in 'everyday bordering' (Yuval Davis, Wemyss and Cassidy 2019) on behalf of the Home Office, as one ESOL professional put it to me: 'Woa, hold on, I'm a language teacher, I'm not going to monitor for the Home Office!'. This new role appended to ESOL provision makes many teachers feel powerless; after pointing out the distinction between ability to communicate and competence in grammatical correctness, Fran added: 'So they're absolutely fluent but couldn't make a past tense to save their life, what do we do?' Such a sentiment was echoed by several other ESOL teachers, who feel caught in a bind and are acutely aware of the stakes when assessing – and sometimes forced to fail – those who need a language certificate to be able to remain in the country.

A lot of emotional labour is required of teachers who seek to support those whose lives hang on the tests:

> you're their best friend, you're their counsellor, you're their … sign for, you know their tutor, everything and it makes that, it makes it very difficult for the tutors because I always say to my staff don't get involved, don't get involved … but what can you do when someone is in distress? (Alan)

The detachment expected of teachers is difficult, if not impossible, to sustain. But there are some rewards; Marianne was invited to accompany one of her students at her citizenship ceremony. Support and solidarities develop between teachers and learners, or among learners themselves, in ways that testify to the productive potential of language learning – a potential that is ruptured by state-imposed testing regimes with high stakes attached to them.

As mentioned above, the current language requirements favour migrants from white settler societies and the educated elite from former colonies or other countries. Indeed, those from majority English speaking countries – therefore exempt from providing evidence of English fluency – might not all have the level of education that ensures the adequate literacy skills to handle the *Life in the UK* study guide in preparation for the citizenship test. As Fran argued, the text in the study guide requires skills 'much higher than [Entry] Level 3 could cope with'; it is more like a 'good GCSE-level' book, according to her (also White 2008). She cited the example of 'Jamaicans' who 'are not literate or whose literacy skills are appalling, and they can't do the Life in the UK test'. Fran used the figure of 'the Jamaican' to point out the inequities of the citizenisation system. Those who were not literate enough to easily pass the citizenship test were likely to fall through the cracks left between the ESOL route and the Life in the UK route. They were not eligible for language classes because they were already at the top level of the speaking and listening skills, but they struggled to pass the test.

This gap was not closed in 2013 by the imposition of *both* evidence of English fluency and passing the LUK test. If anything, failure rates increased from 29 per cent in 2009 (BBC News 2010) to 36 per cent in 2016 (Aru and Lubin 2017). Applicants from poorer countries tend to pass the citizenship test at a lower rate than those from other countries.[11] This confirms the general trend noted by researchers that language and knowledge requirements 'pose a greater burden on nationals of poorer, less educated and non-English-speaking countries' (Ryan 2008 cited in Blinder 2017; also Cameron 2013).

What interests me here is the *figuring* of those who fall through the literacy gap in terms that racialise through language. The figure of 'the Jamaican' has a long history in post-war Britain, one that is associated with violent masculinity and crime. Jamaican patois, for its part, has long since been a 'cultural battleground'

Uncertain citizenship

(Hall et al. 1978: 341; Hewitt 1986; Hebdige 1987) in the cultural politics of race and class. In 2011, historian David Starkey caused public outcry when stating on public television that the white working-class youth 'have become black', citing their use of Jamaican patois as evidence. He contrasted Jamaican patois with Harvard-educated African Caribbean MP David Lammy who Starkey said sounds white (Quinn 2011). This form of languaging combines class and race, where subjects are both classed and racialised by language.

But they are also languaged by race. For Rey Chow (2014: 8), 'the visual and audial significations of the word *tones*' come to bear in languaging. 'The Jamaican' is associated with a particular sound, one that for Fran, is illiterate, and for Starkey is working class and sounds like 'a particular sort of violent, destructive, nihilistic, gangster culture [that] has become the fashion' (cited in Quinn 2011). Similarly, the figure of 'the Asian spouse' evoked by Ann Cryer looms large in fears of other languages spoken in Asian homes and their link to radicalisation. In January 2016, then Prime Minister David Cameron announced plans to inject funds for ESOL classes specifically targeting Asian Muslim spouses. In an interview on the subject, he explained the rationale through the figure of the young Asian boy's 'slide towards radicalisation':

> Think about the young boy growing up in Bradford. His parents came from a village in Pakistan. His mum can't speak English and rarely leaves the home, so he finds it hard to communicate with her, and she doesn't understand what is happening in his life. At the same time, as a teenager he is struggling to identify with western culture. Separate development and accepting practices that go against our values only emphasise differences and can help prompt the search of something to belong to. When that happens, the extremist narrative gives him something – however ridiculous – to believe in.[12]

These gendered figures – the non-English speaking mother, the 'lost' young Asian man – are languaged by race. Ann Cryer could not *hear* the English Northern accent of the youths she was referring to; she could only *see* their Asianness. Skin tones inflect how vocal tones are heard, and in turn, vocal tones inflect how skin tones are seen or imagined. As Chow suggests, the voice is 'de facto an (objectified, artefactual) exterior and surface, not unlike skin, on which is ... inscribed an explicit demand, left over from an unequal historical relation' (2014: 9). In the context that concerns us here, the demand is to speak like 'us' – to speak white English. A noteworthy nuance, however, is that some 'other Englishes' are acceptable – the fluent North American, for example, may be heard as someone who is not *from* Britain, but they are not asked to speak *like* Britons. Some tones are more acceptable than others.

Though Starkey was arguably widely castigated, his statement is telling of enduring ideas of 'good English' that are deeply rooted in class and racial discrimination and that recall the moral panic around Jamaican patois (Hall et al. 1978), or children with other 'mother tongues' in the classroom documented in 1970s and 1980s Britain (e.g. Phillipson 1992). Everyday linguistic racisms are not new, in that sense. But what is different today is that while earlier responses led to forms of institutionalised monolingualism as in the education system, today speaking English is formally tied to citizenship and, by extension, to British nationality, making it legitimate to declare that Britishness and some versions of English fluency racialised as white go hand in hand.

Desire, enervation and speaking otherwise

Jeremy is an Indian-Malaysian British man who I met in 2012. Jeremy strongly identifies as British and speaks fondly of the English language, which he sees as a 'blessing' and 'a wonderful gift of this country to the world'. He tells me how his father encouraged him to learn English and he recalls the following:

> we were still a colony in 1950–55, so it was my primary … secondary school and I had a wonderful English teacher Mrs Scott, I remember [He laughs] Ohh, I practically fell in love with her, she was beautiful and oh, I, I was, I became enamoured with the language after she taught us.

Jeremy's appreciation of the English language as a 'gift to the world' carries the traces of his early encounters with the language under colonial rule, where English language training is steeped in the meanings that language conveys through its association with the superiority of 'standard' (British) English, and its association with the desirable white British 'native speaker' who embodied English culture and language. Jeremy was brought up with the notion that learning English was a passport to England, and he considers it the responsibility of all migrants:

> to make sure [they] master the English language. I stand before you as an example of one who has done this. English is the language spoken here and if we do not learn to read and write it properly, we will always feel we are second-class citizens.

Throughout our conversation, Jeremy oscillated between, on the one hand, worrying about the unequal access to English tuition for migrants because of years of cuts in government funding and the dangers of tethering language to citizenship. On the other hand, he was also waxing lyrical about English language and culture as gifts to the world.

I met several other individuals who were younger than Jeremy, who grew up long after formal decolonisation, and who also spoke fondly of the English language. They were men and women from Pakistan, Iran, Iraq or India, most of whom had been introduced to English at school. Like Jeremy, they came to Britain bearing the oral and audial traces of linguistic imperialism, with their desire for the English language and what it represents.

Khebat was a 27-year old Kurdish man from Iran when I met him in May 2013 in a private language school where he was taking a one-week intensive English language class to try to fulfil the ESOL requirement for ILR – at a cost of £300. He had arrived as an asylum seeker in 2004 and was refused refugee status. He was living in Britain on a three-year exceptional leave to remain visa. Khebat spoke animatedly about his desire for English and England: he said, 'my dream it was learning English, be in England'. I asked him to tell me about that dream: 'when did it start?'

> Khebat: I remember I was in first years in school, imagine about seven years, eight years [old] [...] I used to say to my teacher, just teach me one word, you know? Just please teach me one word, because I don't know I love to learn in English. That's why I come here.
>
> AMF: And it was in England that you wanted to come to, not in the US, it was England?
>
> K: It was proper English yeah.
>
> AMF: Hmm [sounding sceptical] *proper* English ...
>
> K: Proper English, I mean British.

Khebat's dream of coming to Britain where he would find 'proper English' is a manifestation of the endurance of the colonial disciplining of the worldliness of British English. I wonder if his expression of love for the language and for the country – which he repeated several times in the course of our conversation – was a way to outdo what Derrida might call the 'performative contradiction' (Derrida 1998: 3) of his claim to love English and England, but where his very utterances belie his 'deficiency', his 'broken English', his otherness.

The injunction to speak English comes with a promise of recognition, integration and citizenisation. But the promise puts individuals in a protracted position of hope that requires a lot of time and energy to sustain. Khebat again:

> I mean, when I first time arrived … always used to be my dream since young, to speak English, always … [But now] I wanna just leave here this year and go somewhere else, because there's no point, life is getting harder. This is my [inaudible] it's why I come to UK. But when I come here in UK it was fantastic that time, I love to be here but now I don't want to live here I want to run away. […] I mean it's hard to say but I love, I love to live here. I don't understand, this country it doesn't let me come, I don't know why. Always I say to myself, not just me, everybody, I want to go tomorrow but something like holding me back here, you know? It's, it's really crazy.

Khebat is caught up in the relation of cruel optimism, in Lauren Berlant's phrase, that 'exists when something you desire is actually an obstacle to your flourishing' (2011: 1). His desire for Britain has faded as a result of the hardship of trying to fulfil his desire. He is also troubled by the country's rejection of him, leading him to want to leave while he remains drawn to stay. 'Something' is keeping him here.

What also comes across in Khebat's words is the loss of a sense of purpose. There's 'no point' in staying here, he suggests, yet he tries again to find a way to stay in this country, to have a peaceful life running his small business in a Lancashire city. He is tired and has lost faith. His love of England, and of English, has faded after years of moving, working, seeking asylum, paying for language classes and waiting for one visa to run out and applying for the next one. And he is exhausted.

In her book about the unequal global distribution of endurance and exhaustion in late liberalism, Povinelli likens exhaustion to enervation which she describes as 'another form of violence: ... the weakening of the will rather than the killing of life' (2011: 132). Paradoxically, the measures for access to settlement and citizenship were ostensibly designed as tools to facilitate integration and to foster 'life in the UK' (Kiwan 2008). But for many, like Khebat, seeking 'life in the UK' is an exhausting form of cruel optimism. What struck me in Khebat's story is that he invested time, money and energy in taking an intensive ESOL class in the hope of getting the language credentials needed to apply for settlement, *even though he knew* that he was not eligible to apply for settlement as an asylum seeker without refugee status. Yet he persisted. Khebat spoke at length about the hardship of living in Britain, how difficult it is to survive, to get by, to get resident status, let alone citizenship. He spoke of the rules constantly changing; how he submitted to them and felt powerless in the face of them. He was struggling to fit himself into the policy and the mismatch played itself out in the way that he read the requirements for English fluency versus the way that the law read him as a perpetual outsider *regardless* of his English fluency.

But at the end of the day, when asked how he would define himself if he were granted citizenship, he unhesitatingly declared 'British'; 'not Kurdish-British or Iranian-British?' I asked. 'No, I will say I am British. I love to live [here]'. Were he to attend a citizenship ceremony, Khebat would undoubtedly be relieved and extremely happy. At that moment, he reminded me of a self-identified British-Lebanese man I met at a citizenship ceremony who looked at me, all smiles, his eyes welling up as he pounded his chest with a closed fist, telling me how happy he was to be granted British citizenship after 'so long in Britain'.

Khebat also insisted that he *should* be eligible for settlement and citizenship because he is fluent enough. He compared himself to a friend:

> they don't speak English, yeah? They don't do nothing even no been in college but has got British now, and I don't understand how come he has got British which is you have to do, UK Life I mean the test, you know the test in the UK but how can he passed? He don't speak English, he can no write his name and how he's got British. Shame, sometimes I see him I said, phww this is wrong.

'*You* understand me', he added, referring to our conversation as evidence of his adequate fluency. 'I can read English, there's no point to be using my time here, you know, pay three hundred pounds, everything about money now'. Khebat understood himself as having the linguistic capital of the desirable 'integrated' English speaking citizen. Yet Khebat also understood that he is seen as linguistically deficient – he may be anglicised but he is not heard as English (speaking).

Khebat hails from that Anglophone world resulting from linguistic imperialism, which gave rise to 'other Englishes' that challenge global hegemonic English. He came to Britain bearing not only the aural legacies of colonialism, but also its affective imprints. Both Khebat's and Jeremy's accounts are telling of the role of desire in manufacturing the authority of English as an international language. They resonate with Frantz Fanon's evocative account of the Antillean's aspiration to master the French language, which comes with the promise of making him whiter ([1952] 2008: 18). Fanon tracks the kinds of subjectivity created through the spread of language in colonial regimes and how they are tied up in complex languaging relations of desire and repression.

But we can also argue that Khebat is striving for the recognition of his *capability* rather than his linguistic competence (Phipps 2013). *Jus linguarum* is grounded in the neoliberal principles of enhancing one's human capital as a worker, 'participant' in public life and enabler of community cohesion. In contrast, Khebat is showing his capability not at speaking *the* language, but at communicating effectively and at being much more than what the language tests would reveal.

A similar account comes from Nicole, a Filipina refugee who I met in 2013:

> The government is making us dumb saying that we do not speak English. But we run this country! We run the capital! [laughs] We are workers; look at us, we're working in your toilets we're working in your offices we're working to take good care of your old ladies and your sick and your disabled families [...]
>
> But even though Filipinos speak English you know, they couldn't pass the Life in the UK test. Cause it's too ... But they've been in the country working and there's no problem with their job I mean they can communicate they can understand simple English they can understand the rota they can understand the erm erm erm [trails off].

If Khebat is drained, Nicole is angry. She is angry at the deafness to what it means to speak a language that you cannot claim to be your own (Derrida 1998); to work, communicate, listen in another language, day in day out. The minoritisation of other Englishes comes with the minoritisation and devalorisation of the subject who speaks other languages, sometimes several other languages. Like Khebat, Nicole – who acquired British citizenship soon after we met – was naming the raciolinguist ideology whereby the racially minoritised are *made* into linguistically deficient subjects who are perpetually *migratised* as alien to white English Britishness.

Felix is also from the Philippines. He had recently sent off his citizenship application when we met in 2013. He told me about 'simple everyday things', such as:

> when you go to the shop and people sort of look at you and then look at my [white Irish] partner and speak to him first ... But then when I speak to them and they realise 'oh he speaks English'. Then they change sort of behaviour, simple small things like that.

Similarly, when Jeremy speaks in what he qualifies as a good standard English, he is still seen as a foreigner though less of an outsider – an acceptable foreigner. He proudly recalled how on one occasion when we spoke to an audience of citizenship ceremony officials, he was applauded and praised for being 'the kind of citizen we want in this country'. Beyond the content of his speech, which praises the civic values of Britain,[13] Jeremy explains his success as down to his 'good English' – he explains that learning English in Malaysia 'stood him in good stead'. He also understands that as 'Indian looking', the expectation is that he speaks like an Indian man. Jeremy and Felix do not perform language in ways expected of them and they are treated differently as a result – praised for their 'good English'. They are languaged by race, and then re-racialised by language; not deracialised but reminded of and made into 'good Asians'. To paraphrase Sneja Gunew (2017: 26), 'for post-colonial immigrants like [Jeremy] who bear the legacy of a colonial British education this constitutes [a] kind of anomaly': he speaks British English and embraces all that it represents, but he is not of Britain, he is not English, even if he holds British citizenship. As Homi Bhabha might say, he is '*almost the same but not quite*' (1994: 123; emphasis original). *Seeing and hearing are inescapably caught up in the signification of surfaces* – skin surfaces, audial surfaces – that extend and reshape existing logics of exclusion based on race and class.

Together, Jeremy, Khebat, Nicole and Felix show how speaking a language does not mean sharing the same relationship to it. They show a different understanding of what 'good English' is: from the more elitist 'standard' English through to 'broken English' and 'Filipino English', as another Filipino interviewee put it. For Jacques Derrida, the monolingualism of the colonised always signals *other* languages (if only because of accents), and as such, always forces the question of the originality of 'the' language. Derrida writes: '*a* language [e.g. *an* English, like Filipino English or Jamaican patois] will always be called upon to speak about *the* language [*the* British English] – *because* the latter does not exist' (1998: 69; unbracketed emphases Derrida's). In short, there is no original. In this sense, Jeremy's, Khebat's, Nicole's and Felix's 'monolingualism of the other', in Derrida's phrase, reminds us that 'English' is ultimately unlocatable. 'Language is something that no one, not even the master and colonizer, can possess' (Chow 2014: 29).

That said, and perhaps *because* English is unlocatable, what *jus linguarum* does is to solidify language and citizenship in a way that naturalises 'national language' rather than recognising it as a constructed racialised category. If modern citizenship emerged 'in the context of the development of the '"subject capable of property"' (Bhambra 2015: 105; also Brace 2004), then denial of *linguistic* property – of a legitimate ownership or legitimate use of other Englishes and other languages – to multilingual other-English speakers is also denying them citizenship, virtually if not legally.

What is more, the differences between them suggest that sharing a language says nothing about the historical, affective and material connections they might have to that language. Nor does speaking the same national lingua franca shed light on the unequal distribution of 'language' in the 'Anglophone' community and the resulting racialised hierarchies of belonging that ensue. To consider how English as a global and national language is lived and embodied, in such a way that its disappears for some – remember Eric Pickles, David Blunkett and Ann Cryer above – while it is intensely visible, audible and injurious for others, sheds light onto how 'national language' and whiteness are conjoined categories of experience. But to consider English as global *and* national also raises tensions that are constitutive of provincialised English, where anxieties about multilingualism leaking into the public domain are addressed through practices of verbal and audial hygiene that further normalise and naturalise *jus linguarum*. Citizenship ceremonies are a case in point.

The speaking citizen part II: the verbal and audial hygiene of *jus linguarum*

Passing the citizenship test makes one eligible for applying for citizenship (EU applicants) or indefinite leave to remain (non-EU applicants, who are then eligible to apply for citizenship one year later). In this section, I focus on citizenship ceremonies as sites of verbal and audial hygiene that serve to confirm the 'good', 'integrated' English-speaking citizen and to reassure the nation against the unwanted 'noise' of other languages in public spaces.

I begin with the planning of citizenship ceremonies that I observed in the 'nationality team' of a local council that I christened Stadlow Council (see Scene 1). In addition to the formal testing regimes discussed above, informal assessments occur as applicants or new citizens speak to various state actors. In Stadlow, I observed the phone team as they took calls from new citizens signing up for a ceremony. When registrars take calls, they bring up the caller's details on a computer screen as they are talking to them. They also upload an internal 'ceremony form', used for organising and planning the event, and they fill out the caller's details on the form. As they do this, if they consider the caller to be fluent in English they will at some point move their curser to a tick box for 'model citizen'. In doing so, they are identifying this person as someone to be seated in the front row of a ceremony and used as the 'model' that others could mimic.

The 'model citizen' is a bureaucratic tool used by the Stadlow nationality team – and to my knowledge, only by this council – to ensure the smooth and efficient running of ceremonies. But this minor everyday gesture, the simple clicking of the mouse, normalises 'English fluency' *as* model citizenship. The fluent English 'model citizen' is routinised and normalised because it does not appear as a social historical category that grew over time, through hierarchical logics and power relations, and through 'tacit forms of socialization' (Thompson 2005: 81). In the context of *jus linguarum*, the 'model citizen' is a citational practice that naturalises the status of the nationalised lingua franca as an unquestionable necessity for the public good and for becoming British.

When granted citizenship, new citizens receive a letter from the Home Office that instructs them to rehearse the oath of allegiance and citizenship pledge that they will pronounce at the ceremony, and which legally makes them citizens; the texts for both oath and pledge are provided in the letter (and they are reproduced in Scene 4 after this chapter). Many registrars told me that they encourage new citizens to rehearse the texts in advance when they take ceremony bookings; some even do it in a briefing session prior to the formal citizenship ceremony itself, as happened when I acquired British citizenship in 2011. The rehearsal conjures the image of individuals adapting their bodies to speak in English – contorting their lips, tongues, even their vocal cords to pronounce English words. This constitutes what Deborah Cameron calls 'verbal hygiene', which 'refers to all the normative metalinguistic practices through which people attempt to improve languages or regulate their use' (2013: 60). At the ceremony, as they utter the well-rehearsed oath of allegiance and citizenship pledge, the group performatively establish a collective of 'new' English speaking citizens who display discursive and communicative competence in English and 'comply *de facto* with a set of civic ideals' (Gramling 2016: 197; italics original) that have become codified in British law as 'knowledge of life and language' in the UK.

As argued above, language has become a way to signify Britishness that skirts questions of 'blood and soil' by legally codifying language as integral to civic ideals of integration, participation and social mobility. In a citizenship ceremony in a city in the North West, a ceremony dignitary reiterated the principles of *jus linguarum*:

> You can enjoy more of what your adoptive country has to offer you by speaking its language. It will help you to integrate better. Some of you, I'm sure, are very good at speaking the language, but those of you who are not, I would urge you to learn it, because it gives you independence, it gives you the richness and you will appreciate the culture … that you have adopted and the country [that] adopted you.

The common-sense politics of *jus linguarum* draw on assumptions about the necessity for a shared lingua franca that are difficult to contest. But what the politics also do is to make speaking the national lingua franca an obligation for the public good, as well as a measure of one's commitment and willingness to belong. The inducement to speak English to better appreciate their 'adoptive country' reminds the audience not only that they are still foreigners (more in Chapter 5), but also of their linguistic obligation. As already suggested, the promise of English fluency is that it will lead to integration. But it is also marked as a sign of migrants' commitment to Britain; of their worthiness, willingness and effort to integrate (Van Houdt, Suvarierol and Schinkel 2011). In his announcement of new require-ments in 2013, the then immigration minister Mark Harper stated that: 'The government expects that those wishing to become citizens should demonstrate their commitment by learning the English language, as well as having an understanding of British history, culture and traditions' (Home Office 2013b). In turn, 'failed' local cohesion is projected onto the migrants' assumed refusal to speak English. In 2011, Prime Minister David Cameron bemoaned the fact that:

> When large numbers of people arrive in new neighbourhoods, perhaps not all able to speak the same language as those who live there, perhaps not always wanting to integrate, perhaps seeking simply to take advantage of our NHS, paid for by our taxpayers, there is a discomfort and tension in some of our communities. (Cameron 2011b)

I argue elsewhere (2017a) that a constitutive feature of citizenisa-tion is the ambivalent desire–anxiety relationship to new citizens as 'givers' who can also be 'takers'. Cameron's words clearly iterate fears of the unwanted 'taker' whose poor English skills cause disu-nity. His conflation of poor language skills with neighbourhood discomfort and tension renders failed integration as the *responsibility* of migrants who are presumed to be unable or unwilling to speak English.

In contrast, citizenship ceremonies typically celebrate the desirable citizens, the 'givers' who have shown their commitment to the country by successfully passing the tests, and who will 'give back' to the country, in part by sharing their 'culture' in the much celebrated diversity of Britain (more in Chapter 5). One ceremony official from Stadlow Council invoked the multilingualism of the area:

> We speak 130 different languages in this borough and today we've got 18 countries representing … like a mini United Nations, we speak more languages than they speak at Brussels, we've got people from Afghanistan, Bulgaria, Dominica …

Over one hundred languages may well be spoken in the borough, but the myth is that these languages are encouraged in the public domain. Instead, the citizenisation process and its cornerstone *jus linguarum* uphold cultural diversity and acknowledge multilingualism, while discouraging the substantive use of other languages in the public domain (Gramling 2016: 196). In this sense, citizenship ceremonies performatively reassert the 'myth of cosmopolitan monolingualism' (Gramling 2016: 27), which 'is *reactive* in nature as a public policy strategy – rooted, paradoxically, in the recognition that multilingualism has become a societal norm' (Gramling 2016: 196; emphasis added). Such a recognition is at the heart of anxieties about the verbal hygiene of citizenship. The normalisation of fluency in the 'national' language means that this national language as a *historical category* disappears. And this is a historical category that cannot be dissociated from colonial and racial imaginaries.

The idea of verbal hygiene conjures histories of racism, miscegenation and the hygienist ethos driving eugenics. As discussed above, the racially minoritised are assumed to be, and often heard as, linguistically deficient and migrant outsiders. Verbal hygiene is not about audial regimes alone. It connects with visual regimes, and when a racially minoritised subject speaks 'good' English – practises good verbal hygiene – the reaction is one of surprise or praise.

But when considered in the context of ongoing moral panics about other Englishes or other languages, the idea of verbal hygiene extends into what I call 'audial hygiene'. The verbal hygiene required of immigrants is about protecting the audial hygiene of the national public space. Citizenship ceremonies, for example, are stages where an audience of invited guests – usually family or friends related to the new citizens – as well as ceremony officials, witness the performance of an aspirational public sphere of future English speaking 'new' citizens. This is perhaps most evidently displayed at London's 'iconic' citizenship ceremony.

Each year, the London mayoralty holds a pan-London citizenship ceremony that gathers new citizens from the 32 boroughs that comprise Greater London. When asked about how new citizens from the boroughs are selected, one of the organisers told me that:

> it's very random. The Home Office tend to select from the new citizens who have taken the Life in the UK test in case there is media attention and we have people who can barely speak English. It doesn't look good.

Or rather, it doesn't sound good. Thus, the verbal hygienic practices required of new citizens are also about protecting the audial hygiene of the ceremony as a public event. Audial hygiene is a practice of cleansing audial surfaces of undesirable 'poor' English; a form of technology of reassurance that *protects national audial serenity*.

The organiser's concern about media attention must be set in the context of contemporary anxieties about English fluency. Politicians and political commentators from across the political spectrum repeatedly state that speaking English is essential not only to integrate, but also to protect neighbourhoods from discomfort, to protect communities from fragmentation, violence and even terror, and to 'feel British' (Boris Johnson cited in Brooks 2019). Others, like Nigel Farage,[14] speak of feeling estranged in their own country because of hearing other languages on public transport (cited in Hope 2014).[15] Such white anxieties revolve around the perceived minoritisation of the 'national' language – and, by extension, of the nation itself – understood as being under siege by the growing presence of other languages. For Gilles Deleuze, the effect of rendering the national language foreign can potentially open itself to the discovery of the foreignness within it (cited in Gunew 2005: 78). *Jus linguarum* rides on the historical amnesia of linguistic imperialism that enabled the establishment of 'standard English' *through* its relation to foreign languages in foreign lands, not against them.

However, Farage and other politicians and policy-makers do not 'discover' the foreignness that is constitutive of (the) English. Rather, in keeping with the principles of provincialised English and unlike the assumed deterritorialised 'worldliness' of English, when *other* languages are deterritorialised 'from their supposed originating territory they become associated with non-assimilable alterity and danger' (Gunew 2017: 17).

The cumulative effect of English fluency as a marker of 'good' British citizenship and belonging, combined with the stigmatisation of other languages as disturbing national audial serenity, sanctions what can be termed 'everyday linguistic racism', following Philomena Essed (1991).[16] That is, routine or less routine instances where white-bodied English-British individuals feel emboldened to take it upon themselves to punish those who are heard as transgressors and spoilers of the audial surface of the public space. In the weeks and months following Brexit, there was much reporting of Eastern Europeans being violently attacked or even killed after being heard speaking a language other than English in public (Dearden 2016; Lusher 2016). A climate of fear shapes many EU citizens' public behaviours. 'I didn't want to be heard speaking Greek in public because I was aware of the criticism that it might cause', said Ella, who went on to explain how on one occasion when she was walking with a friend's child, she devised an elaborate game to avoid speaking Greek as they passed a group of young people. Foreign language users like Ella exercise practices of verbal hygiene to protect the audial hygiene of presumed non-foreign British English speakers.

It bears repeating that while everyday linguistic racism is not new in Britain, the fears experienced by white-bodied Europeans is compounded by the unravelling of their sense of security *as* white-bodied EU citizens residing in Britain. This is not to undermine their fears and concerns, but rather to situate their specific experience in the broader racist structures of exclusion that shape migration and citizenship regimes which erase, for example, the existence of black Europeans under hegemonic constructions of Europe or 'EU citizenry' (El-Tayeb 2011; Tudor 2018). In turn, everyday linguistic racism against white-bodied EU citizens poses the question of how languaging works here; to what extent do race and language intersect in these instances? It could be argued that these (presumably) European-language speaking subjects are not so much racialised through language as they are *migratised* through language; that is, they are ascribed migrant and *outsider* status within the British national space. Migratism, as Alyosxa Tudor explains, is about 'the power relation that ascribes migration to certain bodies and establishes non-migration as the norm of intelligible national and European belonging' (2018: 1058). Seen in this light, the expulsion of other languages from the public sphere *fixes* the English language in place, securing it *against* multilingualism.

But more than that, the expulsion of presumed white European languages is also about race, for it is an act of purification of white Englishness. Migration and foreignness become additional layers in the linguistic hierarchy of whiteness, along with class, gender, sexuality, ethno-nationalism and race. The violent injunction to speak English is also one that commands to 'speak white'.[17]

Conclusion

In *jus linguarum*, 'language' has accrued meaning in a new and politically binding way through its combined detachment from ethno-nationalism and attachment to ideas of opportunity, civic integration and participation (Gramling 2016: 182). In *jus linguarum*, acquiring the national language is the civic obligation of migrants to ensure social cohesion, and an upskilling opportunity for them to enhance their human capital and increase their chances of social mobility. This chapter unpacks how the contemporary common-sense politics of language and integration has come to be given, and the effects that it has on those forced to learn the language in order to secure settlement or citizenship status and on those who teach them. Using the combined lenses of 'languaging' and 'provincialising English', the chapter argues that this new common-sense politics of language and citizenship normalises the English language as both worldly and naturally rooted in white Britain and Britishness. English is paradoxically hailed as both *the* desirable global language, and as necessary to become and indeed to feel British.

A long view of how current understandings of language and integration have come to be given takes us to the colonial legacies of linguistic imperialism and the establishment of 'standard English' as the prerogative of Britain to define, control and impart. Access to English in the colonies was controlled by colonial administrators and limited to the chosen few. In contrast, a different kind of disciplining takes place in British language requirements today: foreign subjects are not disciplined in terms of their *access* to the English language as much as they are disciplined in terms of their *knowledge* of it.

That knowledge, however, is not equally accessible to all – it *takes time* and hard work to acquire the required skills, and more time to prepare for and complete the LUK test. The language requirements mean that some migrants take more time to complete the citizenisation process than others, depending on their speaking and literacy skills. Some are on a protracted state of uncertainty, indeed anxiety, as they attempt several times to pass the Life in the UK test, or as they struggle to progress from one ESOL level to another. Those from white settler societies and the educated elites from poorer countries are advantaged in this system that privileges linguistic competence rather than capability.

Citizenship *takes place* in the normalisation of English as the national lingua franca, which is shored up by the naturalised status of English as global language that deterritorialises it and deems it the property of the world. These histories reveal how 'standard English' developed *through* its relation to foreign languages in foreign lands, not against them. What is unmarked in contemporary ideas of English as a necessary glue for cohesion is its historical construction as a language that is always in translation (Chow 2014; Gramling 2016), where foreignness is integral to it. Similarly, *jus linguarum* is founded not only on the unspoken inevitability of multilingualism in the world today, but its indispensability. Provincialising English is, on the one hand, the result of histories of linguistic imperialism – domestic and foreign – that contain multilingualism and multilingual speakers within delineated territories and groups. But it is also, on the other hand, the recognition of the indispensability of multilingual-ism in the formation and representation of English as national lingua franca, and the problems of representation that this indispensability creates. The speaking citizen *takes place* at the cross-roads of conflict-ing geographical imaginaries that seek to contain and segregate multilingualism away from public life, to root English decidedly in Britain and in Britishness, and to maintain English as a world language. The much praised and fetishised international mobility of English paradoxically poses a 'problem' to policy-makers when it comes back in the voices and bodies of multilingual speakers, whose right to speak other languages must be disciplined, contained, if not expelled. If standard English developed in response to the spread of English in the British empire, linguistic citizenship developed in response to the spread of other languages in Britain. Other languages (and other Englishes) are spoken *here* because English was *there*. It is in this context that new citizens, as well as immigrants, are compelled to speak English and to exercise verbal hygiene in order to protect the audial hygiene of the nation.

Moreover, these geographical imaginaries congeal around figures such as 'the Jamaican', 'the transnational Muslim wife', or 'the Asian youth' who are languaged by race and racialised by language. The speaking citizen *takes hold* in these figurations that speak of how new and old hierarchies of class, race and gender are woven into the fabric of the politics of language and integration.

More broadly, citizenship *takes hold* in inequalities that have become naturalised through language. A succession of reviews, reports and policies conclude that 'boosting' the English language among migrant minorities will take them out of poverty, segregation, isolation and social immobility. Concealed in these strategies are the unequal conditions under which individuals acquire English as well as the role of the state in creating and reproducing inequalities between the more or less 'integratable' or 'competent'. Instead, this new model of citizenship turns social deficiencies – such as failures in social cohesion – into individual migrants' responsibility rather than a collective responsibility.

Migrants are expected to engage in practices of verbal hygiene, for example in ESOL classes or in rehearsing the oath of allegiance and citizenship pledge in advance of the citizenship ceremony. Citizenship *takes place* when new citizens speak the oath and pledge at the ceremony, collectively performing an aspirational, cosmopolitan, monolingual public sphere of future English-speaking citizens who 'comply *de facto* with a set of civic ideals' (Gramling 2016: 197; italics original). When read against the current climate of anxiety around the incursion of other languages in public life, such displays must also be understood as technologies of reassurance that the national audial serenity will be preserved. Verbal hygiene is also about audial hygiene.

The politics of *jus linguarum* force the question of how inequalities are reconfigured and renamed in citizenisation. This chapter excavates 'racism's shifting modes', as Back, Sinha and Bryan put it (2012: 143), by examining the injurious politics of language and how speaking like a citizen *takes hold* in numerous ways. Consider Nicole, who understands how her Filipino English is cast as a debased, dumbed down affront to the fetishised English language rather than the product of hard work, dedication, skill and desire. *Jus linguarum* marks a shift from post-war anti-immigration politics characterised by a cultural racism that made the non-integratability of some migrants a matter of culture conceived as a fixed property of minoritised groups (Barker 1981). However, Nicole's 'non-belonging' is not the product of her 'culture' that existed *prior* to her arrival. Rather, her non-belonging *is carved out from the very dynamics of the linguistic and racial relations that she is brought into*. If past political debates centred on anxieties about cultural differences and their compatibility with British culture, current debates centre on the 'integration potential' of immigrants and future citizens, indexed in part by language proficiency. Language fluency becomes a marker in new modes of racism that shape hierarchies of belonging and entitlement where linguistic competence is the standard upon which the *value* of foreigners is assessed.

Still, the endurance of linguistic imperialism comes to bear in the voices of those who, like Khebat and Jeremy, are caught up in the complex relations of desire and repression created through the spread of language in colonial and postcolonial systems. Language *took hold* of Jeremy whose initial love for his teacher stood in for his love of Britain and English. Khebat, for his part, despairs at the cruel optimism of the promise of English fluency, where his skills are not enough to give him what he so desires: to acquire British citizenship. Citizenship *takes hold* of Khebat, an asylum seeker without refugee status who is not eligible to apply for settlement, ILR, let alone citizenship, but who still aims for it and citizenises himself in the terms set out by the legal process.

To be sure, Jeremy, Khebat, Nicole and Felix force the question of the unlocatability of English – it is not anyone's property, not even the British. If, following Fran, we were to hear their capability rather than listen for their competence, or if we were to decentre the ownership of English, as Nicole so ardently argues, there may be room for untethering language, citizenship and human value. In the current linguistic climate, however, Khebat, Jeremy, Nicole as well as Felix reveal how regimes of seeing and regimes of hearing intersect in the minoritisation of their other Englishes, where they are and will always be anglicised but also racialised and migratised as '*emphatically* not English' (Bhabha 1994: 125; emphasis original).

In turn, the expulsion of European languages sheds light on a form of exclusion and racialisation that operates through migratism. White-bodied European residents speaking European languages in public are *migratised* through language, that is, they are ascribed migrant and *outsider* status within the British national space. But they are also racialised as not quite white, for the command to speak English is also the command to speak white. Citizenship takes place and takes hold through politics and practices of racial purification that whiten the English language and solidly moor it in white Britain and in white Britishness.

Jus linguarum may be a new model of citizenship, but it is not replacing *jus soli* or *jus sanguinis*. In Britain, English has become highly politicised as part of national belonging and increasingly rooted in territory and identity. Imperial legacies and continuities, along with recent histories of migration in the era of globalisation and neoliberalism, shape policies of language and integration where national language and white English monolingualism are normalised and unmarked as 'naturally' necessary for the public good. Practices of verbal and audial hygiene blend into regimes of seeing and regimes of hearing which combine in shaping what it is to speak like a white English citizen, and what it is that citizens can speak.

Scene 4

Becoming citizen[1]

In January 2014, Aisha became a British citizen. She had arrived from Pakistan in 2002 on a spousal visa. She was a single mother of two when we met. She had divorced from her husband in 2011 and moved to the North West with her children to start a new life.

Aisha went through the process described in previous chapters. She was granted settlement on the basis of marriage two years after her arrival. At the time, she didn't have to take the language or citizenship test for indefinite leave to remain (the law changed later in 2007), and because she applied for citizenship before October 2013, she was eligible for the ESOL (English for Speakers of other Languages) route rather than having to take the Life in the UK (LUK) test.

Upon receiving the letter from the Home Office confirming that she has been granted citizenship, she cried with relief. It had been a long journey, during which time she attended ESOL classes at a local community centre that provided classes for women only. This is where she and I met because Aisha chose to continue the English classes even after obtaining citizenship. 'My English not very good', she said. 'I want to learn, I want to independent, I want to. Because I live here, you know, in UK, because it's here English, because if you can't speak it's difficult.' Studying English was a challenge for Aisha. She found it very difficult to find time to study between her part-time work, child care and housework. But she managed and eventually got her ESOL certificate.

When she told me her ceremony date, I arranged with the registrar – who I'd interviewed some weeks earlier – to attend it as an observer. Aisha had to take an unpaid half-day off work for the ceremony. She invited her ESOL teacher, Marianne, as her guest because she has been 'very helpful, supportive' throughout her application process and generally as her teacher.

On the day of the ceremony, Aisha arrives wearing a beautiful deep red shalwar kameez with a golden rim, and a black hijab. I compliment her on her outfit and she says that she's made an effort because 'this is important for them', meaning the ceremony organisers, 'for respect also of the British culture. It's important for me as well to respect them.'

I ask how she is feeling. Aisha says that she feels nervous because, 'I don't know … Don't know what happen. Very nervous'. I look around the room where individuals and families are waiting, helping themselves to refreshments and cake offered by the Council. Some look nervous. In all the ceremonies I attended, several new citizens were anxious about what the ceremony is 'really' about, with some experiencing it as yet another test (Khan 2018).

The ceremony room is ready. Seventy chairs are arranged in seven rows divided into two sets of five on each side of a passageway. A piece of paper with a person's name is on each chair, along with a card with the texts for the oath (red card) or affirmation (blue card) of allegiance, as well as the citizenship pledge.[2]

At the front of the room, in the left corner, there is a large polished dark oak table where Home Office envelopes holding the individual certificates of naturalisation are piled up. Next to them, a collection of blue boxes, each containing a medal to be presented to the new citizens as a gift from the local authority. Towards the other front corner is a small podium, next to which stands a large photograph of the Queen, which is sitting on an easel positioned in front of a Union Jack hanging from a short pole. Behind these, a large bouquet of fresh flowers provides a splash of colour to the otherwise rather drab room.

I joined Ronnie, the registrar who presided over the ceremony, and sat with him at the front of the ceremony room to have a chat before it began. He looked at the thirty-ish 'new citizens' as they were queuing to register their attendance and he mused:

> I think I realise how lucky we are and what a UK passport does mean in the wider world you know? Doing these ceremonies made me really think about that you know? [pause] My perception of being British is being a lot more proud. It's not until you realise the freedom and the democratic rights that you have in this country that you appreciate

how much freedom you have in order to go about your daily life, without being impinged with, you know, the regime of strict rules, governments and, you know? You don't appreciate it until you've heard people that have come from other countries and say, you don't realise how lucky you are to have your rights. And it's yours. I think that it's everybody's right to have, but not necessarily so in every other country, but you automatically think it's the same, the globe over when it's not so.

People start filing in the room and the new citizens find their seats: those swearing allegiance are on the right, those affirming, on the left. Their guests sit in the rows behind them. The ceremony begins. Ronnie stands and welcomes attendees:

> On behalf of the government, of Her Majesty Queen Elizabeth the Second and B Council, I would like to welcome you all to the ceremony today. For many of you today is the final step in the journey of becoming a British citizen, a process which will welcome you to this nation and welcome you into this community.
>
> Becoming a British citizen is something to celebrate, it means amongst other things the right to live in freedom, the right to religion or to no religion, it means the right to free speech in a democratic society, a right to vote and a right to have a voice in Britain.
>
> The citizenship ceremony is a rite of passage which formally welcomes those who wish to join us into full membership of the British family and into citizenship of the United Kingdom, a state built on a union of nations, beliefs and common civic values and we are here today to extend this welcome to you and to confer the honour of citizenship upon you.

Ronnie then introduces today's 'dignitary', one of the local Deputies to the Lord Lieutenant, 'who is really the representative of the Queen'.

> It's nice, always nice for me to see families and friends and to have children here too and it's always great to see so many nationalities. Today, we have people from Afghanistan, Bangladesh, India, Jamaica and Pakistan. So it's great to be here and to welcome you on behalf of the Queen. [...]
>
> Our population here is a mixture of very diverse backgrounds. Hundreds of years ago people came from Scandinavia and Germany. Many also came from Ireland and Russia and more recently many have come from Eastern and Central Europe and in the last 50 years many from Asia and the Caribbean.

> Our economy and culture have benefited very much from all who have come here. We hope that in return we promise you opportunities.

Following the Deputy Lieutenant's speech, Ronnie presides over the formal section of the ceremony. He invites people to pick up their card and to read after him. He begins with the oath of allegiance, starting with those swearing the oath and then moving to those affirming the oath. He asks each individual to say 'I' and then say their name. Then, the first group are asked to repeat after him to complete the sworn oath of allegiance. He then turns to the 'red team', as he calls them, and does the same. The texts are as follows:

> I [name], swear by Almighty God that on becoming ... [or] I [name], do solemnly, sincerely and truly declare and affirm that on becoming ... [then the text is the same for both] ... a British citizen, I will be faithful and bear true allegiance to Her Majesty Queen Elizabeth the Second, her Heirs and Successors, according to law.

Then follows the citizenship pledge, which all are invited to say together by repeating after him:

> I will give my loyalty to the United Kingdom and respect its rights and freedoms. I will uphold its democratic values. I will observe its laws faithfully and fulfil my duties and obligations as a British citizen.

Ronnie then offers a few words on the significance of the ceremony:

> Thank you, ladies and gentlemen. Today you've publicly acknowledged your UK citizenship in the presence of family and friends. You've made promises and commitments to be a faithful citizen to the Queen and a true and loyal subject to the United Kingdom and may all of our lives be enriched and in turn enrich the lives of others and your communities.

Each individual is then called to approach the podium where they are presented with their certificate of naturalisation and the local gift by the dignitary, with whom most pose for a photograph next to the Queen's photo. The audience applauds each time a person's name is called, but the applause gets rather sparse as time goes on – the ceremonial handing of certificates takes a good half hour, with background music coming from the boombox, for example *Pomp & Circumstance No. 4* by Elgar, or *Country Gardens* by Grainger.

Bridget Byrne (2014) remarks that the citizenship ceremonies are akin to graduation ceremonies and writes of 'citizands' (like 'graduands'). Indeed, Ronnie, like other registrars elsewhere, congratulates the new citizens for their achievement, and the roll call of each person invited to receive their certificate bestowed by a 'dignitary' is very reminiscent of graduation ceremonies.

At the end of the ceremony, everyone is invited to stand and sing the national anthem against the instrumental version coming from the boombox. Ronnie stands very straight and solemn, facing the flag. After the anthem, he concludes:

> Ladies and gentlemen, that is it. Mission completed, and hopefully it wasn't too painful [chuckles from the audience]. Thank you all for coming this morning; thank you for being here. [Applause] If you want some more photographs with the Deputy Lieutenant, there's no charge [chuckles], don't be shy, step forward, otherwise enjoy the rest of your day.

People line up for the photo opportunity with the Deputy Lieutenant and Queen. Aisha is among them; she asks Marianne to take photos from her phone, which she hands to her. After that, Aisha and Marianne go out for tea and cake in the adjoining room, where I join them. She is relieved that it is over. I ask if she will apply for a passport and inform her that she will have to be interviewed. 'What???' she asks, alarmed. I apologise for scaring her and try to reassure her that it is a routine check of identity. 'Don't worry. They only ask questions about you, your address, your children, your parents' names or dates of birth. Things you know already. It's to check your identity'. Marianne chips in to offer more reassurance. Both Marianne and I offer to go with her, but she refuses.

Some weeks later, she comes to the ESOL class with her British passport to show it to everyone. During the break, we talk about the passport application and she says that the interview was fine, 'not scary'. But what was difficult was finding a countersigner because she had not lived in B for that long: 'Difficult for me to … you know, for form, you know sign form somebody know me two years. I had to find somebody know me and my family in B. If I don't have, I can't apply'. Eventually, she was able to ask Marianne. She says that this was easier compared to needing two referees to endorse her citizenship application, which requires them to have known the applicant for at least three years. She notes the additional costs that all this incurred, such as the £20 charge for her GP's signature had she asked him.

*   *   *

Citizenship ceremonies formally anoint individuals with British citizenship. In the narrative arc of the naturalisation process, the ceremony is both the obligatory end-point of the journey to citizenship for all new citizens aged 18 and over (with some exemptions), and the starting point of a new life as a citizen. All ceremonies include the following elements: a registrar as host, a dignitary (Lord Mayor, Deputy Lieutenant or local celebrity/distinguished person), a photograph of Queen Elizabeth II, the British flag, an envelope from the Home Office-UK Visas and Immigration (UKVI) with the documents such as a welcome from the Home Secretary, information about registering to vote or about applying for a passport. Many but not all local authorities also offer a gift to new citizens; the one I encountered the most often was a gold- or silver-plated medal like the one offered to Aisha. One side is embossed with the Union flag with the caption 'To commemorate your UK citizenship'. The other side would be a heraldic symbol representing the Council where the ceremony takes place, for example, the red rose for Lancashire County Council. Some councils also invite someone from the Council to give information about voting registration before the ceremony begins. Ceremonies take place either in a room usually used for weddings or in grander rooms such as the Council chambers. The Queen's photograph and the flag are typically trundled out of a cupboard for the event, along with an audio-playing device for the national anthem.

Ceremonies follow the same format as described above: before the ceremony, individuals must register and confirm their identity, with refreshments available while they wait. The ceremony begins with a welcome from a local registrar, followed by a speech from a 'dignitary', the oath/affirmation of allegiance, the citizenship pledge, the presentation of certificates of naturalisation and local gifts to new citizens, the national anthem, closing remarks and photo opportunities (usually with the Queen's photograph and the dignitary; group photos on special occasions). In some cases, a professional photographer takes snapshots of citizens as they receive their certificate of naturalisation, typically posing with the dignitary next to the photo of the Queen. The photos are then offered for sale after the ceremony. After that, people disperse and vacate the premises.

5

The becoming citizen

Becoming British through registration or naturalisation is – or should be – a significant life event. (Home Office 2002: 32)

Having a British passport is survival. (Nicole, Filipina-British)

I still have the balloon in my room saying 'Congratulations'. It's deflated. (Ella, Greek-British)

Citizenisation policies emphasise citizenship as something to *become* and reward the *becoming citizen* whose citizenship skills and attitudes are deemed fitting with the national community of value. Previous chapters show how 'the becoming citizen' is implicit in understandings of the 'model citizen' who not only must be law abiding,[1] but who must be 'model' in all sorts of other ways – show commitment to setting up residence here, show willingness to integrate, speak English, comply with a set of civic ideals. The previous chapters shed light on processes through which elements of the citizenship ideal are naturalised: intelligibility (of the law, of documents, of subjects), commitment, presence, language. In turn, national insecurities are appeased through curating practices and practices of verbal and audial hygiene. Finally, the previous chapters unpack how these processes and practices articulate, and are articulated through, racial, cultural, religious and class-based exclusions that shore up the distinction between 'migrant' and 'citizen' – a distinction that does not go without critique and challenge from both migrants and citizens.

This chapter takes another angle on the question: 'what is naturalised in naturalisation?' posed in Chapter 1. Rather than focusing on processes, the chapter examines how two of the foundations of citizenship are naturalised and reproduced: the wilful autonomous subject, and birthright. The chapter then unravels these founding principles by going to the global, national and historical inequalities and inequities that they sustain. These principles are unpicked first, by exposing how the value of some citizenships is naturalised through (failed) promises such as 'the good life'; second, by highlighting 'ordinary' practices of becoming otherwise that are not outside but integral to citizenisation and citizenship, and that therefore break open its foreclosures.

The Home Office guide issued to applicants for naturalisation explains what becoming a British citizen means:

> Becoming a British citizen is a significant life event. Apart from allowing you to apply for a British citizen passport [sic], British citizenship gives you the opportunity to participate more fully in the life of your local community. (Home Office 2019a: 3)

The guidance is intimating at the distinction between the instrumental citizen – the one seeking only the passport – and the committed one – who will participate in the life of their community (see Chapter 3). The distinction is framed in terms of active citizenship that suggests that noncitizens are passive and inactive residents. I shall return to this below. What interests me here is how 'becoming British' is grounded in a notion of citizenship that privileges (active) membership to a political community (Yuval-Davis 2011: 48). Nira Yuval-Davis (2011: 12) distinguishes between belonging and the *citizenship politics* of belonging: 'People can "belong" in many different ways and to many different objects of attachment'.

In citizenisation, the politics of belonging and the politics of becoming are deeply entangled and both do 'the dirty work of boundary maintenance' (Favell cited in Yuval-Davis 2011: 20). This applies particularly well to citizenship, which distinguishes between who is included and who is excluded from legal and political membership – 'us' and 'them'. But this volume documents how citizenship is not only experienced but also governed in terms that are not strictly legal or political. Nira Yuval-Davis (2011) and Floya Anthias (2016) have both critically considered the ways in which the legal and political membership that comes with citizenship has come to take a secondary role in favour of the framing of citizenship couched in terms of identity (Anthias 2016: 178–179). The citizenisation process is for most applicants a complicated negotiation of becoming, belonging and identity – insofar as for many, 'nationality' (belonging to a nation) and citizenship (legal status) are blurred. As a result, acquiring a nationality other than the one in which most applicants were born comes with mixed feelings, as we see below.

Becoming and belonging are deeply entangled and each poses questions other than those set by the citizenship politics of belonging. Unlike identity, which fixes who one 'is', with becoming we can ask: becoming what, where and how? Similarly with belonging: belonging to what, where and how? The 'how' question best captures the richness of becoming and belonging: the prescriptions and proscriptions about, but also alternatives to, how one becomes and belongs – temporally, affectively and spatially.

In contrast to belonging, however, becoming has more of a pro-cessual, unfinished character to it (Biehl and Locke 2017a; Khan 2018). Biehl and Locke distinguish between three dimensions of becoming: plasticity; the unknown; time, space and desire. Plastic-ity and the unknown are about the malleable and unpredictable character of human becoming and how 'people belong simultaneously to multiple systems that themselves are made up of people, things, and forces with varying degrees of agentive capacity' (Biehl and Locke 2017b: 5). This resonates with what Nira Yuval-Davis calls multi-layered citizenship (2011: 69), which this chapter explores. Multi-layered citizenship is at once spatial, historical and felt, and enables forms of becoming and belonging that exceed the frames of citizenisation.

The third dimension of becoming outlined by Biehl and Locke (2017b) is that of time, space and desire. The heuristic device of the waiting room used in this volume precisely captures this aspect of becoming that understands the making and unmaking of citizens and of citizenship as operating through multiple and at times contested temporalities, spatialities and affects. To paraphrase Kamran Khan (2018: 26), experiences of becoming unfold in the present, project to the future and are conditioned by the past. Moreover, '[d]esire does not seek a singular, decontextualized object, but a broader world or set of relations in which the object is embedded and becomes meaningful' (Biehl and Locke 2017b: 6). In this sense, becoming British is about citizenship as the presumed object of desire, but it is also about becoming citizen *somewhere*, that is, *in* Britain, which is often contrasted to *elsewhere* – as in Ronnie's musing in Scene 4. As such, citizenship comes with promises that, as this chapter shows, are not always delivered or that are understood and enacted in ways that shed light into ways of becoming *otherwise*.

Much of the chapter draws on scenes from citizenship ceremonies, with scenes from other moments in the citizenisation process making appearances throughout. The chapter includes four sections. It begins with 'choice and desire' and critically considers how citizenship ceremonies assume a wilful, choosing subject that exists prior to the law. The section challenges how 'choice' naturalises a voluntarism that many do not experience. In addition, not only does citizenisation rest on assumptions about individuals choosing citizenship, but it also assumes that they chose migration.

The second section on 'family, reproduction and birthright inequalities' unpacks a much neglected element of empirical research on citizenship attribution: the heteropatriarchal underpinnings of citizenship that reproduce and naturalise gendered, sexualised and racialised understandings of familial arrangements that befit the becoming citizen. These principles also work to sustain birthright citizenship and to preserve the unequal global distribution of the world's riches.

The first two sections set up the frames of reference that underpin citizenship ceremonies, which the two subsequent sections go on to unravel. 'The good life and the pursuit of happiness' argues that this pursuit is entrenched in global inequalities of birthright that direct individuals to what is naturalised as being the cause of happiness (Ahmed 2010): British citizenship. It shows how happiness and the good life combine as a technology of British citizenship (Ahmed 2010) and examines how they are variously mobilised: as a technology of reassurance for citizens who appreciate their 'luck', where their sense of citizenship and of the privileges of 'insiderdom' are secured (Bhattacharyya 2015). In turn, the good life becomes a duty for migrants to enjoy for those 'lucky enough' to be granted citizenship. But from the perspective of the migrant, the promise of the good life and happiness is not always fulfilled.

The final section, 'becoming otherwise', revisits the testing regimes of citizenisation and how they set up forms of becoming through achievement that dictate how one learns to become citizen. I contrast this to 'ordinary' ways of becoming – what some have called 'ordinary citizenship' (Neveu 2015: 148; Staeheli et al. 2012) – excluded from testing regimes, but which are perhaps more meaningful and productive. The section concludes with the 'feeling rules' of citizenship ceremonies, which registrars work hard to make into happy, celebratory events. The section draws out the tensions between the happy celebrations of citizenship and alien feelings. It ends with Sala's story to shed light on the postcolonial becomings that are not only integral to the fetishised certainty of citizenship, but that have the power to undo it.

The chapter concludes by revisiting the generic subject-citizen and the generic 'migrant' produced at ceremonies. It unpacks their limits, edges and hidden layers by outlining how the becoming citizen variously takes place, takes hold and takes time in the waiting room of British citizenship.

Choice and desire

Scene F

On the day you say an oath. You can either swear by God or you can affirm the oath and not say God, it's your choice. What would you prefer to do? With God or without God? [pause] With God okay.

Much has been written about the symbolic significance of the spectacle of new citizens taking the oath of allegiance in citizenship ceremonies, namely for their enactment of choice, indeed of a mutual choice between the nation-state and new citizens (Honig 2001; Coutin 2003; Mazouz 2008; Fortier 2013; Byrne 2014; Aptekar 2015). Oaths have a long history in Western European states and are arguably the 'oldest form of national membership promotion' (Goodman 2014: 29). In British ceremonies today, uttering the oath of allegiance and citizenship pledge formally confirm the new citizens as legally joining the political community. The oath and pledge assert individuals' formal commitment and faithfulness to the state and, in Britain, its reigning monarch. However, a noteworthy feature of the oath and pledge is that the expression of commitment is assessed *in the expression itself*. This is unlike the citizenisation requirements that lead up to the ceremony, which require evidence of commitment – for example between spouses or to the country – and which are measured by evidence of cohabitation, residency, language fluency and the Life in the UK (LUK) test. In the case of naturalisation ceremonies, there are no measures of this commitment to the nation and the state outside of the utterance of that commitment itself (Goodman 2014: 47).

Another noteworthy feature of the British oath of allegiance is the choice individuals are given between a secular or religious version: 'with God or without God', as the Stadlow phone team put it to callers booking their citizenship ceremony. Several ceremony officials noted their surprise to me when seeing Muslims choosing the secular oath, not understanding why those they presumed to be religious because of the hijab, beard or other markers of what 'religious Muslims' look like, would not swear 'with God'. Sala said that she and many other Muslims at her ceremony affirmed rather than swore their allegiance in part because:

> for me and I would think that for some people from my Muslim background, Arab Muslim background, the oath is comparable to a pledge of allegiance to be given to the spiritual political leader of the Muslim community, so it is something very serious.

She goes on to explain this particular understanding of a religious oath as:

> giving your covenant to the ruler. The covenant with God is like the highest, like in Judaism, and then the oath is something to guard for the rest of your life because you're bound by the oath. So, if you promise [in the secular version], it's still serious. But, yeah, it's not as absolute as swearing by Almighty God.

This suggests that for some Muslims – and perhaps other non-Christians, including atheists – the religious oath is cast within a Christian religious matrix that they do not identify with. Moreover, Sala expressed her surprise that the religious oath was even an option for a public ceremony run by a local government:

> I didn't expect a pledge by Almighty God to the Queen; you know, that this would be even thought of as part of the ceremony. Because all public institutions and public relations are governed by this, you know, separation of secular space and religious space. I would understand that the monarchy itself, with the monarch being the head of church, that the monarchy itself in its [own] ceremonies, you know, God might be included. But for all other public relations, why should it be you know asked of me to become a citizen to swear by Almighty God?

In the UK, in addition to citizenship ceremonies, oaths of allegiance to the monarch are performed by members of parliament and certain public servants. All have the option between a religious or secular version. But for Sala, the choice of swearing 'with God' inappropriately blurs the lines between state and Church. However, apparently escaping Sala's notice is that, as Tine Damsholt (2008: 61) points out, non-Christians cannot escape the 'religious matrix' of the British ceremonies if only because of the national anthem which again invokes God. In addition, citizenship ceremonies are rituals that follow the format of Christian religious ceremonies: the alternating standing and sitting, the communal recitation of the oath and pledge, the presiding celebrant, the 'dignitary' who at times represents the absent but omnipresent head of state and head of the Church of England, the photograph of the monarch at the 'altar', and the anointment of citizenship to each individual (Damsholt 2008).

Sofya Aptekar (2015: 83) draws a parallel between US citizenship ceremonies and religious rituals where people engage in a 'collective self-worship' of the nation. In the UK, the 'worship' is not as clearly directed at the nation as it is in the US, as I explain in the third section below. Rather, a form of collective worship to the *state* is staged at ceremonies, or more precisely, as I argue elsewhere (Fortier 2013), they stage a relational politics of desire where the state welcomes desirable citizens who desire the state. The process puts migrants in a position of seeking the state to confirm their subjectivity as suitably desiring of, and desirable to, the state.

The ceremony, then, becomes the site where the mutual choice and desire between the state and its 'new citizens' are dramatised as the culmination of a subject's journey. The becoming citizens befit 'us', the nation, because they confirm the choice-worthiness of 'us' (Honig 2001). When the very first citizenship ceremony was performed in Brent in 2004, it was hailed by Home Secretary David Blunkett as allowing the British public to witness the allegiance of new citizens by sending 'a clear message that those who choose to be part of the [British] family are committing themselves' (Morris and Akbar 2004).

The highly ritualised performance of choice at the citizenship ceremony repeatedly confirms the value of choice and desire through their visible material and embodied performance. Furthermore, this ritualised materialisation of what are otherwise abstract choice and desire, makes them intelligible to the state and to the wider public

(Honig 2001). The enactment of choice at the ceremonies naturalises the choosing subject as prior to citizenship, particularly with the secular version of the oath that emphasises a 'true self' (Damsholt 2008: 67) that seemingly corresponds to the affirmation of 'solemnly, sincerely and truly' declaring one's allegiance to the Queen. In addition, as Bonnie Honig (2001: 95) points out, the citizenship ceremony naturalises the autonomous subject itself:

> by depicting a subject who exists as such prior to the law and is able therefore to consent to it without apparently being always already formed by it. In this regard, the iconic scene of new immigrants taking the pledge of citizenship has an ideological effect. It privileges a choosing subject as a natural subject prior to the law, and it grounds the law in a choice that is its foundation and its raison d'être.

As explained in Chapter 2, the modern conception of citizenship developed along with the development of the self-determining subject capable of property (Brace 2004). Contemporary citizenship ceremonies naturalise that subject, and they also naturalise choice as the originary foundation of the regime and rule of law that new citizens are pledging to abide by. Not only does this marginalise the varied, often violent institutionalised inequalities of the British state and of British citizenship (empire, conquest, slavery, constitutional monarchy), but it also 'recenters the regime on a voluntarism that most citizens and residents never experience directly' (Honig 2001: 95).

'You don't really have a choice', said Ella, who came to Britain from Greece 19 years before we met in 2017. She acquired British citizenship earlier that year, because of the Brexit vote of 2016.

> It feels like kind of blackmail. They force you to do it, and you don't really have a say, you don't really have a choice, and maybe there you feel a little bit like a traitor in the sense that you choose sides or it feels a little bit like you're choosing sides ... But then you kind of have to lower your head and 'ok I'll come over to your side and I'll do as you say, so that you allow me the privilege'.

Ella's sentiments resonate with numerous EU migrants residing in Britain who acquired British citizenship out of fear of losing their rights or being deported (Gentleman 2019b; Weaver and Gentleman 2019). This is a naturalisation by fear, or what some refer to as 'defensive naturalisation', where immigrants seek citizenship to protect their rights in an anti-immigration climate (Ong 2011/2012; Aptekar

2015). In addition, by feeling she was forced to 'take sides', Ella is also hinting at the extent to which nationality and identity are elided in citizenship; an elision that comes with expectations of loyalty. Ella described how she was reluctant to speak about her decision to fellow Greek nationals, one of whom 'vented' his anger at her when he found out. Hostile environments not only create tensions between 'migrants' and 'citizens', but also among migrants.

Moreover, it is not only the choice of becoming citizen that is naturalised at the ceremony: it is also the *choice of migrating* in the first place.[2] Many ceremony officials thank the new citizens for choosing their city or area as a place to live in and settled. At a ceremony in London, a dignitary noted 'the arrival of people from all corners and faiths of the world who chose to make London their home and to build a better future for themselves, their families and their fellow citizens'. While ceremonies create a generic and equivalent subject-citizen, which I return to below, they also create a generic voluntary 'migrant'.

Several migrants I met explained that they came to or are staying in Britain for a variety of reasons – usually to study, to work or to marry. But for others, there was no choice. Sala says that it was not her choice to leave Egypt to study in the UK in the 1990s: 'I wouldn't have left, I would have never left'. Nicole, for her part, reflected on the effect of global inequalities on individual lives. Remarking on her application for British citizenship, Nicole said: 'We are left with no option actually', because in her view, it is the only route to security and safety. Nicole's own parents were forced to emigrate from the Philippines for work – her mother to Dubai, her father to Korea, 'because we don't have a job in the Philippines. So look, I'm am migrant child.' Nicole is the child of a diasporic family, like many of those receiving British citizenship.

Family, reproduction and birthright inequalities

Scene G

On 26 February 2014, Brent Council[3] in North London held the 10th anniversary citizenship ceremony, where Labour MP David Blunkett gave a speech in absentia.[4] In his speech, he said: those of us who are born [in Britain] are citizens from the day of our birth; [we] have no choice. Those who chose to be naturalised citizens are taking a positive step to become part of the family. In fact there's an old saying 'You're born with your family, you choose your friends'. And today you're joining your family and choosing your friends.

Blunkett's seamless move from 'born with your family' to 'joining your family' implies that having chosen Britishness, individuals are now joining the natural national genealogical order of things. As Engin Isin states:

> The extraordinary paradox of the nation-state is perhaps the fact that, although it ideologically constitutes itself as a community of consent and choice beyond family and kinship, it reproduces itself as yet another kind of family through fraternization and birth. (2012: 456)

If adoption is volitional, it also connotes a commitment whereby immigrants tie their destiny to a chosen place. The presumption that people born in another country 'adopt' a different place of residence and its culture is underpinned by the distinction between blood lines and historically situated lines.[5] A transaction occurs between congenital citizenship and 'adopted' citizenship; the territorial base of future births *here* are foregrounded and recrafted, while past births elsewhere are minimised. Indeed, Blunkett concluded his speech by welcoming 'those who are prepared to give their commitment to be part of the country themselves for their children and their grandchildren in generations to come'.

The diffusion of the choice–attribution distinction that the ceremony stages, then, subsumes consensual citizenship within the necessary relationship of citizenship to sexual reproduction and descent. At another ceremony, the presiding registrar congratulated new citizens on taking 'a step that will have lasting repercussions on your lives and of course very much on the lives of your children and their children and on generations of your families in the years to come'. He then added that 'we all have birth mothers' and he went on to declare women to be the 'mothers of the nation'. Such statements conjoin loyalty to the country with reproduction, placing obligations of genealogical intimacy and national perpetuity on the choosing citizens. What Blunkett and others suggest is that by voluntarily joining the British family, new citizens are also inheriting a set of social obligations, including the one to produce future British citizens.

Siobhan Somerville argues that 'naturalization has historically been encumbered with assumptions about a heterosexual, reproductive subject, and so tends to reinforce the model of an organic, sexually reproduced citizenry' (2005: 663; see also Berlant 1997). I argue elsewhere (Fortier 2013) that at our citizenship ceremony, my partner and I were not treated as a same-sex couple but rather as heterosexual friends. But there is more to this story. Since then, I found out that this was not necessarily an omission on the part of the ceremony officials; rather, it is an effect of the documentation that assists them in planning ceremonies. In addition to personal information such as home address or special requirements, registrars receive individuals' certificates of naturalisation from the Home Office, once the latter has approved their citizenship application. Registrars use these certificates to plan their ceremonies; the certificate includes a reference number that indicates if individuals are on their own or 'in a group', as Anna puts it, a registrar from Stadlow Council. Anna assumed that those with the same reference number – which begins with the first letter of a person's surname – were part of a family, which was usually confirmed by the same surname and address. However, if two people were at the same address but different surnames and therefore with different reference numbers, she treated them as individuals; 'the chances are they'll want to come in together. I haven't joined them as a group because they're not under the same reference number but when they call, they could ask to be together'. When I pushed her on this matter, suggesting that couples who are married or in a civil partnership might not have the same surname, Anna said that she had never come across this situation, to which I responded, 'or so you think!'. 'Hmm, yes, that's true', Anna said.

The point is that embedded in the processing system for citizenship are familial assumptions that privilege the patriarchal heterosexual family. While my partner and I, along with a friend who acquired British citizenship on the same day, were treated as a 'group' because we asked to be seated together when we booked our ceremony, we were also treated as three heterosexual friends. This means that we were invited to receive our certificates separately and as individuals rather than as a 'group' or 'family', whereas those who fit the normative family formation were invited together, as a unit. Indeed, in all the ceremonies I observed, I have never witnessed other 'group' formations being recognised as families or friends or otherwise.

Thus, the choosing wilful subject whose existence is assumed prior to the law is also a gendered/sexualised subject. The application forms, referencing and classification systems assume a cisgendered, heterosexual subject, 'single' or part of a patriarchal family, who exists as such prior to becoming citizen. To paraphrase Honig (2001) cited above, the entire process of becoming a citizen has an ideological effect: it privileges a cisgendered/sexualised subject as a natural subject prior to the law, and it grounds the law in the transgenerational transmission of citizenship by birth as the preferred mode of citizenship acquisition and transmission: what Ayelet Shachar (2009) calls 'hereditary citizenship'.

Embedded in 'birthright citizenship' is a coupling of loyalty to the country with reproduction that places obligations of heterosexual intimacy and national perpetuity on the presumed autonomous citizen who has 'chosen' to naturalise. In other words, the insistence on intergenerational reproduction projects the desire for the longevity and continuity of both state and nation onto the imagined bodies of the future descendants of the children present in the room. This renaturalises the heterosexual, reproductive family and its embedding within citizenship. At the citizenship ceremony, *both* gender/sexuality *and* citizenship are *conferred* by the state, as Margo Canaday (2009: 255) suggests. In this sense, the citizenship naturalisation process not only reminds us of the state's authority to award citizenship, but it also reasserts the state's claim to the monopoly on the prerogative to define 'the family'.

Furthermore, the assumption is that families reside in the same country, indeed in the same *household*, whereas most new citizens will have transnational or diasporic family ties and obligations, such as remittances. The household is reactivated in citizenship ceremonies as a site that, as Clare Hemmings argues (2020), can 'only ever see queer as divergence, single mothers as pathology, migrant remittances [and, I would add, family separations] as sad necessity, and single living as selfishness'. There is valuable research on transnational or diasporic families that shows how migration challenges conventional understandings of family formations and intimacy (Bryceson and Vuorela 2002; Goulbourne et al. 2010).[6] But the hardening of citizenship policies, and the growing use of the combined principles of *jus sanguinis* and *jus soli* in Western countries, entrenches the household-bound 'family' as the founding reproductive unit for the nation.

An ontological gap develops, then, between the naturalised localised family and the transnational lives in which people are embedded. The majority of the people I met have siblings and parents still in the country they grew up in. Rahim, a young Kurdish Iraqi refugee, spoke very movingly of his mother who he had not seen in years. He choked up when speaking of his phone calls with her, how he missed her and wished he could 'give back. *How* I give back, I don't know', because he did not have enough income to send her any money. He felt at a loss and dreamt of British citizenship and the ability it will give him to travel to her every year. Transnational family formations might appear commonplace for migration researchers; but they do not feature in legal and everyday understandings of citizenship.

What is even less present in the imaginary of the localised reproductive family are the children left behind by some migrants. Joy sent money to her parents in Thailand not only for them, but for her 13-year-old daughter who they were caring for. Joy said that her daughter is closer to her grandparents than she is to her – and that makes her 'very sad' but she was also matter-of-fact about it. The distance was not only the result of Joy's migration to the UK – it was always part of her and her daughter's life. As the eldest of three children growing up in a very poor family, Joy was forced to work away from home since her young adulthood in order to support her family. Thus, the celebration of the multigenerational family of British citizens erases all forms of transnational family formations and obligations that some countries rely on, such as the Philippines. One dignitary put it this way: 'as you take this very important step in your lives to become a very real part of this country, don't forget to teach your children and your grandchildren what a blessing you all have'.

Racialised conceptions of family formations also shape the imaginary of familial citizenship. At the time of my fieldwork, a joke was circulating within a local council where I attended a few ceremonies. I first heard it from a photographer commissioned by the council to take photos of new citizens during but also after the event, when they often pose with their guest(s) and the dignitary in front of the Queen's photograph. The photographer was addressing a couple from Pakistan where the wife had just become British and her husband was the guest. The photographer said to the husband:

'now that she's British, you'll have to do all the cooking and the cleaning, do you know that?' The husband answered something inaudible and the photographer replied, 'You already do it, do you?' 'Yes', the husband said, interrupting the joke and turning it back on the photographer.

This joke is telling of the racialised assumptions about family formations, particularly when it comes to Asians and Muslims. The photographer was mockingly welcoming the couple to an assumed 'more equal' gender regime (Razack 2004; Lewis 2006) that, as the joke goes, forcibly subjects men to do housework. He was also remaking the couple as racialised migrant others whose 'culture' was not suited for Britain. Integral to the 'family model of the political', as Lynn Hunt (1992) puts it, are racial codings of the politics of intimacy and the fundamental intertwining of the history of sexuality with the history of race (Stoler 2002). In other words, prescribed familial arrangements – just like prescribed love considered in Chapter 3 – is one way of naming and making 'race' and racial difference.

What is more, the system of birthright entitlements and kinship that dominates not only our imagination but also our laws in the allotment of political membership serve to renaturalise 'the "wealth-preserving" aspect of hereditary citizenship' (Shachar and Hirschl 2007: 274; also Shachar 2009) and to preserve the unequal global distribution of the world's riches. While where we are born may be accidental, the unequal distribution of our ensuing life-chances is not. As Sala remarks about her decision to apply for British citizenship, 'you're hostage to fortune as to where you are born ... Why did I have to do this?'

In Chapter 3, I consider how the certificate of naturalisation operates as a birth certificate of sorts and therefore migratises citizenship. However, the framing of citizenisation and the staging of citizenship ceremonies repeatedly reassert the value of British citizenship and its place in the global political economy of inequalities. In this context, birthright citizenship is the favoured means of ensuring the 'birthright transfer of entitlement' (Shachar 2009: 7). Indeed, citizenship has become widely understood as an honour and an opportunity, as states have moved more forcefully and explicitly to institutionalise it as a privilege rather than a right (Goldberg 2002; Bhambra 2015; Kapoor and Narkowicz 2019b). And this privilege is unequally distributed in the world; Lucas, who became British in 2013, likened it to joining a private club, which cost £900 at the time of his application (£1,330 as of February 2020).

In a world where the vast majority of the world population is assigned citizenship by accidents of birth, Shachar (2009) pointedly reminds us that a person's citizenship will greatly influence their life chances; citizenship is very much a 'birthright lottery', as Shachar puts it. While global poverty rates have dropped by half since 2000, one in ten people in the Global South still live on less than the international poverty line of US$1.90 a day. Most of these are in two regions: Southern Asia and sub-Saharan Africa, with the latter counting 42 per cent of its population living below the poverty line. The UN also reports that '[m]ore than 11% of the world population is living in extreme poverty and struggling to fulfil the most basic needs like health, education, and access to water and sanitation, to name a few. There are 122 women aged 25 to 34 living in poverty for every 100 men of the same age group, and more than 160 million children are at risk of continuing to live in extreme poverty by 2030'.[7]

It is in this context that 'the red passport' acquires such a high currency value in the world. Nicole recognised this when she admitted her ambivalence about acquiring British citizenship. 'The only thing I want is survival, you know? Having a British passport is survival.' For many, the appeal of the British passport is the greater mobility that it affords (Byrne 2014; Prabhat 2018). This is a desire that the government dismisses as merely instrumental in favour of participatory membership, as discussed above. But for many, that passport represents so much more; it represents 'the good life'.

The good life and the pursuit of happiness

Because in Pakistan is very small country and very poor people it's not good still in Pakistan. No jobs, no anything, like good for your life. I want to get a good life, happiness with my children, my wife. And I support my back home family as well. (Tariq, migrant on a spousal visa)

Assumptions about the free, autonomous, choosing subject comes with the further assumption that this subject is free to pursue happiness and 'the good life'. But this pursuit is entrenched in global inequalities of the 'accidents of birth' that direct individuals, as Sara Ahmed (2010) argues, to what is naturalised as being the cause of happiness: British citizenship. Migrants pursuing the good life force the interrogation of how ideas of 'the good life' and happiness circulate globally, and which social, cultural and national values are privileged in the process.[8] This section examines the different ways in which happiness and the good life constitute a technology of British citizenship (Ahmed 2010) and how they are variously mobilised. First, I consider how they work as a technology of reassurance for citizens who contemplate their 'luck' at being British. Consequently, the division between migrant/foreigner and citizens is confirmed and a particular version of happiness and the good life naturalised as a feature of British citizenship. As such, the good life becomes a duty to enjoy for those 'lucky enough' to be granted citizenship. Second, I turn to the (failed) promise of the good life and happiness that is attached to British citizenship from the perspective of the subjects of citizenisation.

Luck and citizenship as a technology of reassurance

Harry's musings on 'our' luck cited in Scene 4 capture what many state intermediaries expressed to me in the course of my research. Couched in terms of freedom, democracy and human rights, Harry's realisation was that 'the right to have rights' is not equally available around world. This realisation firmed up his pride in Britain and his confidence in the solidity of British citizenship: 'you don't realise how lucky you are to have your rights', he said, '*and it's yours*'.

Many registrars with experience with the Nationality Checking Service (NCS), Settlement Checking Service (SCS) and citizenship ceremonies stated their awareness of the global disparities of citizenship and its chance distribution. Peter, from a large city council, spoke about how annoyed he got with anti-immigration politics, and how humbling his experience with migrants seeking to settle or to naturalise was. He told me about people getting 'riled up' against immigrants when he talks about his job, and how he likes to educate them about the realities of migrant lives.

> You see people from so many different backgrounds who are escaping whatever they need to for whatever reason and sometimes ... When

you see stories like that, [any anti-immigration argument] all just goes out the window. If you see someone fleeing abuse back in wherever they come from and you see some awful stories. And the applicants feel the need to tell you and it … we don't need to know those stories [as ceremony officials]. We don't need to know why they've been granted access to the country, but they always tell you and you do think: 'I'm so proud to be from a country that's that tolerant and understanding, that we are letting people do this.'

Peter was touched by the pride, happiness, relief and stories of the new citizens he meets. In that sense, citizenisation is transformative for both migrants and citizens. Peter, Harry and others are aware of the inequalities of the birthright lottery. But these inequalities are reproduced in the citizenisation process, and the citizenship ceremony in particular, in ways that reassert their insider status as someone who is 'in a position to define what is acceptable and who can be tolerated and included' (Bhattacharyya 2015: 29). What is more, several registrars acknowledge the 'struggles' that many will have gone through en route to naturalisation. Janine told me that when she presides over a ceremony she always says:

we didn't ask to be born here, we are British just by chance. But many of you will have struggled to pay for citizenship or worked hard or made really great sacrifices to be here, we haven't.

Janine is gesturing not only to the lottery of birth but also to the hurdles that migrants must go through to obtain citizenship. The increasing demands on migrants seeking settlement or citizenship serve 'as a reminder to citizens of their luck in avoiding such [hurdles, and of the] comparative privileges of insider status' (Bhattacharyya 2015: 29) as citizens *place* the good life decidedly *here* and *in* British citizenship.

This is what the citizenship ceremony stages and naturalises – the value of Britishness in a global landscape, confirmed by the gratefulness of the new citizens. Happiness and the good life operate together as a technology of reassurance for citizens like Peter, who find pride in what they perceive as the benevolence of their country. It is gratifying because it gratifies the state, the nation and their representatives by confirming the choice-worthiness of the nation and the state (Honig 2001; Fortier 2013; Byrne 2014; Fortier 2017a). Sitting at the junction of the end of what for many was a long,

hard, painful and costly journey and the beginning of a 'new challenge', as one ceremony official put it, the ceremony fundamentally
conceals the global as well as national hierarchies of citizenship (re)
produced through citizenisation. Nicole saw right through it. For
her, British citizenship is not 'going to save' her and her Filipino
compatriots. Her experience of the ceremony is rather that it is
'upholding imperialism'.

A colleague of Peter's had a slightly different view to his. She
described herself as 'not particularly patriotic' insofar as her experience with applicants and new citizens has not bolstered her sense
of Britishness.

> AMF: So what does it mean for someone who's not particularly
> patriotic to do a citizenship ceremony?
>
> Christine: Erm, cos I mean if they live here, they're just doing something
> to try and make their lives better. So everyone wants to make their
> lives better don't they? So and obviously when they do and you can
> see they're happy about it, it makes you happy. It's just, obviously
> sometimes when they're really happy to be a British citizen I think
> of the other benefits like say you can vote.

Christine is acknowledging the rightful instrumental pursuit of
happiness – they 'just' want to be happy and 'just' want to make
their lives better. Still, this instrumentalism is not without its conditions. The 'desire for just happiness appears to give the other a
certain freedom and yet directs the other toward what is already
agreed to be the cause of happiness' (Ahmed 2010: 133). They live
here because they 'just' want a better life – the matter-of-factness
of Christine's position is grounded in the unquestioned assumption
that British citizenship offers a better life to all.

Other registrars believe that 'we take citizenship for granted. I
realise how lucky we are and what a UK passport does mean in the
wider world', said Lucy, a registrar from a small local council. It is
worth noting that for Lucy and others, citizenship ceremonies or
citizenship pledges should be rolled out to the wider society, for
example in schools. This was an idea mooted by Mark Rimmer, a
champion of citizenship ceremonies, former head of registration
services at the London Borough of Brent and national local government spokesperson on Citizenship and Nationality. Rimmer produced
a report for the Lord Goldsmith Citizenship Review (2008),[9] which

itself was commissioned by then Prime Minister Gordon Brown in 2007. In his report, Rimmer stated that:

> People born and raised in this country are often far too cynical about being British and it seems to be a national pastime to put down British institutions and our way of life. It is far too naive to believe that initiatives like this [citizenship ceremonies] will change attitudes but it might at least make some of our young people stop to think about how lucky we all are to be living in a tolerant and free society. (Rimmer, 2008: 7)

Rimmer proposed that ceremonies not be confined to council chambers or town hall, but that 'iconic' ceremonies take place in public venues or even be part of the citizenship curriculum in schools. Rimmer's report was produced at a time of much national anxiety about the 'weakness' of citizenship (see Chapter 2) and debates about how to enhance the meaning of citizenship as 'a common bond' (Goldsmith 2008: 3; see Fortier 2010, 2013). However, Rimmer's proposal recuperates the narrative of privileged insiderdom: his proposal suggests that the highly ritualised anointment of citizenship to migrants will reassure the nation of its benevolence, tolerance and freedom.

Many registrars and dignitaries encourage new citizens to 'enjoy your rights', in the words of Louise, a dignitary from citizenship ceremony in a city in the North West of England.

> Enjoy your rights and discharge your duties in a responsible way. The best way, in my opinion, to enjoy your rights is to integrate with the society. This does not mean giving up your cultural identity, share your culture with others, and respect and learn others' traditions and cultures as well. Britain has a richness of diversity. Enjoy it, respect it and also learn from it.

Louise concluded her speech with the following:

> So, ladies and gentlemen, welcome to this unique and historic land – a land of true opportunity, which gives everyone a chance to work, to strive and to improve your life. In fact, the sky is your limit. So, let us all appreciate this honour of being granted citizenship of the United Kingdom and work to contribute positively to making our society a place we are proud and happy to live in.

Happiness and enjoying the good life become a duty. In this sense, happiness operates 'as a technology of citizenship, as a way of binding migrants to a national ideal. To be bound *to* happiness is to be bound *by* what has already been established as good' (Ahmed 2010: 133; emphasis original). The gift of citizenship is a gift of a better life that comes with the duty to take advantage of the opportunities offered by that better life. Another ceremony dignitary in another council put it this way: 'It is important that you yourselves set an example to your children by yourselves embracing the opportunities [that your new status offers]'. As a form of neoliberal governance, a central principle of citizenisation is an emphasis on citizenship as a personal responsibility and achievement. Here, this responsibility takes the form of injunctions to be happy. While registrars experience the good life as luck – 'we are lucky' – migrants are told that they are 'the lucky ones' whose responsibility it is to take up the 'opportunity' of the good life and happiness, enjoy it and transmit it. Nowhere in this model is there any suggestion that 'the good life' is not equally accessible to all.

The promise of the good life

The 'conditional happiness' (Ahmed 2010: 133) described above should not distract us from the joy that many experience when awarded British citizenship. Many shed tears of happiness and relief at citizenship ceremonies. If the conditionality of citizenship is embedded in popular consciousness, so is its certainty, which is anchored in ideals of British national belonging and entitlement. Not all citizenships are equal and the reminders of the uncertainty of citizenship simultaneously suture the presumed security of British citizenship, and the worthiness of pursuing it.

Leafing through the guest books available at several citizenship ceremonies gives an indication of the meaningfulness of becoming British for many new citizens.

> I will cherish this day all my life and endeavour to contribute to this country.
>
> I'm really honoured to be what I am now. Thanks!
>
> That drim in my life.
>
> I am happy so much to being British citizen. So, I hope I coming active person to help by my skill and experience this country. Thank you.

[child's handwriting] I very glad to be a British citizen and thank you for the invitation.

The affective economy of citizenisation culminates in a ceremony that binds new citizens in a relationship of gratitude to the state that non-naturalised citizens do not experience. One feature of the waiting room of citizenship is the deferred promise that the struggles to get through the hurdles of citizenisation will be rewarded: eligible migrants[10] 'will have to live with less now in order to live with more in the future' (Povinelli 2011: 99). The promise of happiness and the good life, then, is conditional. Ahmed (2010: 133) points out how '[c]itizenship provides a technology for deciding whose happiness comes first'. The narrative arc of citizenisation places the expectant migrant in a desiring relationship where the terms of desire are dictated by the state. In turn, '[i]f the promise of citizenship is offered as a promise of happiness, then you have to demonstrate that you are a worthy recipient of its promise' (Ahmed 2010: 133; also Fortier 2013).

The testimonies above also intimate that there is an unequal distribution of hope, desire, anxiety that is constitutive of citizenisation's structure of feeling. The 'hurdles' that citizenisation puts in the way of those seeking permanent resident status or citizenship have high stakes not only in terms of legal security and economic stability, but also in terms of emotional costs.

Becoming British 'makes damage', as one respondent in Bridget Byrne's study put it (2014: 118). Ella's story is telling in this regard. On the one hand, despite feeling forced to acquire British citizenship, she expressed surprise at her relief upon confirmation that she was granted citizenship.

Ella: I was surprised to see that my emotional reaction to receiving the letter saying that my application has been accepted. I don't know what it was.

AMF: Emotional reaction as in positive?

Ella: Yeah something more sentimental maybe, like a little bit of approval, a little bit of acceptance, which might be a little bit pathetic you know to feel that I really need that kind of reassurance.

A feature of citizenisation is that it makes it personal. Ella was not alone in finding approval from the state. Others put it differently, some in terms of the deserving versus the undeserving, such as Khebat, introduced in Chapter 4, who considers himself a deserving 'potential' citizen thanks to his English fluency, or Agata who understands her continued residence in Britain to be evidence of her commitment to Britain (see Chapter 3). Indeed, the staging of citizenship ceremonies, where individuals or family units are invited to receive their certificate of naturalisation, symbolically congratulates individuals or families for successfully proving that they are becoming citizens that the state desires.

On the other hand, the anointment of citizenship can leave a sour taste. In contrast to her reaction to the Home Office letter, Ella's sentiments after her citizenship ceremony were less than happy.

> I was feeling a bit numb, not very celebratory. But yeah it came as a surprise that I was feeling a bit upset about the whole thing at the same time as relieved that it was all over and I could stop worrying about it because it had been a year and a bit with constant concern [...]. And yeah ... when I went home and I was by myself, I was feeling a little upset and the next day as well. Now since then it's been I don't know how long, maybe a month, I don't know ... I still have the balloon in my room saying 'Congratulations'. It's deflated.

As seen in previous chapters, the build-up to citizenship is full of curated 'pictures' which include forms, evidence and giving an account of oneself; tests, rehearsals and practices of verbal and audial hygiene; anticipation, protracted waiting, extended temporariness, anxiety, hope and desire. All of this feeds into naturalising British citizenship as a highly valued object of desire. To put it another way, the economic, material, temporal and emotional investment required to acquire British citizenship solidify it as the source of the good life. But as Lauren Berlant has suggested (1997), the very acts and efforts in maintaining these investments become obstacles in one's flourishing and accessing 'the good life'.

As someone who felt she had 'no choice', Ella might have been 'deflated' by the ceremony's insistence that she and others wilfully and happily chose to become British citizens. Moreover, Ella's feelings bear witness to the endless deferral and perpetual conditionality of 'the good life' and belonging.

This deferral is noteworthy when ceremony officials speak in the future tense about what new citizens can and should do in order to become full participants in society, and 'good citizens' as a result. For example:

> the citizenship ceremony is a rite of passage that formally welcomes those who wish to join us into full membership of the British family and into citizenship of the United Kingdom. (Ceremony in London)

> Citizenship should not just mean holding British nationality, it should mean total involvement in British life, in its social networks, in its groups, and organisations that connect citizens to the life of their communities. (Ceremony in a city in the North West of England)

The London welcome migratises new citizens and defers their citizenship by speaking of 'those who *wish* to join us', and both speeches give instructions about what good citizenship should mean and, by inference, when the good life will be achieved. I have argued elsewhere (Fortier 2008: 101) that citizenship ceremonies are a fitting example of the entanglement of technologies of reassurance with technologies of antipathy within the fantasy of national unity, as they demarcate a distinction between the established citizens who need reassuring, the new citizens who need confirmation of their propriety, and the failed citizens – those who do not 'choose to be part of the family' or who fail to 'act British'.

Moreover, as rites of passage, ceremonies are boundary-making performances that demarcate the distance between migrants and citizens in a time-space that casts migrants *outside* of politics and belonging prior to the ceremony. This 'outside' time-space is not only 'a space of non-citizenship where [citizenship] rights and entitlements do not apply' (Bhattacharyya 2015: 28). It is also an *apolitical* time-space that is not understood as politically constituting outsiders and insiders; it is a time-space where migrants are presumably not political and presumably do not engage in acts of citizenship (Bhambra 2015: 105).

However, previous chapters show how individuals, regardless of their citizenship status, variously engage in citizenship acts (Isin and Nielsen 2008) or acquire citizenship skills and knowledge as they navigate the waiting room of citizenship. Sukanya Banerjee's (2010) account of the 'extralegal life of citizenship' in colonial India offers a counterpoint to Chakrabarty's critique of deferred citizenship cited in Chapter 2. Banerjee turns her attention to 'the modes of self-representation [that citizenship] generates even *before* it is codified, the political claims it triggers *because* it is deferred' (2010: 7; emphases added). In the world of citizenisation that places individuals in a state of extended deferral, the duration of which varies, people engage in extra-legal as well as legal self-representations and claims of citizenship *before* it is conferred and *because* it is deferred. Therefore, if ceremonies simultaneously citizenise and migratise the 'new' becoming citizens, these 'new citizens' have already and continue to 'become' otherwise.

Becoming otherwise

Scene H

You should be seen to become involved in your new communities whether it is here or elsewhere in Britain and take on social and moral responsibilities to those communities. In return your new communities should learn to depend on you and draw comfort and support from your dependency on them.

British citizenship ceremonies pay much heed to community participation. While there is room for what Yuval-Davis (2011: 69) calls multi-layered citizenship 'composed of local, regional, national, cross, trans and sometimes supranational' communities of belonging, 'community' grounds an otherwise abstract 'national belonging' to a locality. John Clarke et al. (2014: 125) point out how in Britain community is at once:

the *object* of governance (governing agencies seek to act on communities), the *desired outcome* of governance (dysfunctional areas/people need to become communities) and the *subject* of governance (communities who govern themselves). (emphases original)

This section examines the different versions of multi-layeredness that co-exist in the citizenisation process. By counter posing ways of 'becoming otherwise' against citizenship requirements, narratives and rituals, this section shows that modes of becoming otherwise are not only external to and hidden from formal citizenisation. Rather, becoming otherwise is integral to citizenship and Britishness – it constitutes its very multi-layered fabric. Against the attempts to foreclose what citizenship is and ought to be, becoming otherwise exceeds the terms of belonging that are set by the state, and reveal the splits between state-imposed identity and other identifications, belongings and becomings.

The section includes two subsections. The first considers 'ordinary' citizenship against the heroic or emblematic practices of citizenship that are celebrated as exemplary in citizenship ceremonies, such as participatory democracy or voting. Scholarship on ordinary citizenship sheds light on practices, sites or moments 'that are rendered invisible in mainstream political discourse and research' (Neveu 2015: 148; also Staeheli et al. 2012) Becoming otherwise is about how in their 'ordinary' lives, individuals experience and learn about 'life in the UK', with all its pleasures, pains and disparities.

Second, I unpack the relationship between the local and the national and how it plays out in citizenship ceremonies. Specifically, central governments dispatch 'diversity' to the local, and ceremonies have become tasked with the responsibility to produce unity in diversity. The subsection revolves around Sala's account of her ceremony, and sheds light on how difference functions as a remainder; how it is both watered down and a source of commonality that forces open the edges of British citizenship to embrace, rather than reject, unhappy feelings. Sala's postcolonial becoming speaks volumes of the cost of racist and other exclusions not only to individuals, but to citizenship and Britishness.

Becoming through achievement and the value of the ordinary

'It feels like a graduation ceremony', said Sarah, a registrar from the North West of England. Citizenship ceremonies ritualistically celebrate the individual, autonomous, wilful subject who successfully 'graduated' to the status of citizen. Some authors liken ceremonies not to religious rituals, as discussed above, but to graduation ceremonies – Bridget Byrne (2014) writes of 'citizands', analogous to 'graduands' – where each is invited to receive their certificate and applauded by the audience. The certificate acts as a degree of sorts, marking the successful achievement of test requirements which, as Sarah Goodman (2014: 30) points out, are designed as measures of 'inclusion through achievement'.

Citizenship tests are one of the means devised by governments to redress the 'citizenship deficit' of migrants seeking to settle or to naturalise. Citizenship tests are ideological in the sense that they reflect a system of ideas that forms the basis of economic and political policy: conservative versus liberal ideologies, for example. Any citizenship test is bound to reflect a government's ideology. The first edition of the LUK test designed under Tony Blair's New Labour government aimed at ensuring that migrants have the necessary 'practical knowledge about British life' to equip them 'to take an active role in society' (Home Office 2002: 32). The contents centred on citizenship rights, obligations and the various services at their disposal (how to register with a GP for instance).

The LUK test was subsequently revised in 2013 under the Coalition government, stressing that:

> Citizenship is a privilege and not a right. The Government expects that all those wishing to become British citizens should demonstrate their commitment by learning English and have an understanding of British history, culture and traditions. (Home Office 2013a: 8)

As then Minister for Immigration Mark Harper said:

> We've stripped out mundane information about water meters, how to find train timetables, and using the internet. The new [study guide] rightly focuses on values and principles at the heart of being British. Instead of telling people how to claim benefits it encourages participation in British life. (BBC News 2013)[11]

Two questions arise from this framing of the citizenship test: first, how do citizenship tests operate as mechanisms of inclusion and exclusion not only among the migrant population they target, but within the national population as a whole? Second, what does it mean to 'strip' the test of 'mundane' information, and how does the 'mundane' persist otherwise? What *counts* as 'mundane', when, for whom and under what circumstances?

First, the citizenship test reaches a far wider population than those it targets. A running joke about the citizenship test is that birthright citizens would fail it. The joke is on the presumed 'native' citizens; the introduction of the citizenship test signalled the *conditional* character of citizenship and made those who are already citizens anxious about their right to *claim* citizenship. As mock tests circulate online and individuals give it a shot – some registrars had done so and confessed, with embarrassed laughter, that they failed – the laughter can also be read as an anxious feeling that 'we' could also be dispossessed of citizenship and be like 'them'.

In 2012, former Prime Minister David Cameron infamously failed to say what the Magna Carta is or to identify the composer of 'Rule Britannia!' on the David Letterman US talk show. 'You have found me out. That is bad, I have ended my career on your show tonight', he joked (Dathan 2015). While Cameron's authority might have been jeopardised, his citizenship was not. The laughter is telling of the power asymmetries between citizens and migrants seeking citizen-like status, because non-naturalised citizens can be secure in the reality that they are not expected to take the test, and thus can be secure in their sense of rightful status and rightful presence in their country of residence. What the Cameron story shows is that Britons – even the Prime Minister whose government was responsible for raising the requirements on the language and citizenship test in 2013 – cannot live up to the idea of what constitutes 'knowledge' of British life, but they hold others to account about it. Malika, a Pakistani woman on a spousal visa who I met in an ESOL class, understood that citizens do not have to go through the test and consequently found their assumption that it is easy to be insolent:

> the other Life in UK test, they say take test, not too much hard. Because here, the citizens here, the people, the UK people, they don't know what these questions. When asked what is citizenship they don't know anything. They don't know. The test, too much hard.

At a time when the uncertainty of citizenship is normalised and reaches the population as a whole, the hardening of requirements for migrants is a way to secure the distinction between migrants/ noncitizens and citizens, to secure the *idea* of citizenship as stable and certain, and, crucially, to ensure that migrants '*learn their place in the world*' (Bhattacharyya 2015: 14; emphasis added).

That said, these same migrants act differently upon their position 'inside' and 'outside' the citizenisation process, and with different effects (Bassel, Monforte and Khan. 2018: 233). This takes me to the second point about how the 'mundane' persists and has value. For Aisha, obtaining citizenship and continuing with ESOL classes was a way to achieve more independence. ESOL and naturalisation were instrumental in her personal life and in her rejection of patriarchal authority – she had divorced her abusive husband and family-in-law some years earlier. Aisha is but one example that flies in the face of the figure of the submissive Muslim woman forcefully confined to her home and unable to speak English and whose children are at risk of radicalisation as a result – a figure mobilised by several politicians through the years, from Ann Cryer in 2001 (cited in Blackledge 2005: 98–103) to David Blunkett (2002) to David Cameron in 2016 (cited in Mason and Sherwood 2016; see Chapter 4).

For all the value attributed to Britain's 'long and illustrious history' (Home Office 2017), participatory democracy, and various facts and figures about traditions, festivals and population statistics, others find valuable information from what Harper dismissed as 'mundane'.[12] Maya did the first version of the citizenship test, about which she said: 'I just don't think [the citizenship test] is useful in any way'. But she added that:

> the only sections I personally found interesting was, you know, laws regarding maternity leave, or if you have kids at what age are you allowed to leave them alone. That was before we had kids, but this was practical information which you needed to know, but everything else was just, I just memorised and just forgotten.

Tamara, for her part, said that she learned about 'how you buy a house in Scotland'. Tamara and Maya are speaking about elements of 'ordinary' life that many take for granted, but which are extra-ordinary for those who do not have the 'right' legal status to get a mortgage or a job, let alone be eligible for maternity leave (Staeheli et al. 2012).

Likewise, ESOL classes or the citizenship test are useful, practical sources of learning for most. Changuna, a permanent resident from India who was seeking to acquire British citizenship, spoke of ESOL as a way to improve her English in order to:

> do my British passport and computer and learn how to work or something, yeah. And then help my children with their homework. My eldest, she's 11 and her homework is very hard now, yeah it's very hard. She's helping me when I was doing my homework most of the time I'll ask for spelling, but her homework is very hard. I can help on maths because I like maths … Sometime when my children are doing study I'll just sit with them and doing mine. After seven, for an hour, yeah. We all sitting together, reading because my children get reading from school, spelling and homework.

For Changuna, ESOL classes are a stepping stone to 'other routes of progression' (Khan 2018: 40), to other qualifications, to jobs, as well as to share study time with her children. For Aisha, ESOL is also a place to make friends and where she can build her confidence: 'My confidence low. And like, I'm think, I want to just like learn English because I go to see doctor, for my son', who requires continuous medical attention.

ESOL classes can be spaces of becoming (Baynham and Simpson cited in Khan 2018: 40); not becoming 'British' but becoming an 'ordinary' resident. ESOL classes are not end points in the 'achievement' of settlement or citizenship. According to Dina Kiwan (2008), who was a member of the 'Life in the UK Advisory Group',[13] the English language requirement is not intended to be a hurdle to the acquisition of citizenship; rather, it is the first step to communicating and participating with one's fellow citizens, learning and integrating into a new culture. For Kiwan, the test was designed as a technique of the self through which individuals equipped themselves with the necessary knowledge to begin their integrative journey into 'life in the UK'.

In contrast, Melanie Cooke (2009: 75) points out that linking ESOL classes and eligibility for citizenship means that the speaking and listening tests conducted at the end of each level 'have been transformed, in the eyes of students needing evidence for their application for citizenship, into *de facto* nationality tests and therefore [become] very high stakes tests indeed, and the cause of much anxiety and stress' (Cooke 2009: 76). During my fieldwork I met several learners who spoke of their stress and nervousness at having to progress a level (as the rules were at the time). For example Tariq, from Pakistan, said how it made him nervous to be put in level three: 'the teacher, he told me, he think me level three, but I, I quite nervous. Because very high level this for me. I want to come here for learn and pass this test and get certificate British applied citizen. Level three high level for me.'

Moreover, the stakes attached to ESOL tests raise the anxiety of many learners who are not eligible for settlement or citizenship, such as Khebat who undertook an intensive language class in order to get a language fluency certificate event though he knew that he was not eligible for settlement because of his status as an asylum seeker with an exceptional leave to remain visa. The rules changed just a few months after we met, which means that his certificate, which he paid £300 for, would be invalid if he became or were to become eligible for Indefinite Leave to Remain (ILR) or citizenship after October 2013, and he would have to do another test, perhaps take another class. People like Khebat are pushed to the edges of life, somewhere between here and there as they anxiously wait for either a positive change of status that will grant them the right to remain, or a negative change that will deport them back to the countries they fled. But they endure, they persist. 'You carry on', Khebat said. 'It's not broken my back. I know I've got something to stay here and I've got something to fight for'.

There is more to learning a language or completing a citizenship test than learning about 'the values and principles at the heart of being British' that Harper insisted upon. The issue is not only that the language and LUK tests have become increasingly restrictive and therefore departed from the original intentions behind them (Byrne 2016). As argued in Chapter 1, the world of citizenisation relies on testing regimes that depend on social and political claims about who and what ought to be tested (Davies 2014) and concomitantly, who and what should not. Other modes of learning and becoming are bracketed out and those with less of the 'right' cultural capital are disadvantaged (Prabhat 2018). Moreover, the previous chapter shows how a conflation occurs between testing results and moral claims 'regarding the "worth" of humans' (Davies 2014: 16) – for example where speaking English has become evidence of a commitment and willingness to integrate, that is, of 'good citizenship'. As a result, what lies 'at the heart of being British' are repeated attempts to foreclose ways of becoming otherwise and to push some to the edges of worthy humanity.

Postcolonial becomings

> I like to say that the ceremony should be like a group hug. (Ken, Stadlow Council)

> I couldn't eat, I couldn't swallow, I felt like I was choking honestly. Maybe this is a bit too dramatic, but I don't know what came over me. (Sala, arriving at her citizenship ceremony)

Citizenship ceremonies in Britain are distinctly local, usually intimate affairs; they are intimate when contrasted to some US ceremonies that may include hundreds of new citizens (Aptekar 2015), and local when contrasted to other countries where ceremonies privilege national membership above all (Byrne 2014; Aptekar 2015). In Britain, ceremony officials take much pride in planning and running the events, which all include an account of the local (immigration) history, landmarks, sometimes local music (for example something from the Beatles in Liverpool), or references to other distinctive features, for example Cumbria's landscape, Lancashire's industrial history or Brent's super-diversity.

All ceremonies place much emphasis on local diversity. A striking element of these local claims to diversity is that 'the local' has become the place where the multicultural resides. It is worth remembering that current citizenisation processes in Europe developed or tightened at a time when national leaders dismissed multiculturalism as a failed project that hinders rather than enables integration and community cohesion. Anxieties about the perceived divisiveness of 'identity politics' underpin policies of *local* cohesion founded on the idea of diversity, rather than difference, as a source of integration. As I argue elsewhere (Fortier 2008), this vision is one that favours the transcendence of differences and dilution of oppositional politics in favour of an anonymised and universalised notion of 'diversity' where 'difference' is generic: 'we are all different', 'we are all ethnics', 'we are all migrants', hence, 'we' are all the same (also Coutin 2003).

The demise of national multiculturalism came with its dispatch to the local community. Following on from this, local citizenship ceremonies have taken on the task of making diversity a source of unity (Coutin 2003: 115). Ceremony officials will typically refer to their area's 'long history of welcoming people to settle here', and where minoritised communities have 'enriched' the local life with their cultures, skills and talents.

The paradox of the citizenship ceremony is that it creates generic and equivalent subject-citizens but whose 'difference' is both a matter of privatised proclivities and of collective enrichment. Individuals are welcome to enjoy their entry into universal citizenry based on rights, freedoms and duties – 'the good life' – while officials hasten to remind them of their foreign origins (Mazouz 2008: 92). A staple feature of ceremonies is the list: every ceremony official recites the list of countries 'represented' at each ceremony. In doing so, new citizens are migratised again, reminded of their origins, but not asked their story. In turn, the list serves to confirm the *British* citizenship of those entitled to bestow citizenship to migrants.

In contrast to other countries such as the US, new citizens are encouraged to remain 'aware of your heritage' and to share it with their children and with 'others' (as Louise suggests above). 'Do not sacrifice your own culture', as one dignitary stated. But this comes with the condition to:

> be tolerant of the different ways of your neighbours. You need to set an example with your community by taking full part in our democracy. This is now your country; look after it and protect it.

Attachment to 'their' culture and heritage is clearly delineated in terms of how one behaves in the public sphere, and by extension, what the public sphere should look like. As John Clarke et al. argue (2014: 128), '[t]he turn to "community" as a governing strategy both seeks to accommodate diversity and, at the same time, separate it from the politics that identified difference, inequality and exclusion as political issues'. This is accomplished in citizenship ceremonies by demanding that 'new citizens' formally declare their Britishness via values and allegiance (with the pledge and oath), which comes with the condition of a degree of ethnic dis/identification. As Ken put is, 'less of a sense self and more of a sense of community'. Within the vision of British tolerance and diversity, there is an assumed freedom, movement and choice offered to British citizens; one which allows, indeed prescribes, a detachment from *some* ethnic identifications and differences in favour of the attachment to an idealised abstract 'post-ethnic' British citizen (Fortier 2008; see Chapter 4).

The confinement of diversity as a matter of local management has another effect. As Sarah Mazouz (2008: 98) suggests, the schema of ceremonies distinguishes between the logic of the state on the one hand, which solemnly presents the benevolence, generosity and grandeur of the UK as a tolerant liberal democracy and constitutional monarchy. The confinement of diversity to the local comes with erasures of the violent histories that enabled the various self-presentations of localities: the North West as 'the cradle of the industrial revolution', for example. None of the ceremonies I attended makes any reference to the empire, colonialism, slavery or to histories of racism and anti-racist opposition (also Byrne 2012).

On the other hand, and in contrast to the logic of the state, the logic of the local is one where officials are more attentive to valorising proximity and conviviality. As Ken said to me, 'I like to say that the ceremony should be like a group hug'. Registrars indeed put a lot of effort in ensuring that ceremonies are welcoming, pleasurable and celebratory. Their emotional labour is rewarded with the smiling, tearful, grateful guests. Aisha acknowledged that the ceremony was as much 'for them' as it was for her (Scene 4). Perhaps *because* of their position as intermediaries of the state who meet applicants on a regular basis, ceremony officials recognise that, as Ronnie said, 'they're not here for the ride, you know, and to take, take, take. They're here to give, give, give really'. Ronnie put his finger on the state's ambivalent xenophilic/xenophobic relationship to migrants, where the 'xenophilic insistence that immigrants are givers to the nation itself feeds the xenophobic anxiety that they might really be takers from it' (Honig 2001: 99). This ambivalence between desire and anxiety is an organising feature of citizenisation measures, which are designed to separate the 'givers' from the 'takers'. The presumption is that those awarded citizenship have fulfilled the requirements of desirability. Still, some registrars told me about how they find themselves having to defend new citizens to some dignitaries who would privately admonish those with poor English skills and question how they 'achieved' citizenship. Even when 'naturalised', some citizens remain suspect to some and therefore are re-migratised as undesirable outsiders. Some registrars resist this and undertake the labour of educating the sceptics and indeed admonishing them for their lack of appreciation of the costs – financial, labour, emotional – of acquiring British citizenship. While this 'education' remains within the framework of 'luck' discussed above, it is worth noting that those who are conscripted by the state to assess and welcome new citizens enact the state in different ways.

The effort to create a 'happy atmosphere', however, comes with 'feeling rules' (Hochschild 2003: 82) where all are expected to display the 'correct feelings' (Byrne 2014). The aim of the registrars is to produce a 'community of feeling', in Mabel Berezin's (2002: 39) phrase, where intermediaries of the state 'believe in the emotional energy' that the ritual of ceremonies generates, regardless of the outcome which, as seen with Ella, may be a negative feeling. Citizenisation casts applicants and new citizens in the role of desiring the state in a meaningful way, through behaviour or feeling (Goodman 2014). However, as a staged and scripted process, citizenisation also opens up possibilities for dissociations and 'as if' enactments of citizenship throughout, culminating in the citizenship ceremony. The highly staged character of the ceremony allows for the utterance of allegiance in an 'as if' fashion, in the absence of the identificatory and emotional energy assumed in the oath. In the words of Jacqueline Rose (1996: 9), '[y]ou mould your acts and gestures to a persona that deep down you know isn't really there'.

Sala's story is very telling in this regard. Her account of her own citizenship ceremony was fraught with mixed feelings that resulted from her belonging to Britain through historical and personal colonial connections (Prabhat 2018: 58). Her words are worth reproducing at length in Scene J.

Scene J

I arrived early and as I went into the townhall. I saw all the people standing outside. And I noticed that again all of us except one person are either African or Asian people. And as we went into the townhall, it was like a back door and you go through a staircase and it felt like we are it. The first thing that came to mind is that this is all configured by colonial relations, and that we [are] the colonial subjects with, you know, post-independence [of former colonies]. This Britain remained the horizon of ... it has more superior education, better, you know? If you want to improve you want to be like your coloniser.

And it was very painful to realise this because all my life, although my father talked about his own direct experience of colonisation, he also admired British authors, British thinkers, British culture, British education, and his dream in life was for me to come here and get a PhD from here. He wanted me to be a scientist.

So, I was fulfilling my father's dream, but then thinking about my father and the tension in what he was feeling about loving British culture maybe more than Arab culture. He himself lived in Britain for a few years, but he turned down the citizenship because he had the right, he was married to a British woman, he had the right to apply then in the '60s. But he had to give up his Egyptian nationality according to Egyptian law, so he refused to give up his Egyptian nationality and eventually left Britain and lived in the Middle East, different countries in the Middle East. So I thought: I'm fulfilling my father's dream. But maybe one of the reasons why I delayed and delayed in applying for British citizenship is because I thought I don't want to do something that my father thought was inexcusable, to give up your own identity, even though I don't have to give up the Egyptian nationality now, but it felt a bit strange to want to become British. It felt like: why do I have to in order to protect myself and to be able to travel and to be able to live my life? I have a sense of myself as being more international, not a global citizen, but as someone who has belonging in different places. And invested in a wider world rather than a particular nation. And I'd love to live that through my own life, but it's very difficult when you're applying for visas and British passport. The British passport is one of the [top] two passports [in the world] and the Egyptian passport is maybe number 150th.[14] So you also lament the fact that these things are so complicated and you're hostage to fortune as to where you are born and so it makes you think about the arbitrary nature of how the world is organised. Why did I have to do this?

Anyway ... so on the stairs I started to feel very emotional, remembering my father ... So yeah I was thinking as we were going up the stairs and thinking this is a very different situation, but it's the same power relations more or less. And I started to feel really emotional as we went into the hall and the County Sheriff emerged in his full, you know, what appears as military [outfit]. I don't know if it has any other historical roots in the UK, but it felt like very formal and with military connotations that this is the uniform of the empire, the empire is still here. And [the Sheriff] was very sweet but then I started to feel really really upset about complying and coming here and I was going through difficult emotions I think. And in order not to [cry], I started to type on my mobile, just to appear busy and to hide my tears.

Sala's moving story captures so many layers that are constitutive of British citizenship. As a daughter of the empire, she explains her presence and attraction to Britain as a desire to emulate the ruler. Her words conjure Homi Bhabha's (1994: 122) theory of colonial mimicry, which in order to be effective, he argues, 'must continually produce its slippage, its excess, its difference'.

> [C]olonial mimicry is the desire for a reformed, recognizable Other, *as a subject of a difference that is almost the same, but not quite.* ... [M]imicry emerges as the representation of a difference that is itself a process of disavowal. (emphasis original)

Sala's struggle with her feelings are in part about not knowing what to do with them – or rather, *knowing* that she cannot display them, if only to avoid drawing undesired attention or having to explain them. Her struggle goes at the heart of the split between becoming British and identifying as other, as different. But more than that. Her self-enforced silence is the one that expects the minoritised to remain silent about the disavowal required of them – disavowal of a past, a history, as well as of racism, homophobia, sexism, disablism, class inequalities and other forms of exclusion and discrimination. Citizenship ceremonies are indeed not so much for new citizens as they are for the state and the nation; a celebration of the ideal of integration where there is no place for unhappiness (Ahmed 2010: 158). Sala was tapping into the deep sadness of a (post)colonial subject's sense of belonging. In becoming 'the becoming citizen', Sala is torn up by what feels like a disavowal of her Egyptian identity and a betrayal of her father. But even in her quiet sorrow, Sala was refusing to put that history behind her, while she was also refusing to be cast as the 'suffering migrant' who cannot let go of that history (Ahmed 2010). Sala is not 'suffering': she is *refusing* to erase that history as well as the presence of racism in Britain. She is refusing to become an 'affect alien', in Ahmed's phrase, by doing something with her alien affect (Ahmed 2010: 158). Even if that affect was silenced in the townhall, she wrote about it, spoke about it, named it. And then, she met the County Sheriff's Egyptian mother-in-law, as recounted in Scene K

Scene K

She came to me with so much eagerness. She said I'm Egyptian, and I still didn't take her seriously because she looked European, she looked yeah, she didn't look typically Egyptian. She said I'm Egyptian and I asked her when did you leave? She said in 1956. I thought: OK they left when Nasser evacuated the British, so this was the independence. She was 21 by the time she left. And she said Egypt was my home. But the passion she spoke with about Egypt was stunning, was amazing. I mean I don't feel about Egypt the way she does. She said I was born there, I lived there. I asked her if she spoke Arabic. She spoke a bit of Arabic, she said I don't speak it anymore, she spoke perfect posh English. And so we talked; she was so sincere that I was moved. She said well I always felt Egyptian, I wouldn't have left had I not been forced to leave, all my friends, all my life. She idealised Egypt; the Egypt she described is an Egypt I recognised from my mother's stories about the golden age of the 1950s and the 1960s.

She made me think that there's someone here. I mean it shifted things around because it destabilised my 'us and them' thinking in my head. There was this British woman who is coming here as part of the ceremony, as part of the officialdom, she was like helping the Sheriff with the ceremony, and she didn't feel British at all and she felt completely Egyptian. And so ... there is nothing purist here about the whole thing. You know the person who's one of the people confirming the citizenship on me is herself not feeling British and herself feeling more Egyptian than I am. Things eased for me [then] and I took things a bit more lightly.

[After the ceremony, they resumed their conversation] She was in tears, well she was in tears when I talked to her the first time, she was in tears again and she said I left with my bag, you know a suitcase of few of my clothes, no money, nothing, I found myself in Cairo airport coming to England. And I thought that doesn't sound right, and I asked her what was her maiden name in Egypt and she told me, and then I realised: I said you belong to the Jewish community or she said I belong to the Jewish community, I can't remember whether I asked her or she said it. Then I realised she's *Egyptian* Egyptian.

This chance encounter turned things around for Sala, made things lighter, making her realise that things are not as 'pure' as they might appear. Sala was able to redirect her sorrow and turn it into some kind of comfort grounded in a shared difference and shared distance from Britishness. What comforted Sala was not simply meeting a person she at first thought was white British. It was that this woman stood for the state while dis-identifying from it. This was somewhat amazing for Sala, and it brought home the reality of the texture of Britain and Britishness that is far from 'pure'.

This is what happens to difference when it is erased in naturalisation – it becomes a remainder, as Susan Bibler Coutin (2003) suggests. A remainder that leads 'the authenticity of naturalized identities to be questioned', but that also enables migrants' 'refusals to consign "difference" to the private sphere, where it becomes a source of commonality, challenges the requirement that public citizenship assume a generic form' (2003: 521). Sala's story speaks volumes of migrant lives, migrant belongings, migrant becomings, *migrant-citizens*: where they are, what holds them, what their temporalities are. Their histories and stories do not disappear in citizenisation, nor *could* they or should they. Their becoming otherwise is not simply making Britishness become otherwise; it is unveiling how

Britain is, and always has been, brim full of 'other' becomings. Something different, not accounted for that is foreclosed by the process, but not totally closed off because these forms of becoming otherwise not only erupt from or exceed the frames of reference. They are already integral and *necessary* to them, and therefore also have the power to disrupt and unravel them.

Conclusion

Britain's postcolonial citizenship exists through a logic akin to processes of provincialisation described by Chakrabarty: it acknowledges the indispensability of the (postcolonial) racially minoritised to representations of Britishness and British citizenship, 'and yet struggles with the problems of representation that this indispensability invariably creates' (Chakrabarty 2007: 22). Moreover, this 'representation' is both about how British citizenship is imagined and depicted – for example, in the LUK test – and how officials 'represent' the state – as in the County Sheriff's Egyptian mother-in-law. Identificatory splits develop not only between 'new' citizens and the state, but also within the state itself: indeed, this chapter shows the various ways in which registrars or other officials enact the citizenship ceremony, which reveal that states do not operate in unified ways.

Ideals of citizenship as stable and certain are sustained through push and pull dynamics usually associated with migration. Citizenship is not equally distributed in the world, and its reproduction through principles of inheritance ensures that these inequalities endure. Citizenships from the Global North acquire a value and currency that attracts citizens from the Global South. In this sense, accusations of 'instrumentalism' waged against migrants obscure the ways in which states themselves are instrumental about preserving the value of their citizenships, for example by tightening citizenisation processes for political gains.[15]

But migrants (like intermediaries of the state) are not without agency or reflexivity about their 'pull' towards citizenship, and their ways of becoming citizen unravel the parameters of 'good' and 'happy' citizenship. This chapter asks how one becomes and belongs from the point of view of those directly involved in the citizenisation process, particularly in citizenship ceremonies but also in ESOL classes. The chapter counterposes their experiences and enactments against institutional structures and political discourses, thereby exposing the limits of, but also alternatives to, prescriptions and proscriptions about how one becomes and belongs – temporally, spatially, affectively.

Citizenship *takes time* in its perpetual deferral. Citizenship ceremonies welcome new citizens in the future tense where details about how to become full participants in and members of their communities reinstate the conditionality of citizenship, becoming and 'the good life'. More broadly, citizenisation processes position individuals in a state of extended deferral, the duration of which varies. As a result, people engage in extra-legal as well as legal self-representations and claims of citizenship *before* it is conferred and *because* it is deferred (Banerjee 2010: 7). Therefore, if ceremonies simultaneously citizenise and migratise the 'new' becoming citizens, these 'new citizens' have already and continue to 'become' otherwise.

They become otherwise through a range of 'mundane' practices and encounters that were dismissed by Cameron's coalition government. ESOL classes, for example, are spaces of becoming where individuals are there not only to 'become' British, but rather as part of a trajectory that is assumed 'ordinary' by most citizens: to acquire skills and other qualifications in order to get a job or to take part in 'ordinary' family activities such as helping children with their homework. Such 'ordinary' features of life are extra-ordinary for those who do not have the 'right' legal status, or the 'right' cultural or social capital.

But citizenship *takes time* also in its simultaneous disavowal of and reliance on postcolonial citizens. On the one hand, the postcolonial citizen is bound to silence and to negate histories of violence and discrimination. On the other hand, she is enjoined to represent and confirm the present benevolence of the tolerant state while embodying local diversity. This is one way in which citizenship *takes place*: the disjunction between the logic of the state and the logic of the local, where the former is characterised by solemnly and formally legitimating the UK as a tolerant liberal democracy and constitutional monarchy.

The logic of the local, for its part, is one that celebrates diversity; a diversity that central governments have dispatched away from 'the nation' and into 'the local'. In citizenship ceremonies, migrants are reminded of their origins in the obligatory list of countries, which registrars read out to positively signal the 'rich' diversity of the local. For all the good intentions behind this ritual, this vision emanates from national politics that favour the dilution of difference in favour of an anonymised and universalised notion of 'diversity' where 'difference' is generic.

Difference is consigned to the private domain and cast at the margins of neoliberal citizenship. Citizenisation is a boundary-making process that delineates the distance between migrants and citizens in a *time-space* that casts 'migrants' *outside* of politics and belonging prior to the ceremony, and even still at the ceremony. This 'outside' time-space is a space where citizenship 'rights and entitlements do not apply' (Bhattacharyya 2015: 28). It is also an *apolitical* time-space that is not understood as *itself* politically constituted, and as *itself* constituting outsiders and insiders. By making difference a remainder to diversity's universality, citizenisation ensures that migrants and naturalised citizens know 'their place in the world' (Bhattacharyya 2015: 14). The paradox of the citizenship ceremonies is that they create generic and equivalent subject-citizens but whose 'difference' is both a matter of privatised proclivities and of collective enrichment.

Citizenship ceremonies *take hold* through a local logic of xenophilia that acts as a counterpoint to the xenophobic anxiety of the state and hostile anti-immigration politics. In contrast to ceremonial gestures, local officials are more attentive to valorising proximity, intimacy and conviviality. Their intention on making ceremonies a joyful event – making them like a 'group hug' – is motivated in part by their awareness that many arrive at these events feeling nervous and anxious. At the same time, when understood in the broader context of the politics of diversity and citizenship, this framing also comes with 'feeling rules' that contain 'alien affects' (Ahmed 2010) of anger, unhappiness, disappointment in favour of the duty of happiness and gratitude.

The promise of the good life and happiness 'pull' many to aspire for the 'red passport' and places them in a relationship of desire for and gratitude to the state that citizens do not experience. Or, in the view of several registrars, that citizens do not experience *enough*. Here, the logic of 'luck' operates alongside happiness and the good life as a technology that confirms British citizenship as the source of that luck, happiness and the good life. At the same time, it secures citizens in their own sense of insider status and their 'luck' at not having to be in 'the waiting room', like 'them'.

Citizenisation leads to ceremonies that produce a generic voluntary subject-citizen who exists prior to the law. Moreover, citizenship ceremonies also produce the generic voluntary *migrant* who chooses to come to and reside in Britain. The distinction between naturalisation as choice versus birthright as ascription conceals the global inequalities of 'hereditary citizenship' (Shachar 2009), while it shores up ideals of choice as equally available to all. Citizenship ceremonies uphold this distinction by noting the difference between 'we' who have no choice, and 'you', who chose 'us', where 'you' hold up a mirror and confirm the choice-worthiness of 'us'.

Birthright citizenship remains the privileged mode of citizenship transmission and it is embedded in racialised familial assumptions that privilege the reproductive patriarchal 'more equal' heterosexual family. At the citizenship ceremony, *both* gender/sexuality *and* citizenship are *conferred* by the state (Canaday 2009: 255). What is more, citizenship ceremonies *place* citizenship decidedly in Britain, where reproductive obligations must occur decidedly here rather than in the diasporic spaces that many families inhabit.

The impulse of citizenisation processes is to counter what are cast as external forces in order to assert the certainty of citizenship. However, the experiences, choices and actions of *migrant-citizens* reveal the extent to which citizenship *takes place, takes hold* and *takes time otherwise*. They do so by re-signifying the 'ordinariness' and extra-ordinariness of becoming, belonging and citizenship, by exposing the empty promise of the good life and happiness because of their perpetual deferral, or by unravelling the constitutive and necessary postcolonial presence within citizenship, Britishness or the British state. By becoming otherwise, migrant-citizens are refusing to remain alienated by doing something with their difference, their 'extra-ordinary' trajectories, their lack of choice and their alien affects. Those who are 'bracketed' in the citizenisation process are not passively waiting: they are actively reconfiguring what it means not only to become, but to be a (British) citizen.

Conclusion –
Lessons from the waiting room:
citizenisation and migratisation

> Do they really know the agony they put people in? Do they really
> know the effect they have on people's life? Why do they treat these
> kinds of issues in this inhumane detached manner? Do they really
> realise … [pause] When someone who's waiting to know if they can
> stay or not …[trails off]. (Tamara, Lebanese national waiting to apply
> for citizenship)

'Tell me your story.' This is how I started each interview with migrants
and applicants. They would tell me about their dreams, hopes,
difficult and sometimes dangerous journeys, their dealings with the
Home Office, their lives in the UK, their longing for those left behind
and for 'the good life'. Their stories span a range of routes and
timespans, some much easier than others.

The stories of institutional actors – those I call intermediaries of
the state – and some British citizens with foreign spouses are also
heard in this book. These individuals were transformed by their
experiences of meeting or living with migrants, and migration policies
variously encroached on their working or private lives. Registrars
and ESOL (English for Speakers of other Languages) professionals
are conscripted into the national and transnational fields of professionals charged with everyday bordering in the name of securitising
the state and its national culture (Bigo 2002). These responsibilities
indubitably position them as 'citizens' endowed with the authority
to ask for and scrutinise migrants. These are responsibilities which
many enact with as much care and compassion as they can, given
the constraints imposed on their roles.

But other stories are also told in this book. The story of documents,
as they circulate and generate actions, reactions and relations in
and beyond the waiting room of citizenship. The story of language,

of the English language in particular, and its historical formation as a 'global' good that is also a marker of national belonging and commitment. The story of historical and bureaucratic processes and technologies that naturalise not only the ideal of citizenship as the 'gold standard' but also categories, norms, locales: the reproductive heterosexual family formation, romantic love, coupledom, 'residence', white English monolingualism, birthright, the state, the nation. This is also the story of traces, of what is left behind, discarded, erased, omitted, in transactional relations whereby outsiders are made into insiders, but also when insiders are made into outsiders – remember Charlotte's daughter Katie, or Paul's realisation that his mobility is now controlled.

Citizenisation is part of the neoliberal retooling of state authority within a global capitalist market that favours 'flexible citizenship' (Ong 1999) to enable more adaptable, moveable people. Citizenisation policies developed as means to contain that very adaptability and secure it more firmly to singular territorialised national cultures of value. Citizenship today is a tool in everyday bordering (Yuval-Davis, Wemyss and Cassidy 2019), between and within state boundaries, and its parameters are intimately entwined with migration. But this book also documents how citizenship confines migration within the global market of 'free labour' that pre-emptively determines the 'citizenship potential' of some and discards the rest as less integratable from the outset (Bhattacharyya 2015). Chapter 1 situates citizenisation – which encompasses what is usually referred to as 'integration and naturalisation' measures – within the broader neoliberal world of 'managed migration' that skillifies and depoliticises citizenship in favour of measuring the integration potential of migrants in both economic and social, cultural terms. Citizenship is depoliticised insofar as it is less about rights and obligations than it is about skills and opportunities and framed as a matter of security, market interests, household governance and civic ideals. Citizenisation policies emphasise citizenship as something to *become* rather than a status to acquire, and they reward the *becoming citizen* whose citizenship skills and attitudes are deemed fitting with the national community of values (Anderson 2013).

However, citizenship is *intensely* politicised as a necessary means to ensure that citizens are protected from external threats, and that migrants with citizenship potential are or will be 'safe' citizens for the state and their fellow citizens (Weber 2008). Moreover, citizenship is intensely politicised under the cloak of 'objective' tests aimed at redressing the citizenship deficit of migrants by educating them into the national community of values: 'inclusion through achievement' (Goodman 2014: 30). But such values remain expressed through racialised, gendered, sexualised and culturalised technologies of love and commitment (Chapter 3), language (Chapter 4), religion (Chapter 5). Chapter 3 shows how all applicants for settlement or citizenship must give an account of themselves, as all are set on the legal course towards citizenship that renders them continuously accountable. But the terms of accountability remain framed in ways that advantage those with the right cultural capital. Migrants are required to tell their story in the institutional, bureaucratic, legal and cultural terms of their country of immigration.

What does the telling of these stories do, then? Scrutinising life in the waiting room of citizenship enables an analysis of how citizenisation *takes time, takes place* and *takes hold* in ways that conform, exceed and confound the frames of reference laid out in citizenisation policies. Analysing the social life of citizenisation sheds light on how the distribution of power and inequality through time, space and affect/bodies works to enact multiple conceptions of citizenship or the state–citizen relationship.

Citizenisation brings forth contested *temporalities*. The 'heteronomous times' (Cwerner 2001) of citizenisation result from a politics of waiting where who is to wait, how and what for are defined by, but also define, status – migrants on different visas, or citizens who control the time and timing of, and charge for, checking services, for example. Experiences of time reveal the asynchronicities of citizenisation, where subjective experiences of time – protracted waiting for example – differ significantly from the bureaucratic time and timing of documents. Crucially, taking the long view citizenisation brings forth the hidden and contested histories of citizenship. Chapter 2 retraces how the idea that British citizenship is 'weak' results from a long history of power tied to imperialism and colonialism. As a 'global institution' (Karatani 2003), Britain was and is part of the international political and economic landscape where citizenship is continuously redefined. The relatively late arrival of a specifically *national* British citizenship, then, was more about *citizenising Britain* than it was about redressing a historical weakness; it was about equipping the British state with the technology of citizenship in the process of further hardening the borders of British nationality and nationhood.

Bridget Anderson writes that 'the Migrant qua migrant has no history, but rather, an origin' (Anderson 2013: 179). Colonial pasts and presents that shape citizenship regimes today are absent from citizenisation, but they are not absent from the migrant-citizens. They resurface in the bodies and voices of postcolonial migrants and citizens – for instance whose other languages and other Englishes are here because English was there (Chapter 4). As seen in Chapter 5, citizenship ceremonies reduce migrants to their origins in the list that signals local diversity but dehistoricises, and consequently depoliticises, difference and inequality. Against nativist rootings of citizenship, migrants *have* stories and histories that are intimately connected to British citizenship; stories that have always shaped, and continue to shape, what it means to 'become' British.

Citizenisation is exemplary of the ways in which uncertainty constitutes instruments of neoliberal governing, where the promise of resolution is always deferred. The promise of 'certain' citizenship is deferred throughout the citizenisation process, including the citizenship ceremony, were migrants are instructed about the conditions for achieving 'the good life': evidencing one's rightful presence or substantiating one's liaison with a citizen, speaking English and, for 'new citizens', the duties of happiness, gratitude, political participation and community orientation. But precisely because migrants are consigned to varying states of extended deferral, they learn ways of becoming otherwise that extend what it means to be citizen.

Becoming British also takes place in contested *spatialities*: the impulse of citizenisation processes is to firmly emplace subjects within national cultural territories. They do so through governing mobility such as residence requirements or Home Office letters that require immediate action; or through testing regimes that favour those with the 'right' cultural capital for 'life' and language in the UK; or through reasserting and reproducing birthright as the privileged route to citizenship transmission and reproduction. Citizenship takes place through imaginative geographies that distinguish between 'good' and 'bad' places for citizenship. Narratives of 'luck', which come from a place of recognition of 'the migrant', their histories and stories, still remain grounded in the understanding that 'good citizenship' happens in Britain. The circulation of narratives of luck and the good life are revealing of how citizenship is not only a national system of inclusion/exclusion. It is also a global system of unequal distribution of the world's riches (Shachar and Hirschl 2007; Shachar 2009).

But migrant-citizens confound established understandings of citizenship by becoming and belonging otherwise, if only by enduring the social and physical immobility of protracted waiting. A majority of migrant-citizens have diasporic lives, families and obligations that exist harmoniously with localised belongings; ESOL classes are spaces of becoming otherwise that are not reducible to 'becoming British'; migrants work, live, learn English in ways that extend the terms of 'becoming citizen'. The ways of becoming and belonging of the migrants I met cannot be reduced to 'the logic of job, family, and citizenship' of citizenisation, where the assumption is that the state can determine, detect and select migrants with the 'right' motivations, values and plans (Anderson 2013: 180). For all the inequities embedded in citizenisation, the migrants I met all shared the desire for 'the good life' that fulfils the need for subsistence, for relations of mutual care and support, and imagined futures of full inclusion rather than a world where the right to exclude prevails (Anderson 2013: 180–181).

In addition to contested spatialities and temporalities, citizenisation takes us to the multiple ways in which it *takes hold*. Citizenisation operates from, and reproduces, the premise of the generic, autonomous free and wilful subject which lies at the foundation of modern conceptions of citizenship (Chapter 2). Citizenisation naturalises the choosing citizen-subject as existing prior to the law by concealing the role of the law in defining the terms of that choice and how to express it. 'Choice' is naturalised as a feature of naturalisation that congratulates not only voluntary citizen, but also the voluntary migrant. The narrative arc of citizenisation takes hold of the value of citizenship and holds it down by emphasising the choosing, voluntary migrant-citizen who choses to come 'here' and to become one of 'us'.

Following on from this, the feeling rules of citizenisation dictate how citizenship should be imparted and received. Registrars put a lot of effort into ensuring that ceremonies are welcoming, pleasurable and celebratory. The idea of the 'group hug' that one registrar aims to convey captures the ways in which local registrars feel compelled to reassure and hold new citizens, and to collectivise the event in a manner that includes new as well as long established citizens. It suggests a form of intimacy that contrasts with the formality of the state.

The 'feeling rules' (Hochschild 2003: 82) of citizenship are organised around an economy of feelings: the production, circulation and distribution of legitimate feelings for and within the nation, where the burden of that labour largely falls upon migrants: Agata was at pains to show her 'commitment' to living in Britain, while the registrar she met was at pains to ensure that such an abstract feeling could be documented. Discrepant feelings arise between subjective experiences of citizenisation and the institutional structures of feeling and feeling rules. Migrants can find themselves in a relationship of cruel optimism to citizenship, where the object of desire is also an obstacle to fulfilling that desire: remember Khebat's love of English, Tariq's desire for the good life, or Nabaz's hope for 'that piece of paper'. Documents, language requirements and the promise of happiness combine in reifying citizenship as the ultimate but ultimately deferred object of desire. Desire, hope, anxiety, gratitude are unevenly distributed in the waiting room of citizenship. In other words, the distribution of power and inequality through affect is another way in which citizenship takes hold.

Moreover, the politics of affect also place migrants in a position to make citizens feel better. From the outset, citizenisation measures target those whose 'integration potential' has been pre-emptively assessed. In return, these migrants must reassure the state of their commitment to integrate by undertaking appropriate measures, whether that is to curate the right documents or be 'model citizens' that will ease the job of state intermediaries and case workers, or practise verbal and audial hygiene to protect national serenity. Citizenisation also takes hold of subjects when registrars read bodies against identity documents or read off bodies for signs of true or fake love. These various technologies – of modelling, of love, of commitment – are designed and deployed with racially, culturally and class coded expectations of love, gender equality, familial arrangements, commitment, 'good English' or the ownership of property.

More than 'just' exploring how citizenship and citizens are made and unmade in citizenisation, this book also touches on how the state, as well as state–citizen relations, are 'made up' (Cooper 2015), not only in the sense of how they are imagined, but also in the sense of how they are variously actualised in the enactment of the policy requirements around documenting, speaking, becoming and naturalising citizens. The state, then, is not a monolithic entity; it is enacted and imagined differently by different actors as they navigate the complex legal, policy and social landscape of citizenisation. In that sense, the authority of the state relies on relational dynamics that reassert both the subject ('migrant' or 'citizen') *and* the state as social subjects, as 'actors' and agents in people's everyday lives (Chalfin 2008). The state is omnipresent in migrants' lives, in the form of letters, forms, webpages, certificates that confer the authority of the state to demand actions and reactions, to confirm one's status and to remind subjects of their place as migrants or migrant-citizens.

Intermediaries of the state, for their part, have expectations about state propriety while they also conjure an invisible, amorphous state as the unknow decision-maker whose reasoning they cannot access; the 'they' that Tamara speaks of in the epigraph above. But throughout the citizenisation process, the state also reproduces *itself* for itself. In a world where the state is alien and distant from the people it is meant to represent, Jacqueline Rose (1996) argues, it is aware of its fragility, as well as of its own intransigence insofar as authority is always under threat of its own demise. This requires the state to always 'make *sure* of itself' (Rose 1996: 8, emphasis original), for example, by confirming and indeed increasing its presence and authority in the citizenisation process.

State policies of citizenisation arise from states' ambivalent relationship to migrants and to migration. A 'desire–anxiety' nexus mediates the state–citizen relationship where migrants are required to desire the state and be desirable to the state, in terms set by the state. In turn, state anxieties take the form of the ambivalent xenophilic/xenophobic relationship to immigrants discussed in Chapter 5 and which underpin the process of distinguishing between 'givers' and 'takers'. But another anxiety feeds into the state's mobilisation of citizenship, which is the fear that citizenship is not appealing to others – indeed, one of the concerns addressed by the Goldsmith Review (2008) was how to provide those with permanent resident status with 'a compelling route to citizenship' (Goldsmith 2008:

79). Citizenisation, then, becomes another means to tackle the 'choiceworthiness of us' and to 'have that sense refurbished' (Honig 2001: 13). Citizenisation enlists migrants into a relation of desire for the state, which in turns confirms the authority of the state to define the terms of that desire and to bestow citizenship to the desirable desiring citizens. There is an instrumentality in citizenisation that is not only about instrumentalising citizenship to fulfil market interests (Kundnani 2007; Vink and de Groot 2010; see Chapter 1). What previous chapters document is how the instrumentality of citizens and the instrumentality of the state are in tension in the citizenisation process. Home Office guidance repeatedly asserts that citizenship should mean more than 'just' acquiring a passport, disqualifying such views as 'merely' instrumental. In turn, however, states instrumentalise *migrants* to repeatedly shore up, sustain and naturalise the 'value' of citizenship and the privileges of insider status. In citizenisation, migrants are instrumentalised as *both* subjects of communication and objects of information.

However, the information they communicate reaches beyond the frames of citizenisation. Life in the waiting room is a space where migrants mobilise the remainders of difference that have been histori-cally and procedurally cast out of citizenship: remainders of race, gender, sexuality and class that privatise and depoliticise 'difference' and inequalities within a watered-down celebration of diversity. However, the remainders of difference also open up ways of *rethinking* citizenship, 'migranthood' and their relationship to each other through enactments of *documenting otherwise* by telling the story of migration rather than justifying the presence of migrants; *speaking otherwise* that shows capability rather than competence and that embraces multilingualism and other Englishes; and *becoming otherwise*, in 'ordinary' encounters and spaces, and in mobilising 'difference' not as an alien or suffering 'identity' but as space of becoming and belonging that is shaped through shared stories, histories, inequalities, struggles and inclusions.

* * *

This book travels along with migrants, citizens and intermediaries of the state in their travails and turbulences as they meet, move through and are moved by the waiting room of citizenship. Their stories teach us something about how it is only through the lens of migration and the migrant that we can fully appreciate how citizenship operates, today more than at any other time. Papadopoulos, Stephenson and Tsianos (2008: xviii) speak of the 'autonomy of migration' as a tool:

> to jettison the ubiquitous notions of the migrant as either a useful worker or as a victim. Instead of conceiving of migrational movements as derivatives of social, cultural and economic structures, the autonomy of migration lens reveals migration to be a constituent creative force which fuels social, cultural and economic transformations. Migration can be understood as a force which evades the policing practices of subjectivity.

Migration can also be understood as a force that not only evades, but that reshapes what it means to be a citizen or migrant subject. To think about the pervasiveness and constitutive force of migration in today's world is more than normalising migration as no longer an exception (Papadopoulos, Stephenson and Tsianos 2008; Nail 2015; Hui 2016). It is to normalise migration as part and parcel of people's lives and imaginaries (Fortier 2012), regardless of their migration status. This requires investigations into how, regardless of status, substance or location, subjects constitute themselves, or are constituted, as migrants.

What emerges from this study is that citizenisation and migratisation work together in ways that converge and diverge. The aims of citizenisation are to redress the citizenship deficit of migrants in view of enabling and enhancing their integration potential. However, migrants are repeatedly migratised and decitizenised throughout citizenisation, including when they are 'naturalised'; migrants are assumed to inhabit an apolitical time-space where citizenship rights and obligations do not apply, where their *other* citizenship(s) 'is unmade by being made unworkable' (Nyers 2013: 38), and where they do not engage in 'citizenship acts' – therefore underestimating the extent to which citizenisation itself in a constellation of 'acts of citizenship', while also concealing the political construction of migrants as noncitizen outsiders.

Turning the lens of migration on citizenship sheds light on how citizenship and citizens are migratised as well – how migration encroaches into people's lives, but also how citizenship itself *is* an immigration status (Yeo 2018) – and the history of British citizenship is a case in point. In addition, migratisation can take the form of migratism, which 'ascribes migration to certain bodies and establishes non-migration as the norm of intelligible national and European belonging' (Tudor 2018: 1058). Racially minoritised subjects are presumed outsiders even when citizens; or racially majoritised but linguistically minoritised subjects such as white-bodied Europeans are expelled from the British nation. Through intertwined regimes of seeing and regimes of hearing, migratism and racism together enable the disappearance of 'whiteness' and 'nativism' as unmarked historically constructed categories that developed through histories of domination. Such erasures are normalised in bureaucratic processes that underpin evidence-based methodologies of documentation, or common sense politics of *jus linguarum* and 'the good life'.

Against migratism, to think about citizenisation and migratisation together is to acknowledge the indispensability of migration to citizenship and to acknowledge the problems *about* and limits *of* citizenship that this indispensability invariably brings to the fore. Migratising citizenship forces the recognition that migrant lives and belongings exceed the constraining politics of citizenship and instead can release the potential of citizenship itself: that of multi-layered belongings that span not only geographical scales (Yuval-Davis 2011), but that recognise desires and searches for the good life beyond fixed 'identities' – gendered, sexual, racial, class, ableist, national, cultural, religious, ethnic – and that foreground living with difference where inequalities are a collective, not individualised, responsibility.

Postscript

When I started writing this book, the major uncertainty *around* citizenship in Britain was Brexit. However, the effects of Brexit are not confined to Britain. They must be understood within the world of citizenisation and migratisation, as well as within the global rise of nationalisms and right-wing populisms that place citizenship at the heart of controlling and defining who belongs and who does not. While the outcomes of Brexit remain unknown even as I write these lines a few months before the 31 December 2020 deadline, the likelihood is that citizenship will become even more difficult to get and easier to lose, while the net of precarity and uncertainty widens and is likely to catch a much wider population.

As I began this book, the Windrush scandal had just brought to light the deep uncertainty *of* citizenship. This uncertainty has become even more salient as I end this book during the COVID-19 global pandemic. COVID-19 has become the object of competing introspective nationalisms and racisms that further highlight the precarity and fragility of citizenship as we witness the closing of borders, the importance of visa status, of residency and of living conditions. COVID-19 spotlights how people in the (perpetual) waiting room of citizenship are treated differently – living in crowded accommodation or in detention, on working visas without access to social benefits, as 'key workers' with precarious statuses or as their spouses. It also sheds lights on inequalities of citizenship and the failed promise of 'the good life', as we see indigenous (United Nations 2020) and racially minoritised citizens disproportionately affected by the disease. In short, the pandemic foregrounds long-standing global and national inequalities in the distribution of 'full' citizenship and the concurrent growth of precarious statuses that render the racially minoritised poor more disposable.

What is more, international Black Lives Matter (BLM) protests that erupted in the wake of George Floyd's murder by US police, forced the recognition of militarised policing and forced questions about the politics of memorialisation that celebrate the colonial administrators and profiteers of slavery and racial capitalism. The inequalities and uncertainties of citizenship and the ways in which citizenisation and migratisation function in the contemporary world are made raw by the coalescence of the pandemic with the BLM protests, which have been used in further attempts to control the movement of people within localities as well as across borders.

Studying citizenisation and migratisation and how they work together calls for the consideration of how shared local, national and global trends congeal and take form in specific social, political and historical contexts. My hope is that forensic examinations of the perpetuation of nativist, sedentarist politics of belonging and entitlement will not only make it more difficult to turn away from the inequalities they foster and reinforce, but that these examinations will contribute tools to help unravel these injustices and find alternatives to citizenship that embrace migration and difference as constitutive creative forces of all social life.

Notes

Introduction

1 Indicative references include: Gillespie and O'Loughlin 2009; Kostakopoulou 2010; Pykett 2010; Vora 2013; Clarke et al. 2014; Abrahamian 2015; Kapoor 2015; Pulinx and Van Avermaet 2015; Balta and Altan-Olcay 2016; Engel 2016; Džankić 2019; Vandevoordt and Verschraegen 2019.
2 Indicative references include: Evans 1993; Soysal 1995; Kymlicka 1995; Lister 1997; Linklater 1998; Ong 1999; Bell and Binnie 2000; Faist 2001; Johnston 2001; Plummer 2003; Mookherjee 2005; Motomura 2006; Auvachez 2009; Fortier 2010; Johnson 2010; Fitzgerald 2017; Sadiq 2017; El-Enany 2020.
3 Denizenship was coined by Tomas Hammar (1990) to refer to a category of foreigners with long-term residency who possess extensive rights, which, in many respects, are comparable to those of citizens (also Soysal 1995; Bosniak 2006). The history of denizenship goes back further than generally acknowledged, as Karatani (2003) shows in his history of British citizenship. We return to this briefly in Chapter 2.
4 In the case of EU citizens residing in the UK, campaigners expressed fears that they are at risk of becoming 'illegal' due to shortages of government support for advising and processing settlement applications (Proctor 2020).
5 The 'Windrush generation' refers to Citizens of the United Kingdom and Colonies who came to Britain between 1948 and 1973, who had the right of abode, the right to work and leave to remain, but the government did not automatically issue them documents to prove their rightful presence. Nor did the Home Office keep records (Williams 2020: 24). 'Windrush' refers to the HMT Empire Windrush, a ship that docked at Tilbury Docks, Essex, on 21 June 1948, with 1,027 official passengers on board. Of these, 802 stated their last country of residence was in the Caribbean. The Windrush 'has come to symbolise

post-war Caribbean migration to the UK at the end of the empire' (Williams 2020: 24).

6 The phrase was used by Theresa May in 2012 when she announced a new immigration policy intended to, in her words, 'create, here in Britain, a really hostile environment for illegal immigrants' (Goodfellow 2019). Her policy was implemented in the Immigration Act 2014 and Immigration Act 2016. Among other things, the policy includes requirements for landlords, National Health Services, charities, community interest companies, and banks to carry out ID checks on individuals seeking their services. The policy also supported strategies such as 'Go Home' vans as a way to encourage voluntary deportation (cf. Jones et al. 2017).

7 While 55 individuals were wrongfully subjected to hostile environment sanctions (Williams 2020: 25).

8 In 2018, the fee for naturalisation was £1,330. The waiver applies to all those from Commonwealth countries who arrived in the UK between 1948 and 1973.

9 For example, I argue elsewhere that British politics of multiculturalism make tolerance and diversity a distinctly British value, which in turn makes Britain a distinctive national setting that enables 'diversity' to thrive (Fortier 2008).

10 I am inspired by Ruben Andersson's (2014a) use of scenes from his fieldwork in his ethnography of clandestine migration.

Scene 1

1 Up to 31 December 2020, EU nationals have lifetime family reunion rights with no restrictions. From 31 December 2020, EU nationals will be treated like British nationals and will need to meet the income threshold required of the Britain-based spouse (set at £18,600 in May 2019).

2 The Home Office Guidance summarises the required standard as follows: 'A person at ESOL Entry 3 is able to follow straightforward spoken explanations and instructions and hold a conversation on a familiar topic' (Blackledge 2005: 224).

3 A B1 level of English is above the 'basic user' level and called 'independent user' in the CEFR and is described by Cambridge ESOL as: 'Can understand the main points of clear standard input on familiar matters regularly encountered in work, school, leisure, etc.' (Council of Europe 2001: 23).

4 See also www.gov.uk/english-language/exemptions [last accessed 4 December 2019].

5 Migrants came from: Australia, Brazil, Canada, Egypt, Germany, Greece, India, Italy, Iraq, Iran, Lebanon, Mexico, Pakistan, Philippines, Switzerland, Thailand.

6 I asked all participants 'what languages do you speak?', where 'speaking' was not qualified. Thus, the answers provided are based on self-assessment. In addition to English, the languages listed by applicants were: Arabic, Austrian, Dutch, Filipino, French, German, Greek, Gujarati, Hindi, Ilocano, Italian, Japanese, Kurdish, Persian, Portuguese, Punjabi, Sorani, Spanish, Tagalog, Thai, Turkish, Urdu.

7 It is beyond the scope of this volume to discuss how exceptions are to be used in qualitative research such as this. Suffice to say that it poses the question of the effects that setting parameters have on selective sampling which are necessary, to be sure, to ensure a modicum of common ground that can be taken as given, but which should not stop researchers from expanding their field to allow for the unexpected to arise. 'Exceptions' and the unexpected are more often than not rich sources of knowledge that take us in new directions.

Chapter 1

1 *Today* programme, BBC Radio 4, 24 March 2016. While Wallonia introduced an integration decree before Flanders, it did not originally include language or citizenship 'orientation' requirements. The capital region of Brussels, for its part, introduced an integration strategy in 2017. See the European Website on Integration available at: https://ec.europa.eu/migrant-integration/governance/belgium [last accessed 9 April 2020].

2 Other authors offer different translation of *inburgering* used in Dutch or Flemish. For van Oers (2008), it means integration, while Pulinx and Van Avermaet (2015) and Schinkel (2010) translate it as 'becoming a citizen' or 'becoming-citizen'. Foblets (2006) uses 'citizenise' and 'citizenisation'.

3 It is worth noting that in the US, 'naturalisation' was introduced in the late eighteenth century by the colonial government as a system *outside* of the feudal system of 'natural allegiance', or 'birth within the king's ligeance' (Karatani 2003: 17). Naturalisation in the US introduced a system based on will and consent, rather than based on birth.

4 In the US – the context that concerns Smith and Eisenach – the pledge of allegiance that is commonly recited in schools, in public meetings, congressional sessions, etc., refers to the US Republic as 'one nation under God'. In republics like France, a loyalty oath to the Republic's

values is secular. In a constitutional monarchy such as the UK, oaths of allegiance are sworn to the monarch, and are performed by members of parliament, certain public servants and by new citizens at the citizenship ceremony. All have the option between a religious or secular version. For more on the oath in the British context, see Chapter 5.

5 Indicatively Feldman 2005; Bauböck et al. 2006; Bloemraad 2006; Extra, Spotti and Van Avermaet 2009; Bauböck and Joppke 2010; Calder, Cole and Seglow 2010; Ersanilli and Koopmans 2010; Kostakopoulou 2010; Vink and de Groot 2010; de Leeuw and van Wichelen 2012; Koopmans, Michalowski and Waibel 2012; Kiwan 2013a; Goodman 2014; Aptekar 2015.

6 There is also considerable debate around whether integration measures 'thicken' citizenship by foregrounding a cultural content, or whether they produce a 'citizenship light' (Joppke 2010). Much of this discussion follows the classic distinction between civic and ethnic nationalism and extends it into citizenship. In contrast, the framework developed here seeks to challenge that distinction – citizenship (like nationalism) *always* contains both 'civic' and 'ethnic' elements – by examining how the distinction itself is naturalised in citizenisation measures, and what effects it has on social relations.

7 Honig 2001; Coutin 2003; Damsholt 2008; Mazouz 2008; Fassin and Mazouz 2009; Byrne 2014; Kipling 2015; Ossipow and Felder 2015.

8 Etzioni 2007; McNamara and Shohamy 2008; Wright 2008; Extra, Spotti and Van Avermaet 2009; Hogan-Brun, Mar-Molinero and Stevenson 2009; Han, Starkey and Green 2010; Slade and Möllering 2010; Joppke 2013; Kiwan 2013a; Byrne 2016.

9 On the former, Cosgrave 2011; Bassel, Montforte and Khan 2018; Khan 2018; Prabhat 2018. On the latter, Helbling 2008.

10 I am inspired here by Charis Thompson's (2005) examination of processes of socialisation, normalisation, naturalisation and subjectification in her ethnography of assisted reproductive technology clinics. For a discussion of my use of her work, see Fortier 2017b.

11 Recent discussions about the 'instrumental turn' (Joppke 2019) of citizenship focus on individual strategies for acquiring citizenship (Harpaz and Mateos 2019). The focus on the discussion in this chapter is rather on broad shifts in citizenship policies that instrumentalise it in the name of economic and cultural interests.

12 The active citizenship agenda was introduced in 1988 under the Thatcher government by the then Home Secretary Douglas Hurd and carried over under successive governments led by Conservatives and New Labour.

13 Though that history is different in Britain. See Chapter 2 for a detailed account of the specificity of citizenship in Britain.

14 Available at: www.sajidjavid.com/news/conservative-party-conference-speech-2018 [last accessed 10 April 2020].

15 Javid is alluding to the grooming gangs in Rochdale, where nine Asian men were found guilty of child sexual exploitation and abuse of vulnerable young girls. As of December 2018, three men were stripped of their British citizenship and were facing deportation to Pakistan after they served their sentence. A fourth man's appeal was yet to be adjudicated.

16 Williams's distinction between 'household' as a primarily economic unit and 'home' as a social one omits the history of household governance and its conception in scholarship – particularly International Relations scholarship. Patricia Owens (2015) pointedly argues that the very concept of 'household governance' conflates 'household' with 'the social', and in turn uncritically naturalises 'the social' as a site of domesticating power. For critical engagements with Owens' work, see the symposium on her book in *The Disorder of Things*, January 2016 https://thedisorderofthings.com/2016/01/04/economy-of-force/ [last accessed 31 May 2019], and the special section on Owen's book in *Security Dialogue* 47(3) July 2016.

17 E.g. the *Optionsregelung*, also known as §29 of the German Citizenship Act (see Winter 2014). For country by country information, see the country profiles available from the Global Governance Programme at the European Institute http://globalcit.eu/country-profiles/ [last accessed 3 September 2018].

18 Chakrabarty is referring to John Stuart Mill's argument about self-rule as the highest form of government, but one which some people were to arrive at later than others. Chakrabarty goes on to show how colonial settings such as India refused the very premise of this historicism, refused to 'learn the art of waiting'.

19 Other government agents who are invisible to applicants also play a role in the waiting room, such as UKVI agents who advise registrars over the phone, or UKVI case workers who will process applications and make the final decision.

20 Thank you to Leah Bassel for pushing me on this point.

Chapter 2

1 Parliamentarians, members of police forces, Scouts and girl guides, as well as 'new' citizens must declare an oath of allegiance to the Crown (see more in Chapter 3).

2 These early forms of denizenship are akin to contemporary forms of fast-track (partial) citizenship for wealthy investors that many countries offer. See Abrahamian 2015.

3 British-born subjects who voluntarily naturalised in another country became aliens and lost the rights and privileges that came with subject-hood to the sovereign, including land ownership. It is worth noting that the 'free subject' was male (and white as we see later); women married to British subjects who choose to naturalise abroad, and their children under 21, would also lose their subject status.

4 Available at: https://babel.hathitrust.org/cgi/pt?id=umn.31951002090 907t;view=1up;seq=1 [last accessed 6 March 2019].

5 For example, Chinese were refused naturalisation in New South Wales (1888), and Natal's Immigration Restrictions Act 1897 had the appear-ance of not distinguishing between migrants, but in practice enabled immigration officers to refuse entry to free Indians on the basis of property ownership and literacy in a European language (Anderson 2013: 34). Australia's 1901 'White Australia' policy emulated Natal's 1897 immigration act.

6 In effect, the principle of indelible allegiance persisted even after its legal abolishment in 1870 (Karatani 2003: 95).

7 They were called Colonial Conferences up to 1907 and were replaced after the Second World War by Commonwealth Prime Ministers' Conferences (1944 until 1969) and then Commonwealth Heads of Government Meetings since 1971.

8 Indeed, the government reasoned that including non-European countries in the Commonwealth, and extending to countries in Asia and Africa, Britain could '[demonstrate] to the world that our proclaimed policy for the Colonial peoples is not an empty boast, and that independent status in the Commonwealth is not, in practice, reserved for peoples of European descent' (Creech Jones, Secretary of State for the Colonies in 1947, cited in Karatani 2003: 112).

9 With the exception of the Irish who were in theory aliens but who were treated like citizens. See Hansen 2000: 100, n. 1; and Karatani 2003: 117–118.

10 The ship 'brought 1,027 official passengers, of which 802 stated their last country of residence was in the Caribbean' (Williams 2020: 24).

11 There is considerable debate about the Conservative government's reac-tion to Amin's ejection of Asians. Whether Edward Heath stood his ground and ensured that the UK and other nations welcomed the Asians fleeing Uganda or whether he bowed to Enoch Powell's anti-immigration politics, the fact remains that anti-immigration politics mobilised and crystallised racist conceptions of citizenship, which were foundational to subsequent developments in British citizenship law.

12 It is worth noting that globally, *jus soli* has been on the decline since the second half of the twentieth century by restricting citizenship to those born to legal citizens or permanent residents – e.g. Thailand 1972, Chile 1980, Australia 1986, South Africa 1995 Cambodia 1996, Hong Kong 1997, Ireland 2005, New Zealand 2006. India and Malta abolished *jus soli* altogether in 1987 and 1989 respectively (from Gramling 2016: 199).

13 It is worth reminding that the Act was adopted under Margaret Thatcher's prime ministership, who associated immigration, which was racially coded as black, with the deterioration of Britain and British neighbourhoods.

14 For a detailed explanation of my concept of citizenisation, see Chapter 1.

15 Labour MP David Blunkett oversaw the implementation of the citizenship curriculum in schools in England and Wales when he was Education Secretary, and he subsequently introduced new citizenisation measures aimed at immigrants in his role as Home Secretary. In both cases, he called on Sir Bernard Crick to chair the committees respectively tasked with conducting a policy review of citizenship education (the Crick Advisory Group on Education for Citizenship and the Teaching of Democracy in Schools), and with developing proposals for language and citizenship education for immigrants applying for naturalisation (the Life in the United Kingdom Advisory Group). See Kiwan 2013b.

16 The active citizenship agenda was introduced in 1988 under the Thatcher government by the then Home Secretary Douglas Hurd and carried over under successive governments led by Conservatives and New Labour.

17 This refers to civil disturbances that took place in Oldham, Burnley and Bradford (Northern England), between May and July 2001. Widely reported as 'race riots', the disturbances involved large numbers of people from different backgrounds – especially young men – and resulted in the destruction of property and attacks on individuals. The confrontations were largely between Asian youths and the police, where the former were angry at the failure of the latter to protect them from recent racist attacks and threats perpetrated by racist groups such as the British National Party (BNP).

18 This law enabled Home Secretary Sajid Javid to deprive Shamima Begum of her citizenship in early 2019 even though in effect it rendered her stateless, thereby contravening international law.

Chapter 3

1 Some readers might notice the nod to James C. Scott's *Seeing Like a State* (1998). However, as I go on to explain, registrars, UKVI case

workers and applicants do not check, read or indeed see like the state in as uniform a way as Scott's theory might suggest. Registrars, UKVI case workers, language teachers and applicants will variously work in the same general direction, alongside, or completely counter to, 'state reasoning'.

2 I use 'picture' rather than 'story' – the latter used by some authors describing the asylum seeking process (e.g. Gill 2014) – because the requirements that punctuate the citizenisation process are more perfunctory, fragmentary, amount to a constellation of documents that together give a picture – a bit like a collage.

3 Registrars are 'street-level bureaucrats' insofar as they engage in face-to-face encounters with citizens or residents and mediate between them and the state. But they do not have the level of discretion and power that Michael Lipsky (2010) attributes to them. While registrars must be knowledgeable of relevant legislation and make decisions within the limits awarded to statutory registration duties, their decision powers are not the same as the teachers, social workers or judges concerned in Lipsky's research. For example, registrars can help in the selection of documents submitted for a naturalisation application, but they have no authority on whether that application is accepted or rejected. This is unlike the decision-making authority that judges, social workers or teachers have over litigants, families or students for instance. Moreover, UKVI case workers acknowledged that the checking services facilitated their job to the extent that they would receive a package that is already checked and organised, saving them the trouble to do so. For these reasons, and when it comes to NCS and SCS in particular, I consider registrars to act more as intermediaries of the state.

4 This followed the model of the passport checking service offered by the Post Office.

5 Interview conducted in May 2019 with a staff from Libraries Connected, a national organisation established in June 2018 to support and promote public libraries in the country.

6 Thank you to Jonathan Darling for pointing out how 'making up' has particular meaning in the context of curating applicants' pictures.

7 For the purposes of this book, the most relevant legal categories are: Tiers 1 and 2 (so called 'economic migrants'), EU nationals, spousal visas and refugees. The first two are eligible for Indefinite Leave to Remain (ILR) providing that they have evidence of 'continuous residence', that is, of 'living and working in the UK for 5 years and spent no more than 180 days outside the UK in any 12 months'. Individuals from the EU, EEA or Switzerland can apply for 'permanent residence' status or 'settled status' after living in the UK for five years. For those on

spousal visas, their eligibility for ILR was extended from two years to five years in 2013, which is why the training session described in Scene 2 took place. As for asylum seekers, they become 'refugees' under the UK legal system when they are granted asylum, with leave to remain for five years at the end of which they must apply for ILR under the Settlement Protection route – SET (Protection). To acquire citizenship, the requirement is normally that the applicant has lived in the UK for 12 months after receiving ILR or equivalent.

8 This was prior to October 2013; see Scene 1.

9 What I wish to emphasise here is that beyond its legal definition, naturalisation is part of a wider cultural formation in which citizenship 'makes sense'.

10 See Chapter 4 on citizenship and regimes of hearing.

11 However, Charlotte also revealed that Katie was not recognised as Australian either. It is beyond the scope of this chapter to go into the details of the Australian citizenship laws but suffice to say that had Charlotte not been able to prove Katie's British citizenship, Katie could have been legally stateless.

12 'Since July 2012, UK citizens and settled residents applying to bring a non-EEA partner to the country must meet a minimum income requirement of £18,600 per year before tax. The threshold is higher for those who are also sponsoring children' (Vargas-Silva 2016: 2).

13 Thank you again to Jonathan Darling for making the connection with the broader algorithmic politics of border control and association rules identified by Amoore.

14 As explained in Chapter 2, it was not until 2006 that children born of unmarried 'settled' (or British) fathers, or indeed recognised as a man's or 'second female parent's' child under the Human Fertilisation and Embryology Acts 1990 and 2008 (Home Office 2019b: 5), could acquire British citizenship. Still, the condition of marriage still applies to children born between 1 January 1983 and 1 July 2006 of a foreign parent where only the father has settled status.

15 This was before the Brexit vote and before new settlement and pre-settlement statuses implemented for EU residents in the UK. She was legally a 'resident' by virtue of having resided in the county for more than five years.

16 The White Paper on nationality, immigration and asylum published in 2002 has a chapter dedicated to amendments in marriage and family migration laws. While the chapter is not specifically focused on 'arranged marriages', it is noteworthy that it opens with a reference to 'genuine arranged marriages' which, the documents states, were disadvantaged by the 'primary purpose' rule that prevented foreign spouses from entering

the country under false pretences. Abolishing this rule is framed as recognition of the desire of 'many ethnic groups' to arrange marriages between individuals of 'a similar cultural background'. The paragraph then concludes with what can be only be read as a reassuring note: 'As time goes on, we expect the number of arranged marriages between UK children and those living abroad to decline. Instead, parents will seek to choose a suitable partner for their children from among their own communities in this country' (Home Office 2002: para. 7.1 p. 99).

17 At the time, more flexible rules on spousal visas applied for EU residents with non-EU or EEA spouses seeking entry in the UK.

18 Thank you to Jonathan Darling drawing my attention to this other aspect of self-curation.

Chapter 4

1 The legal terminology for 'right' (of blood, of territory or, in Gramling's phrase, of languages), has two accepted Latin spellings: *ius* or *jus*. Gramling adheres to the first, while I use the second throughout this book, in line with much of the English language scholarship on citizenship.

2 For a similar line of questioning with regards to whiteness, see Ahmed 2007.

3 In an interview on BBC Radio Four's *Today* programme, 18 January 2016.

4 The riots were triggered by BNP activists taunting local residents with fascist and racist abuse.

5 For example, David Blunkett (2002), David Cameron in January 2016 (see Mason and Sherwood 2016).

6 Which Tove Skutnabb-Kangas coined as 'ideologies, structures, and practices which are used to legitimate, effectuate, regulate, and reproduce an unequal division of power and resources (both material and immaterial) between groups which are defined on the basis of language' (1988: 13; also Phillipson 1992: 47). I extend this to include forms of discrimination and inequalities based on language practices and uses.

7 As a reminder: *all* applicants for settlement are 'expected *both* to pass the Life in the UK test (LUK) *and* to have an English speaking and listening qualification at B1 CEFR or above' (Home Office, 2013a; emphasis added). Those exempt from showing an English speaking and listening qualification are those who obtained a degree taught in English and nationals from majority English speaking countries (white settler societies and countries in the West Indies) (Home Office, 2013a: Appendix).

8   It is beyond the scope of this chapter to address the history and status of Welsh and Scottish Gaelic in the UK. Suffice to say that historically, and through its relation to the empire, the status of Welsh, Scottish Gaelic as well as other 'national' languages such as Irish or Cornish have been minoritised as minor to English as the language of the United Kingdom.

9   'I think learning the language … the freedom it gives if you can communicate and … it can give you equality. The control men can sometime have over women because they can't go to the doctors on their own, they can't shop on their own and it's a means of control which means they can't complain to anybody, they can't talk to anybody, they're isolated so I think from that point of view … I don't say this in a patronising way. Some of them are excellent at this language cos they are doctors and academics and lots of different people there who have been in this country a long time. But I say this mainly for the women whose first language is not English, especially women from Asian countries so I do say that they should be a bit more … it is important for women to get that message from somebody else to … take the initiative to learn the language.'

10 The BSA survey does not systematically repeat the same questions from year to year, which is why more recent data on this particular question is not available. For the 2014 survey, see Taylor (2014).

11 The latest comprehensive government statistics available that offer a breakdown of success rate by country of origin cover the years 2009–2014 and are available at: www.gov.uk/government/publications/knowledge-of-language-and-life-in-the-uk-test-results-2009-to-2014 [last accessed 30 September 2020].

12 *Today* programme, BBC Radio 4, 18 January 2016.

13 Jeremy shared the speech with me, in which he spoke of his loyalty to the UK and to the Crown: 'When I became a citizen, I gave my complete loyalty to the UK. And I have never regretted that. Because by respecting the rights and freedoms of this country, and upholding its democratic values, I have not only fulfilled my duties and obligations as a British citizen, but as a truly loyal subject of Her Majesty.'

14 Former leader of the right-wing UKIP party, and leader of the Brexit party at the time of writing.

15 'Do I think parts of Britain are a foreign land? I got the train the other night, it was rush hour, from Charing Cross. It was a stopper going out and we stopped at London Bridge, New Cross, Hither Green, it was not til we got past Grove Park that I could hear English being audibly spoken in the carriage. Does that make me feel slightly awkward? Yes it does' (Farage cited in Hope 2014).

16 Essed defines everyday racism as connecting structural racism with routine situations in everyday life, whereby 'the consciously or unconsciously felt security of belonging to the group in power, plus the expectation that other groups members will give (passive) consent, empowers individual members of the dominant group in their acts or beliefs against the dominated group' (1991: 40).

17 As a Québécoise living in Britain, I've been haunted in the course of my research into linguistic imperialism by Michèle Lalonde's 1968 poem written in French but bearing the English title 'Speak White', which became a rallying cry of the Québécois nationalist movement in the late 1960s and well into the 1970s. It is beyond the scope of this chapter to elaborate on my critical relationship to this poem, which was written as postcolonial declaration against British and French imperialisms, while it was later weaponised against minorities in neocolonial politics of French nationalist Québec. But I cannot use that phrase without acknowledging the legacy of these post/neo-imperial politics in my linguistic positioning within the Anglophone and Francophone worlds (see Scene 3).

Scene 4

1 The scene depicted here is a composite that draws on interviews and observations.

2 New citizens are given the option of a religious or secular oath of allegiance when booking their ceremony. More on this in Chapter 5.

Chapter 5

1 In the legal process, the 'good character' criterion is where one must declare any breach of the law. Criminal offences in British nationality law span unpaid road traffic fines through to genocide, crimes against humanity, war crimes and terrorism. Therefore, a person who failed to pay several parking tickets and a genocidal dictator may all be refused citizenship on the grounds of failing the good character criterion (Anderson 2013: 107). What is more, the good character requirement may be couched primarily in legal terms, but individuals have been refused settlement or citizenship due to mistakes they made in their tax returns that they legally corrected (see Hill 2018; Mohdin and Wong 2018; and Right to Remain 2018). This suggests that the hostile environment created by Theresa May during her term as Home

Secretary (2010–2016) has enabled a looser and broader interpretation of 'good character' – which is already notoriously vague in nationality law – and forces migrants to be more 'becoming' than non-migrant sections of the population. What is more, the broader definition of 'good character' comes with the similar broadening of 'bad character', which has become a principle reason for citizenship refusals in recent years and which operates as a racialised mechanism of amorphous restrictions and constraints upon the lives and opportunities of non-white denizens. (Kapoor and Narkowicz 2019a).

2 It is beyond the scope of this chapter to elaborate on the problematic distinction in much migration scholarship between 'free' and 'forced' migration. Rhadika Mongia (2018: 9) pointedly argues that this separation 'produces a reified understanding of "freedom" as equivalent to consent embodied in a contract – the very understanding of "freedom" propagated by the state conjoined with discourses of political economy. This assumption has largely restricted analysis of state regulation firmly within the sphere of "free" migration. As a result, despite the involvement of states in managing, facilitating, and, eventually, rendering illegal "unfree" and "semi-free" movements, such moments of state regulation are excised from histories and theories of state regulation of migration that have come to focus only on migrations termed "free."'

3 This is the only ceremony that is not anonymised because it was open to a broader public and reported in local papers. Mark Rimmer, then Head Registrar at Brent Council, kindly invited me when I contacted him about it.

4 Blunkett was Home Secretary and champion of the new citizenship acquisition process in 2001 and attended the first ceremony, which also took place in Brent, in 2004.

5 But as Charlotte's story reminds us (Chapter 3), genealogical links are fragile and can be erased by the state if a child is adopted by foreign parents.

6 It is worth adding that although not necessarily transnational, the experience of several non-migrant families today include multi-locality and some measure of mobility – children travelling between homes – that also challenge conventional understandings of the stable, nuclear family residing in the same household or even in the same geographical location.

7 From United Nations 'Ending Poverty', available at: www.un.org/en/sections/issues-depth/poverty/ [last accessed 12 November 2019].

8 The good life, then, extends beyond economic pursuits. See Katie Wright (2012), who extends literature on migration and development by refocusing the analysis away from financial and social remittances

to how wider notions of 'living well' are constructed globally and how they travel.

9 The Goldsmith Review was commissioned to 'enhance the meaning and significance of citizenship as the common bond that binds us together' (Goldsmith 2008: 3). This was by no means the first review of citizenship ordered by a government: in 1990 for example, the Conservative government set up the Commission on Citizenship which laid out plans to develop 'active citizenship' in its report *Encouraging Citizenship* (Commission on Citizenship 1990). However, in contrast to its predecessors, the Goldsmith Review put much emphasis on naturalisation and encouraging long-standing foreign residents with permanent resident status to acquire British citizenship. In doing so, the Goldsmith Review brought 'migrants' 'centre stage in debates about what it means to be British' (Anderson 2013: 102). Indeed, in addition to Rimmer's report, Goldsmith commissioned two others 'to stimulate discussion': 'Mentoring for New Migrants' and 'Becoming a British Citizen' (Goldsmith 2008: 4).

10 It bears reminding that the citizenisation process which is the focus of this book already establishes those who are deemed eligible for 'the good life' and separates them from others who are not.

11 As of November 2019, the Conservative government was undertaking a consultation about current requirements in view of revising them again (Easton 2019).

12 A small minority of those I met, like Sala, enjoyed studying the history section of the Conservative government version of the citizenship test – 'of course, I'm a historian!', she said with laughter.

13 This group had the remit to develop proposals for language and citizenship courses and tests for immigrants applying for British citizenship. It was chaired by Bernard Crick, who had previously chaired the Advisory Group on Citizenship (1998) that led to the citizenship curriculum in schools in England and Wales. See Chapter 2.

14 Sala may be referring to Passportindex.org, where in 2019 the UK's 'power rank' was 5th and Egypt's was 76th. The power rank is measured by a passport's mobility score, that is, the extent to which its holder requires visas or not to visit other countries.

15 Moreover, citizenship is instrumentalised in migration policies determined by market interests, where fast-tracked passports are offered to rich investor migrants who are not accused of instrumentalism.

References

Abrahamian, Atossa Araxia (2015) *Cosmopolites: The Coming of the Global Citizen*, New York: Columbia Global Reports.

Abrams, Philip (1977 [1988]) 'Notes on the difficulty of studying the state', *Journal of Historical Sociology* 1(1): 58–89.

Advisory Group on Citizenship (1998) *Education for Citizenship and the Teaching of Democracy in Schools*, London: Qualifications and Curriculum Authority.

Ahmad, Ali Nobil (2008) 'Dead men working: Time and space in London's (illegal) migrant economy', *Work, Employment and Society* 22(2): 301–318.

Ahmed, Sara (2007) 'A phenomenology of whiteness', *Feminist Theory* 8(2): 149–168.

Ahmed, Sara (2010) *The Promise of Happiness*, Durham, NC: Duke University Press.

Ahmed, Sara (2012) *On Being Included: Racism and Diversity in Institutional Life*, Durham, NC: Duke University Press.

Alim, H. Samy (2016) 'Introducing raciolinguistics: Racing language and languaging race in hyperracial times'. In: H. S. Alim, J. R. Rickford and A. F. Ball (eds) *Raciolinguistics: How Language Shapes Our Ideas About Race*, Oxford: Oxford University Press, pp. 1–30.

Alim, H. Samy, John. R. Rickford and Arnetha F. Ball (eds) (2016) *Raciolinguistics: How Language Shapes Our Ideas About Race*, Oxford: Oxford University Press.

Allsopp, Jennifer, Elaine Chase and Mary Mitchell (2015) 'The tactics of time and status: Young people's experiences of building futures while subject to immigration control in Britain', *Journal of Refugee Studies* 28(2): 163–182.

Amoore, Louise (2006) 'Biometric borders: Governing mobilities in the war on terror', *Political Geography* 25: 336–351.

Amoore, Louise (2009) 'Algorithmic war: Everyday geographies of the war on terror', *Antipode: A Radical Journal of Geography* 41: 49–69.

Amoore, Louise and Marieke de Goede (2008) 'Transactions after 9/11: The banal face of the preemptive strike', *Transactions of the Institute of British Geographers* 33: 173–185.

Amunátegui Perelló, Carlos (2018) 'Race and nation: On *ius sanguinis* and the origins of a racist national perspective', *Fundamina* 24(2): 1–20.

Anderson, Benedict (1991) *Imagined Communities*, London: Verso.

Anderson, Bridget (2013) *Us and Them? The Dangerous Politics of Immigration Control*, Oxford: Oxford University Press.

Anderson, Bridget (2019) 'New directions in migration studies: Towards methodological de-nationalism', *Comparative Migration Studies* 7(article 36): 1–13.

Anderson, Bridget (2020) 'And about time too …: Migration, documentation and temporalities'. In: S. Horton and J. Heyman (eds) *Paper Trails: Migrants, Documents and Legal Insecurity in the Global North*, Durham, NC: Duke University Press, pp. 53–72.

Andersson, Ruben (2014a) *Illegality, Inc. Clandestine Migration and the Business of Bordering Europe*, Oakland, CA: University of California Press.

Andersson, Ruben (2014b) 'Time and the migrant other: European border controls and the temporal economics of illegality', *American Anthropologist* 116(4): 795–809.

Anthias, Floya (2016) 'Interconnecting boundaries of identity and belonging and hierarchy-making within transnational mobility studies: Framing inequalities', *Current Sociology Monograph* 64(2): 172–190.

Aptekar, Sofya (2015) *The Road to Citizenship: What Naturalization Means for Immigrants in the United States*, New Brunswick, NJ: Rutgers University Press.

Aru, Debora and Rhian Lubin (2017) '1 in 3 people fail the British Citizenship test – but would you pass? Try our quiz', *The Mirror*, 18 June. Available at: www.mirror.co.uk/news/uk-news/1–3-people-fail-british-10643413 [last accessed 15 August 2019].

Auvachez, Élise (2009) 'Supranational citizenship building and the United Nations: Is the UN engaged in a "citizenisation" process?', *Global Governance* 15(1): 43–66.

Baas, Michiel and Brenda S. A. Yeoh (eds) (2019) 'Special issue: Migration studies and critical temporalities', *Current Sociology Monograph* 67(2).

Back, Les, Shamser Sinha and with Charlene Bryan (2012) 'New hierarchies of belonging', *European Journal of Cultural Studies* 15(2): 139–154.

Balibar, Etienne (1991) 'The nation form: History and ideology'. In: E. Balibar and I. Wallerstein, *Race, Nation, Class: Ambiguous Identities*, London: Verso, pp. 86–105.

Balta, Evren and Özlen Altan-Olcay (2016) 'Strategic citizens of America: Transnational inequalities and transformation of citizenship', *Citizenship Studies* 39(6): 939–957.

Banerjee, Sukanya (2010) *Becoming Imperial Citizens: Indians in the Late-Victorian Empire*, Durham, NC: Duke University Press.

Barad, Karen (2003) 'Posthumanist performativity: Toward an understanding of how matter comes to matter', *Signs: Journal of Women in Culture and Society* 28(31): 801–831.

Barker, Martin (1981) *The New Racism. Conservatives and the Ideology of the Tribe*, London: Junction Books.

Bassel, Leah, Pierre Monforte and Kamran Khan (2018) 'Making political citizens: Migrants narratives of naturalization in the United Kingdom', *Citizenship Studies* 22(3): 225–242.

Bauböck, Rainer and Christian Joppke (eds) (2010) *How Liberal Are Citizenship Tests?*, Florence: Robert Schuman Centre for Advanced Studies, EUI.

Bauböck, Rainer, Eva Ersbøll, Kees Groenendijk and Harald Waldrauch (eds) (2006) *Acquisition and Loss of Nationality: Policies and Trends in 15 European States*, 2 Vols, Amsterdam: Amsterdam University Press.

BBC News (2010) 'British citizenship test: One in three immigrants fails', 27 May. Available at: http://news.bbc.co.uk/1/hi/8707152.stm [last accessed 25 September 2019].

BBC News (2013) 'UK citizenship test "to cover Britain's greats"', *BBC News*, 28 January. Available at: www.bbc.co.uk/news/uk-21221773 [last accessed 29 March 2019].

Bell, David and Jon Binnie (2000) *The Sexual Citizen: Queer Politics and Beyond*, Cambridge: Polity.

Bennett, Jane (2010) *Vibrant Matter: A Political Ecology of Things*, Durham, NC: Duke University Press.

Berezin, Mabel (2002) 'Secure states: Towards a political sociology of emotions'. In: J. Barbalet (ed.) *Emotions and Sociology*, Oxford: Blackwell, pp. 33–52.

Berlant, Lauren (1997) *The Queen of America Goes to Washington City*, Durham, NC and London: Duke University Press.

Berlant, Lauren (2011) *Cruel Optimism*, Durham NC: Duke University Press.

Bhabha, Homi (1994) *The Location of Culture*, London: Routledge.

Bhambra, Gurminder (2015) 'Citizens and others: The constitution of citizenship through exclusion', *Alternatives: Global, Local, Political* 40(2): 102–114.

Bhatt, Ibrar (2014) 'Curation as digital literacy practice', *Ibrar's Space: Musings on Language, Literacies, Higher Education, and Technologies*, 21 May. Available at: https://ibrarspace.net/2014/05/21/curation-as-a-digital-literacy-practice/ [last accessed 16 April 2020].

Bhattacharyya, Gargi (2015) *Crisis, Austerity and Everyday Life: Living in a Time of Diminishing Expectations*, Basingstoke: Palgrave Macmillan.

Biehl, João and Peter Locke (eds) (2017a) *Unfinished: The Anthropology of Becoming*, Durham, NC: Duke University Press.

Biehl, João and Peter Locke (2017b) 'Introduction: Ethnographic sensorium'. In: J. Biehl and P. Locke (eds) *Unfinished: The Anthropology of Becoming*, Durham, NC: Duke University Press, pp. 1–38.

Bigo, Didier (2002) 'Security and immigration: Toward a critique of the governmentality of unease', *Alternatives* 27(1 supplement): 63–92.

Bissell, David (2007) 'Animating suspension: Waiting for mobilities', *Mobilities* 2(2): 277–298.

Bissell, David and Gillian Fuller (2009) 'The revenge of the still', *M/C Journal: A Journal of Media and Culture* 12(1). Available at: http://journal.media-culture.org.au/index.php/mcjournal/article/view/136 [Last accessed 14 April 2020].

Blackledge, Adrian (2005) *Discourse and Power in a Multilingual World*, Amsterdam: John Benjamins.

Blinder, Scott (2017) *Briefing, Naturalisation as a British Citizen: Concepts and Trends*, Oxford: Migration Observatory, University of Oxford.

Blinder, Scott (2018) *Briefing, Naturalisation as a British Citizen: Concepts and Trends*, Oxford: Migration Observatory, University of Oxford.

Bloemraad, Irene (2006) *Becoming Citizen: Incorporating Immigrants and Refugees in the United States and Canada*, Berkeley, CA: University of California Press.

Bloom, Tendayi (2015) 'The business of noncitizenship', *Citizenship Studies* 19(8): 892–906.

Blunkett, David (2002) 'Integration with diversity: Globalisation and the renewal of democracy and civil society'. In: P Griffith and M. Leonard (eds) *Reclaiming Britishness: Living Together After 11 September and the Rise of the Right*, London: Foreign Policy Centre, pp. 65–77.

Bosniak, Linda (2006) *The Citizen and the Alien: Dilemmas of Contemporary Membership*, Princeton, NJ and Oxford: Princeton University Press.

Bourdieu, Pierre and Luc Boltanski (1975) 'Le fétichisme de la langue', *Actes de la recherche en sciences sociales* 1(4): 2–32.

Brace, Laura (2004) *The Politics of Property: Labour, Freedom and Belonging*, Edinburgh: Edinburgh University Press.

Brah, Avtar (1996) *Cartographies of Diaspora*, London: Routledge.

Brooks, Libby (2019) 'Johnson pledges to make all immigrants learn English', *The Guardian*, 10 July. Available at: www.theguardian.com/politics/2019/jul/05/johnson-pledges-to-make-all-immigrants-learn-english?CMP=Share_iOSApp_Other [last accessed 21 September 2019].

Brooks, Thom (2016) *Becoming British: UK Citizenship Examined*, London: Biteback Publishing.

Brown, Wendy (2015) *Undoing the Demos: Neoliberalism's Stealth Revolution*, New York: Zone Books.

Brutt-Griffler, Janina (2002) *World English: A Study of Its Development*, Clevedon: Multilingual Matters Press.

Bryceson, Deborah and Ulla Vuorela (eds) (2002) *The Transnational Family: New European Frontiers and Global Networks*, Oxford: Berg.

Butler, Judith (1997) *The Psychic Life of Power*, Stanford, CA: Stanford University Press.

Butler, Judith (2005) *Giving and Account of Oneself*, New York: Fordham University Press.

Byrne, Bridget (2012) 'A local welcome? Narrations of nation and citizenship in UK citizenship ceremonies', *Citizenship Studies* 16(3/4): 531–544.

Byrne, Bridget (2014) *Making Citizens: Public Rituals and Personal Journeys to Citizenship*, Basingstoke: Palgrave Macmillan.

Byrne, Bridget (2016) 'Testing times: The place of the citizenship test in the UK immigration regime and new citizens' responses to it', *Sociology* 1–16. Online First DOI: 10.1177/0038038515622908.

Byrne, B. (2017) 'British values: An oath without meaning?', *Manchester Policy Blogs*, http://blog.policy.manchester.ac.uk/ethnicity/2017/01/british-values-an-oath-without-meaning/ [last accessed 12 October 2020].

Calder, Gideon, Phillip Cole and Jonathan Seglow (eds) (2010) *Citizenship Acquisition and National Belonging*, Basingstoke: Palgrave Macmillan.

Cameron, David (2011a) 'PM's speech at Munich Security Conference', 5 February. Available at: www.gov.uk/government/speeches/pms-speech-at-munich-security-conference [last accessed 10 April 2020].

Cameron, David (2011b) 'David Cameron on immigration: full text of the speech', *The Guardian*, 14 April. Available at: www.theguardian.com/politics/2011/apr/14/david-cameron-immigration-speech-full-text [last accessed 13 April 2020].

Cameron, David (2011c) 'Prime Minister's Speech on Immigration [given at the Institute of Government]', 10 October. Available at: www.gov.uk/government/speeches/prime-ministers-speech-on-immigration [last accessed 13 April 2020].

Cameron, Deborah (2013) 'The one, the many and the other: Representing multi-and mono-lingualism in post-9/11verbal hygiene', *Critical Multilingualism Studies* 1(2): 59–77.

Canaday, Margot (2009) *The Straight State: Sexuality and Citizenship in Twentieth Century America*, Princeton, NJ: Princeton University Press.

Caplan, Jane and John Torpey (eds) (2001) *Documenting Individual Identity: The Development of State Practices in the Modern World*, Princeton, NJ and Oxford: Princeton University Press.

Casey, Louise (2016) *The Casey Review. A Review into Opportunity and Integration*, London: Department for Communities and Local Government.

Chakrabarty, Dipesh (2007) *Provincializing Europe: Postcolonial Thought and Historical Difference* (New Edition), Princeton, NJ: Princeton University Press.

Chalfin, Brenda (2008) 'Sovereigns and citizens in close encounter: Airport anthropology and customs regimes in neoliberal Ghana', *American Ethnologist* 35(4): 519–538.

Charalambous, Constadina, Panayiota Charalambous, Kamran Khan and Ben Rampton (2015) 'WP177: Sociolinguistics & security', *Working Papers in Urban Language and Literacies*, London: Kings College.

Chow, Rey (2014) *Not Like a Native Speaker: On Languaging as a Postcolonial Experience*, New York: Columbia University Press.

Clarke, John, Dave Bainton, Noemi Lendvai and Paul Stubbs (2015) *Making Policy Move: Towards a Politics of Translation and Assemblage*, Bristol: Policy Press.

Clarke, John, Kathleen Coll, Evelina Dagnino and Cahterine Nevey (2014) *Disputing Citizenship*, Bristol: Policy Press.

Coetzee-Van Rooy, Susan (2016) 'Multilingualism and social cohesion: Insights from South African students (1998, 2010, 2015)', *International Journal of the Sociology of Language* 242: 239–265.

Commission on Citizenship (1990) *Encouraging Citizenship: Report of the Commission on Citizenship*, London: HMSO.

Conlon, Deirdre (2011) 'Waiting: Feminist perspectives on the spacings/timings of migrants (im)mobility', *Gender, Place and Culture: A Journal of Feminist Geography* 18(3): 353–360.

Cooke, Melanie (2009) 'Barrier or entitlement? The language and citizenship agenda in the United Kingdom', *Language Assessment Quarterly* 6(1): 71–77.

Cooper, Davina (2015) 'Bringing the state up conceptually: Forging a body politics through anti-gay Christian refusal', *Feminist Theory* 6(1): 87–107.

Cosgrave, Catherine (2011) *Living in Limbo: Migrants' Experiences of Applying for Naturalisation in Ireland*, Dublin: Immigrant Council of Ireland.

Council of Europe (2001) *Common European Framework of Reference for Languages: Learning, Teaching, Assessment*, Strasbourg: Language Policy Unit.

Coutin, Susan Bibler (2003) 'Cultural logics of belonging and movement: transnationalism, naturalization and U.S. immigration politics', *American Ethnologist* 39(4): 508–526.

Crerar, Pippa, Anne Perkins, Amelia Gentleman (2018) 'Windrush generation will get UK citizenship, says Amber Rudd', *The Guardian*, 23 April. Available at: www.theguardian.com/uk-news/2018/apr/23/windrush-generation-will-get-uk-citizenship-says-amber-rudd [last accessed 8 April 2020].

Cresswell, Tim (2010) 'Towards a politics of mobility', *Environment and Planning D: Society and Space* 28(1): 17–31.

Crowley, Tony ([1989] 2003) *Standard English and the Politics of Language* (2nd edn), Houndmills: Palgrave-Macmillan.

Cwerner, Saolo B. (2001) 'The times of migration', *Journal of Ethnic and Migration Studies* 27(1): 7–36.

Damsholt, Tine (2008) 'Making citizens: on the genealogy of citizenship ceremonies'. In: P. Mouritsen and K. E. Jørgensen (eds) *Constituting Communities: Political Solutions to Cultural Conflict*, Basingstoke: Palgrave Macmillan, pp. 53–72.

D'Aoust, Anne-Marie (2013) 'In the name of love: Marriage migration, governmentality, and technologies of love', *International Political Sociology* 7(3): 258–274.

D'Aoust, Anne-Marie (2018) 'A moral economy of suspicion: Love and marriage migration management practices in the United Kingdom', *Environment and Planning D: Society and Space* 36(1): 40–59.

Darling, Jonathan (2014) 'Another letter from the Home Office: Reading the material politics of asylum', *Environment and Planning D: Society and Space* 32(3): 484–500.

Dathan, Matt (2015) 'David Cameron champions Magna Carta but in 2012 he didn't know what it meant when he appeared on David Letterman's Late Show', *The Independent*, 15 June. Available at: www.independent.co.uk/news/uk/politics/david-cameron-champions-magna-carta-but-in-2012-he-didnt-know-what-it-meant-when-he-appeared-on-10320601.html [last accessed 22 November 2019].

Dauvergne, Catherine (2007) 'Citizenship with a vengeance', *Theoretical Inquiries in Law* 8(2): 484–508.

Davies, William (2014) *The Limits of Neoliberalism: Authority, Sovereignty, and the Logic of Competition*, London: Sage.

Dearden, Lizzie (2016) 'UK student stabbed in neck for speaking Polish describes brutal post-Brexit assault in Telford', *The Independent*, 20 September. Available at: www.independent.co.uk/news/uk/crime/uk-student-stabbed-in-neck-for-speaking-polish-brutal-post-brexit-assault-telford-donnington-park-a7319181.html [last accessed 15 June 2020].

de Genova, Nicholas (2010) 'The queer politics of migration: Reflections on "illegality" and incorrigibility', *Studies in Social Justice* 4(2): 101–126.

de Leeuw, Marc and Sonja van Wichelen (2012) 'Civilizing migrants: Integration, culture and citizenship', *European Journal of Cultural Studies* 15(2): 195–210.

Department for Communities and Local Government (2012) *Creating the Conditions for Integration*, London: Department for Communities and Local Government.

Derrida, Jacques (1998) *Monolingualism of the Other OR The Prosthesis of Origin*, Stanford, CA: Stanford University Press.

Desmond, Matthew (2014) 'Relational ethnography', *Theory & Society* 43(5): 547–579.

de Wilde, Mandy and Jan Willem Duyvendak (2016) 'Engineering community spirit: The pre-figurative politics of affective citizenship in Dutch local governance', *Citizenship Studies* 20(8): 973–993.

Dobson, Rachael (2020) 'Local government and practice ontologies: Agency, resistance and sector speaks in homelessness services', *Local Government Studies*, DOI: 10.1080/03003930.2020.1729748: 1–22.

Dummett, Ann (1994) 'The acquisition of British citizenship: From imperial traditions to national definitions'. In: R. Bauböck (ed.) *From Aliens to Citizens: Redefining the Status of Immigrants in Europe*, Aldershot: Avebury, pp. 75–84.

Dummett, Ann and Andrew Nicol (1990) *Subjects, Citizens, Aliens and Others: Nationality and Immigration Law*, London: Weidenfeld and Nicolson.

Džankić, Jelena (2019) *The Global Market for Investor Citizenship*, Basingstoke: Palgrave Macmillan.

Easton, Mark (2019) 'Citizenship test: How hard should it be to become British?', *BBC News*, 30 August. Available at: www.bbc.co.uk/news/uk-49485612 [last accessed 22 November 2019].

Eisenach, Eldon (1999) 'Liberal citizenship and American national identity', *Studies in American Political Development* 13(1): 198–215.

El-Enany, Nadine (2020) *(B)ordering Britain: Law, Race and Empire*, Manchester: Manchester University Press.

Elliott, Alice (2016) 'Paused subjects: Waiting for migration in North Africa', *Time and Society* 25(1): 102–116.

Ellis, Elizabeth (2006) 'Monolingualism: The unmarked case', *Estudios de Sociolingüística* 7(2): 173–196.

El-Tayeb, Fatima (2011) *European Others: Queering Ethnicity in Postnational Europe*, Minneapolis: University of Minnesota Press.

Engel, Stephen M. (2016) *Fragmented Citizens: The Changing Landscape of Gay and Lesbian Lives*, New York: New York University Press.

Ersanilli, Evelyn and Ruud Koopmans (2010) 'Rewarding integration? Citizenship regulations and the socio-cultural integration of immigrants in the Netherlands, France and Germany', *Journal of Ethnic and Migration Studies* 36(5): 773–791.

Essed, Philomena (1991) *Understanding Everyday Racism*, London: Sage.

Etzioni, Amitai (2007) 'Citizenship tests: A comparative, communitarian perspective', *Political Quarterly* 78(3): 353–363.

Evans, David (1993) *Sexual Citizenship: The Material Construction of Sexuality*, London: Routledge.

Extra, Guus, Massimiliano Spotti and Piet Van Avermaet (eds) (2009) *Language Testing, Migration and Citizenship: Cross-National Perspectives on Integration Regimes*, London: Continuum.

Faist, Thomas (2001) 'Social citizenship in the European Union: nested membership', *Journal of Common Market Studies* 39(1): 39–60.

Fanon, Frantz ([1952] 2008) *Black Skin White Masks*, London: Pluto

Fassin, Didier (2013) 'The precarious truth of asylum', *Public Culture* 69(1): 39–63.

Fassin, Didier and Sarah Mazouz (2009) 'Qu'est-ce que devenir français? La naturalisation comme rite d'institution républicain', *Revue française de sociologie* 5(50): 37–64.

Feldman, Gregory (2005) 'Essential crises: A performative approach to migrants, minorities, and the European nation-state', *Anthropological Quarterly* 78(1): 213–246.

Feldman, Gregory (2011) 'Illuminating the apparatus: Steps towards a nonlocal ethnography of global governance'. In: C. Shore, S. Wright and D. Però (eds) *Policy Worlds. Anthropology and the Analysis of Contemporary Power*, Oxford: Berghahn Books, pp. 32–49.

Fernandez-Reino, Mariña, and Madeleine Sumption (2020) *Briefing: Citizenship and naturalisation for migrants in the UK*, Oxford: Migration Observatory, University of Oxford.

Fitzgerald, David Scott (2017) 'The history of racialized citizenship', In: A. Shachar, R. Bauböck, I. Bloemraad and. M. Vink (eds) *The Oxford Handbook of Citizenship*, Oxford: Oxford University Press, pp. 129–152.

Foblets, Marie-Claire (2006) 'Legal aspects of the multicultural society: Tensions and challenges for policy making'. In: L. Leen d'Haenens, M.

Hooghe, D. Vanheule and H. Gezduci (eds) *New Citizens, New Policies? Developments in Diversity Policy in Canada and Flanders*, Gent: Academia Press, pp. 89–104.

Fortier, Anne-Marie (2003) 'Global migranthood, whiteness and the anxieties of (in)visibility'. In: C. Harzig and D. Juteau (eds) *The Social Construction of Diversity: Recasting the Master Narrative of Industrial Nations*, Oxford and New York: Berghahn Books, pp. 227–246.

Fortier, Anne-Marie (2008) *Multicultural Horizons: Diversity and the Limits of the Civil Nation*, London: Routledge.

Fortier, Anne-Marie (2010) 'Proximity by design? Affective citizenship and the management of unease', *Citizenship Studies* 14(1): 17–30.

Fortier, Anne-Marie (2012) 'The migration imaginary and the politics of personhood'. In: M. Messer, R. Shroeder, and R. Wodak (eds) *Migrations: Interdisciplinary Perspectives*, Vienna: Springer Science + Business Media, pp. 31–41.

Fortier, Anne-Marie (2013) 'What's the big deal? Naturalisation and the politics of desire', *Citizenship Studies* 17 (6–7): 697–711.

Fortier, Anne-Marie (2017a) 'The psychic life of policy: Desire, anxiety and "citizenisation" in Britain', *Critical Social Policy* 37(1): 3–21.

Fortier, Anne-Marie (2017b) 'The social life of citizenisation and naturalisation: Outlining an analytical framework', *COLLeGIUM: Studies Across Disciplines in the Humanities and Social Sciences* 23: 12–30.

Fortier, Anne-Marie (2018) 'On (not) speaking English: colonial legacies in language requirements for British citizenship', *Sociology* 52(6): 1254 –1269.

Foucault, Michel (1979) *Discipline and Punish: The Birth of the Prison*, New York: Vintage.

Foucault, Michel (2008) *The Birth of Biopolitics: Lectures at the Collège de France, 1978—1979* (trans. Graham Burchell), Basingstoke: Palgrave Macmillan.

Fuglerud, Oivind (2004) 'Constructing exclusion: The micro-sociology of an immigration department', *Social Anthropology* 12(1): 25–40.

Gentleman, Amelia (2019a) *The Windrush Betrayal: Exposing the Hostile Environment*, London: Guardian Faber.

Gentleman, Amelia (2019b) '"I've been here 50 years": The EU citizens struggling for the right to stay in Britain', *The Guardian*, 25 October. Available at: www.theguardian.com/politics/2019/oct/08/ive-been-here-50-years-the-eu-citizens-struggling-for-the-right-to-stay-in-britain [last accessed 8 November 2019].

Gerken, Christina (2013) *Model Immigrants and Undesirable Aliens: The Cost of Immigration Reform in the 1990s*, Minneapolis, MN: University of Minnesota Press.

Giblin, Connor (2018) 'What does the Windrush scandal reveal about British citizenship and its relation to empire?', unpublished essay, Sociology Department, Lancaster University.

Gill, Nick (2009) 'Longing for stillness: The forced movement of asylum seekers', *M/C Journal: A Journal of Media and Culture* 12(1). Available at:

http://journal.media-culture.org.au/index.php/mcjournal/article/view/123 [last accessed 13 April 2020].

Gill, Nick (2014) 'Forms that form'. In: N. Thrift, A. Tickell, S. Woolgar and W. Rupp (eds) *Globalization in Practice*, Oxford: Oxford University Press, pp. 231–235.

Gillespie, Marie and Ben O'Loughlin (2009) 'Precarious citizenship: Multiculturalism, media and social insecurity', In: P. Noxolo and J. Huysmans (eds) *Community, Citizenship and the War on Terror: Security and Insecurity*, Basingstoke: Palgrave Macmillan, pp. 89–112.

Gilroy, Paul (1993) *The Black Atlantic: Modernity and Double Consciousness*, London: Verso.

Glass, Andrew (2018) 'Bush creates Homeland Security Department, Nov. 26, 2002', *Politico*, 26 November. Available at: www.politico.com/story/2018/11/26/this-day-in-politics-november-26–1012269 [last accessed 10 April 2020].

Glissant, Édouard (1989) *Caribbean Discourse*, Charlottesville, VA: University of Virginia Press.

Goldberg, David Theo (2002) *The Racial State*, Oxford: Blackwell.

Goldsmith, Peter (Lord) (2008) *Citizenship: Our Common Bond*, London: Department of Justice.

Goodfellow, Maya (2019) *Hostile Environment: How Immigrants Became Scapegoats*, London: Verso.

Goodman, Sara Wallace (2014) *Immigration and Membership Politics in Western Europe*, Cambridge: Cambridge University Press.

Goulbourne, Harry, Tracey Reynolds, John Solomos and Elisabetta Zontini (2010) *Transnational Families: Ethnicities, Identities, and Social Capital*, Abingdon and New York: Routledge.

Gramling, David (2016) *The Invention of Monolingualism*, London: Bloomsbury.

Gray, Herman and Macarena Gómez-Barris (eds) (2010) *Toward a Sociology of the Trace*, Minneapolis, MN: Minnesota University Press.

Grewal, Inderpal (1996) *Home and Harem: Nation, Gender, Empire and the Cultures of Travel*, Durham, NC: Duke University Press.

Griffiths, Melanie (2014) 'Out of time: The temporal uncertainties of refused asylum seekers and immigration detainees', *Journal of Ethnic and Migration Studies* 40(12): 1991–2009.

Griffiths, Melanie, Ali Rogers and Bridget Anderson (2013) 'Migration, time and temporalities: Review and prospect', *COMPAS Research Resources Paper*, Oxford: COMPAS, University of Oxford.

Guillaume, Xavier and Jef Huysmans (2013) 'Introduction: Citizenship and security'. In: X. Guillaume and J. Huysmans (eds) *Citizenship and Security: The Constitution of Political Being*, Abingdon: Routledge, pp. 1–17.

Gunew, Sneja (2005) 'Stammering "country" pedagogies: Sickness for and of the home', *Journal of Australian Studies* 29(86): 71–82.

Gunew, Sneja (2017) *Post-multicultural Writers as Neo-Cosmopolitan Mediators*, New York: Anthem Press.

Hage, Ghassan (ed.) (2009a) *Waiting*, Melbourne: Melbourne University Press.

Hage, Ghassan (2009b) 'Introduction'. In: G. Hage (ed.) *Waiting*, Melbourne: Melbourne University Press, pp. 1–12.

Hagelund, Anniken and Kaja Reegård (2011) '"Changing teams": A participant perspective on citizenship ceremonies', *Citizenship Studies* 15(6–7): 735–748.

Hall, Stuart, Chas Critcher, Tony Jefferson, John Clarke and Brian Roberts (1978) *Policing the Crisis: Mugging, the State, and Law and Order*, London: Macmillan.

Hammar, Tomas (1990) *Democracy and the Nation State*, Aldershot: Avebury.

Han, Christine, Hugh Starkey and Andy Green (2010) 'The politics of ESOL (English for speakers of other languages): Implications for citizenship and social justice', *International Journal of Lifelong Learning* 29(1): 63–76.

Hansen, Randall (2000) *Citizenship and Immigration in Post-War Britain: The Institutional Origins of a Multicultural Nation*, Oxford: Oxford University Press.

Harpaz, Yossi and Pablo Mateos (2019) 'Strategic citizenship: Negotiating membership in the age of dual nationality', *Journal of Ethnic and Migration Studies* 45(6): 843–857.

Haugen, Einar (1966) 'Dialect, language, nation', *American Anthropologist* 68(4): 922–935.

Heater, Derek (2006) *Citizenship in Britain: A History*, Edinburgh: Edinburgh University Press.

Hebdige, Dick (1987) *Cut 'n' Mix: Culture, Identity and Caribbean Music*, London: Routledge.

Helbling, Marc (2008) *Practising Citizenship and Heterogeneous Nationhood: Naturalisations in Swiss Municipalities*, Amsterdam: Amsterdam University Press.

Heller, Monica and Bonnie McElhinny (2017) *Language, Capitalism, Colonialism*, Toronto: University of Toronto Press.

Hemmings, Clare (2020) 'Revisiting virality (after Eve Sedgwick)', *Feminist Review Blog Series Confronting the Household*, 26 May. Available at: https://femrev.wordpress.com/2020/05/26/revisiting-virality-after-eve-sedgwick/#_edn1 [last accessed 26 June 2020].

Hewitt, Roger (1986) *White Talk, Black Talk: Inter-racial Friendship and Communication Amongst Adolescents*, Cambridge: Cambridge University Press.

Hill, Amelia (2018) 'At least 1,000 highly skilled migrants wrongly face deportation, experts reveal: Home Office accused of 'abusing' section of Immigration Act designed to tackle terrorism', *The Guardian*, 6 May. Available at: www.theguardian.com/uk-news/2018/may/06/at-least-1000-highly-skilled-migrants-wrongly-face-deportation-experts-reveal [last accessed 9 July 2019].

Hitchcock, Peter (2001) 'Decolonizing (the) English', *South Atlantic Quarterly* 100(3): 749–771.

Hochschild, Arlie Russel (2003) *The Commercialization of Intimate Life: Notes from Home and Work*, Berkeley, CA: University of California Press.

Hodder, Ian (2000) 'The interpretation of documents and material culture'. In: N. Denzin and Y. Lincoln (eds) *Handbook of Qualitative Research* (2nd edn), Thousand Oaks, CA: Sage, pp. 703–717.

Hogan-Brun, Gabrielle, Clare Mar-Molinero and Patrick Stevenson (eds) (2009) *Discourses on Language and Integration: Critical Perspectives on Language Testing Regimes in Europe*, Amsterdam: John Benjamins.

Home Office (2002) *Secure Borders, Safe Haven: Integration with Diversity in Modern Britain*, Norwich: The Stationary Office.

Home Office (2007) *Life in the United Kingdom: A Journey to Citizenship*, Norwich: The Stationary Office.

Home Office (2013a) *Knowledge of Language and Life in the UK for Settlement and Naturalisation: Statement of Intent, Changes to the Requirement from October 2013*, London: Home Office.

Home Office (2013b) 'Tougher language requirements announced for British citizenship'. Available at: www.gov.uk/government/news/tougher-language-requirements-announced-for-british-citizenship [last accessed 19 September 2019].

Home Office (2017) *Life in the United Kingdom: A Guide for New Residents* (3rd edn), Norwich: The Stationary Office.

Home Office (2019a) *Guide AN: Naturalisation Booklet – The Requirements*, London: Home Office.

Home Office (2019b) *Nationality Policy: Children of Unmarried Parents*, London: Home Office.

Honig, Bonnie (2001) *Democracy and the Foreigner*, Princeton, NJ: Princeton University Press.

Hope, Christopher (2014) 'Mass immigration has left Britain "unrecognisable", says Nigel Farage', *The Telegraph*, 28 February. Available at: www.telegraph.co.uk/news/politics/ukip/10668996/Mass-immigration-has-left-Britain-unrecognisable-says-Nigel-Farage.html [last accessed 23 August 2019].

Horton, Sarah B. and Josiah Heyman (eds) (2020) *Paper Trails: Migrants, Documents and Legal Insecurity in the Global North*, Durham, NC: Duke University Press.

Hughes, Sarah M. and Peter Forman (2017) 'A material politics of citizenship: The potential of circulating materials from UK Immigration Removal Centres', *Citizenship Studies* 1–18.

Hui, Allison (2016) 'The boundaries of interdisciplinary fields: Temporalities shaping the past and future of dialogue between migration and mobilities research', *Mobilities* 11(1): 66–82.

Hull, Matthew S. (2012) 'Documents and bureaucracy', *Annual Review of Anthropology* 41: 251–267.

Hunt, Lynn (1992) *The Family Romance of the French Revolution*, London: Routledge.

Hunter, Shona (2008) 'Living documents: A feminist psychosocial approach to the relational politics of policy documentation', *Critical Social Policy* 28(4): 506–528.

Hunter, Shona (2015) *Power, Politics and the Emotions: Impossible Governance?*, London and New York: Routledge.

Huntington, Samuel (1996) *The Clash of Civilizations and the Remaking of World Order*, New York: Simon & Shuster.

Hyatt, Susan Brin (2011) 'What was neoliberalism and what comes next? The transformation of citizenship in the law-and-order state'. In: C. Shore, S. Wright and D. Però (eds) *Policy Worlds: Anthropology and the Analysis of Contemporary Power*, Oxford: Berghahn, pp. 105–129.

Isin, Engin (2009) 'Citizenship in flux: The figure of the activist citizen', *Subjectivity* 29(1): 367–388.

Isin, Engin (2012) 'Citizens without nations', *Environment and Planning D: Society and Space* 30(3): 450–467.

Isin, Engin (2015) 'Citizenship's empire'. In: E. Isin (ed.) *Citizenship After Orientalism: Transforming Political Theory*, Basingstoke: Palgrave Macmillan, pp. 263–281.

Isin, Engin and Bryan S. Turner (2007) 'Investigating citizenship: An agenda for citizenship studies', *Citizenship Studies* 11(1): 5–17.

Isin, Engin and Greg Nielsen (eds) (2008) *Acts of Citizenship*, London: Zed Books.

Isin, Engin and Peter Nyers (2014) 'Introduction: Globalising citizenship studies'. In: E. Isin and P. Nyers (eds) *Routledge Handbook of Global Citizenship Studies*, London: Routledge, pp. 1–11.

Janeja, Manpreet K. and Andreas Bandak (eds) (2018) *Ethnographies of Waiting: Doubt, Hope and Uncertainty*, London: Bloomsbury.

Janoski, Thomas (2010) *The Ironies of Citizenship: Naturalization and Integration in Industrialized Countries*, Cambridge: Cambridge University Press.

Jeffrey, Craig (2010) *Timepass: Youth, Class and the Politics of Waiting in India*, Stanford, CA: Stanford University Press.

Jessop, Bob (2019) 'Ordoliberalism and neoliberalization: Governing through order or disorder', *Critical Sociology*, OnlineFirst DOI: 10.1177/0896920519834068.

Johnson, Carol (2002) 'Heteronormative citizenship and the politics of passing', *Sexualities* 5(3): 317–336.

Johnson, Carol (2010) 'The politics of affective citizenship: From Blair to Obama', *Citizenship Studies* 14(5): 495–509.

Johnston, Paul (2001) 'The emergence of transnational citizenship among Mexican immigrants in California', In: T. Aleinikoff and D. Klusmeyer (eds) *Citizenship Today: Global Perspectives and Practices*, Washington, DC: Carnegie Endowment for International Peace, pp. 254–277.

Jones, Hannah, Yasmin Gunaratnam, Gargi Bhatacharyya, William Davies, Sukhwant Dhaliwal, Kirsten Forkert, Emma Jackson and Roiyah Saltus

(2017) *Go Home? The Politics of Immigration Controversies*, Manchester: Manchester University Press.

Joppke, Christian (2010) *Citizenship and Immigration*, Cambridge: Polity.

Joppke, Christian (2013) 'Through the European looking glass: Citizenship tests in the USA, Australia and Canada', *Citizenship Studies* 17(1): 1–15.

Joppke, Christian (2019) 'The instrumental turn of citizenship', *Journal of Ethnic and Migration Studies* 45(6): 858–878.

Kapoor, Nisha (2015) 'Removing the right to have rights', *Studies in Ethnicity and Nationalism* 15(1): 105–110.

Kapoor, Nisha and Kasia Narkowicz (2019a) 'Characterising citizenship: Race, criminalisation and the extension of internal borders', *Sociology* 53(4): 652–670.

Kapoor, Nisha and Kasia Narkowicz (2019b) 'Unmaking citizens: Passport removals, pre-emptive policing and the reimagining of colonial governmentalities', *Journal of Ethnic and Racial Studies* 42(16): 46–62.

Karatani, Rieko (2003) *Defining British Citizenship: Empire, Commonwealth and Modern Britain*, London: Frank Cass.

Khan, Kamran (2014) 'WP130: Citizenship, securitization and suspicion in UK ESOL policy', *Working Papers in Urban Language and Literacies*, London: Kings College.

Khan, Kamran (2018) *Becoming a Citizen: Linguistic Trials and Negotiations in the UK*, London: Bloomsbury Academic.

Kipling, Kate (2015) 'Making British citizens: The role of citizenship ceremonies and tests in integration and belonging', unpublished PhD thesis, Department of Geography, University of Leeds.

Kiwan, Dina (2008) 'A journey to citizenship in the United Kingdom', *International Journal of Multicultural Societies* 10(1): 60–75.

Kiwan, Dina (ed.) (2013a) *Naturalization Policies, Education and Citizenship*, Basingstoke: Palgrave Macmillan.

Kiwan, Dina (2013b) 'Learning to be British? Education and naturalization in the UK'. In: D. Kiwan (ed.) *Naturalization Policies, Education and Citizenship*, Basingstoke: Palgrave Macmillan, pp. 25–49.

Kofman, Eleonore (2005) 'Citizenship, migration and the reassertion of national identity', *Citizenship Studies* 9(5): 453–467.

Koopmans, Ruud, Ines Michalowski and Stine Waibel (2012) 'Citizenship rights for immigrants: National political processes and cross-national convergence in Western Europe, 1980–2001', *American Journal of Sociology* 117(4): 1202–1245.

Kostakopoulou, Dora (2006) 'Thick, thin and thinner patriotisms: Is this all there is?', *Oxford Journal of Legal Studies* 26(1): 73–106.

Kostakopoulou, Dora (2008) *The Future Governance of Citizenship*, Cambridge: Cambridge University Press.

Kostakopoulou, Dora (2010) 'Matters of control: Integration tests, naturalisation reform and probationary citizenship in the United Kingdom', *Journal of Ethnic and Migration Studies* 36(5): 829–846.

Krzyzanowski, Michal and Ruth Wodak (2010) 'Hegemonic multilingualism in/of the EU institutions: An inside–outside perspective on European language policies and practices'. In: H. Böhringer, C. Hülmbauer and E. Vetter (eds) *Mehrsprachigkeit aus der Perspektive zweier EU-Projekte: DYLAN meets LINEE*, Frankfurt am Main: Peter Lang, pp. 115–135.

Kundnani, Arun (2007) *The End of Tolerance: Racism in 21st Century Britain*, London: Pluto.

Kymlicka, Will (1995) *Multicultural Citizenship: A Liberal Theory of Minority Rights*, Oxford: Clarendon Press.

Law, John (2004) *After Method: Mess in Social Science Research*, London: Routledge.

Linklater, Andrew (1998) 'Cosmopolitan citizenship', *Citizenship Studies* 2(1): 23–41.

Lewis, Gail (2006) 'Imaginaries of Europe, technologies of gender, economies of power', *European Journal of Women's Studies* 13(2): 87–102.

Lewis, Gail (2010) 'Animating hatreds: research encounters, organisational secrets, emotional truths'. In: R. Ryan-Flood and R. Gill (eds) *Secrecy and Silence in the Research Process: Feminist Reflections*, London: Routledge, pp. 211–227.

Lipsky, Michael (2010) *Street-Level Bureaucracy: Dilemmas of the Individual in Public Services. Thirtieth Anniversary Expanded Edition*, New York: Russel Sage Foundation.

Lister, Ruth (1997) *Citizenship: Feminist Perspectives*, Basingstoke: Palgrave.

Lorey, Isabell (2015) *State of Insecurity: Government of the Precarious*, London: Verso.

Low, Eugenia (2000) 'The concept of citizenship in twentieth-century Britain: Analysing contexts of development'. In: P. Catterall, W. Kaiser and U. Walton-Jordan U (eds) *Reforming the Constitution: Debates in Twentieth-Century Britain*, London: Frank Cass, pp. 179–200.

Löwenheim, Oded and Orit Gazit (2009) 'Power and examination: a critique of citizenship tests', *Security Dialogue* 40(2): 145–167.

Lusher, Adam (2016) 'Racism unleashed: True extent of the 'explosion of blatant hate' that followed Brexit result revealed', *The Independent*, 28 July. Available at: www.independent.co.uk/news/uk/politics/brexit-racism-uk-post-referendum-racism-hate-crime-eu-referendum-racism-unleashed-poland-racist-a7160786.html [last accessed 15 June 2020].

Makoni, Sinfree and Alastair Pennycook (2007) 'Disinventing and reconstituting languages'. In: S. Makoni and A. Pennycook (eds) *Disinventing and Reconstituting Languages*, Clevedon: Multilingual Matters, pp. 1–41.

Mason, Rowena and Harriet Sherwood (2016) 'Migrant spouses who fail English test may have to leave UK, says Cameron', *The Guardian*, 18 January. Available at: www.theguardian.com/uk-news/2016/jan/18/pm-migrant-spouses-who-fail-english-test-may-have-to-leave-uk [last accessed 24 March 2016].

Mavelli, Luca (2018) 'Citizenship for sale and the neoliberal political economy of belonging', *International Studies Quarterly* 62(3): 482–493.

Mazouz, Sarah (2008) 'Une célébration paradoxale: Les cérémonies de remise des décrets de naturalisation', *Genèses* 70(1): 88–105.

McClintock, Anne (1995) *Imperial Leather: Race, Gender and Sexuality in the Colonial Contest*, London and New York: Routledge.

McNamara, Tim and Elana Shohamy (2008) 'Language tests and human rights', *International Journal of Applied Linguistics* 18(1): 89–95.

Mezzadra, Sandro and Brett Neilson (2013) *Border as Method or, the Multiplication of Labor*, Durham, NC: Duke University Press.

Mignolo, Walter (2006) 'Citizenship, knowledge, and the limits of humanity', *American Literary History* 18(2): 312–331.

Millar, Jeffrey Darren (2014) 'The revaluation of the national language in a post-national era: Language policy and the governance of migration and citizenship', unpublished doctoral thesis, Doctor of Philosophy: Linguistics, York University.

Ministry of Housing, Communities and Local Government (2018) *Integrated Communities Strategy Green Paper*, London: HM Government publications.

Ministry of Housing, Communities and Local Government (2019) *Integrated Communities Action Plan*, London: HM Government publications.

Mohdin, Aamna and Joon Ian Wong (2018), Britain is using simple tax errors as a reason to deport migrants, 17 May. Available at: https://qz.com/1275866/the-british-government-is-using-simple-tax-errors-as-a-reason-to-deport-migrants/ [last accessed 9 July 2019].

Mol, Annemarie (2002) *The Body Multiple: Ontology in Medical Practice*, Durham, NC: Duke University Press.

Mongia, Rhadika (2018) *Indian Migration and Empire: A Colonial Genealogy of the Modern State*, Durham, NC: Duke University Press.

Mookherjee, Monica (2005) 'Affective citizenship: feminism, postcolonialism and the politics of recognition', *Critical Review of International Social and Political Philosophy* 8(1): 31–50.

Morris, Nigel and Akbar, Arifa (2004) 'Phil Collins and God Save the Queen: the soundtrack to becoming British', *The Independent*, 27 February. Available at: www.independent.co.uk/news/uk/this-britain/phil-collins-and-god-save-the-queen-the-soundtrack-to-becoming-british-71195.html [last accessed 9 July 2019].

Motomura, Hiroshi (2006) *Americans in Waiting: The Lost Story of Immigration and Citizenship in the United States*, Oxford: Oxford University Press.

Mountz, Alison, Richard Wright, Ines Miyares and Adrian J. Bailey (2002) 'Lives in limbo: Temporary protected status and immigrant identities', *Global Networks* 2(4): 335–356.

Nail, Thomas (2015) *The Figure of the Migrant*, Stanford, CA: Stanford University Press.

Navaro-Yashin, Yael (2002) *Faces of the State: Secularism and Public Life in Turkey*, Princeton, NJ: Princeton University Press.

Navaro-Yashin, Yael (2007) 'Make-believe papers, legal forms and the counterfeit: Affective interactions between documents and people in Britain and Cyprus', *Anthropological Theory* 7(1): 79–98.

Neveu, Catherine (2015) 'Of ordinariness and citizenship processes', *Citizenship Studies* 19(2): 141–154.

Newman, Janet (2013) 'Performing new worlds? Policy, politics and creative labour in hard times', *Policy and Politics* 41(4): 515–532.

Ngũgĩ wa Thiong'o (1986) *Decolonising the Mind*, London: Heinemann Educational.

NIACE and LLU (2010 [2006]) *Citizenship Materials for ESOL Learners*, Leicester: NIACE.

Ní Mhurchú, Aoileann (2014) *Ambiguous Citizenship in an Age of Global Migration*, Edinburgh: Edinburgh University Press.

Nyers, Peter (ed.) (2009) *Securitizations of Citizenship*, New York: Routledge.

Nyers, Peter (2013) 'Liberating irregularity: No borders, temporality, citizenship'. In: X. Guillaume and J. Huysmans (eds) *Citizenship and Security: The Constitution of Political Being*, London: Routledge, pp. 37–52.

Ong, Aihwa (1999) *Flexible Citizenship: The Cultural Logics of Transnationality*, Durham, NC and London: Duke University Press.

Ong, Aihwa (2006) *Neoliberalism as Exception: Mutations in Citizenship and Sovereignty*, Durham, NC: Duke University Press.

Ong, Paul M. (2011/2012) 'Defensive naturalization and anti-immigrant sentiment: Chinese immigrants in three primate metropolises', *Asian American Policy Review* 22: 39–55.

Ossipow, Laurence and Maxime Felder (2015) 'Ethnography of a political ritual: Speeches given to new Swiss citizens by representatives of the state', *Citizenship Studies* 19(3–4): 233–247.

Ossman, Susan (2007) 'Introduction'. In: S. Ossman (ed.) *Places We Share: Migration, Subjectivity, and Global Mobility*, Lanham, MD: Lexington Books, pp. 1–16.

Owens, Patricia (2015) *Economy of Force: Counterinsurgency and the Historical Rise of the Social*, Cambridge: Cambridge University Press.

Papadopoulos, Dimitris, Niamh Stephenson and Vassilis Tsianos (2008) *Escape Routes: Control and Subversion in the Twenty-first Century*, London: Pluto.

Pennycook, Alastair (1994) *The Cultural Politics of English as an International Language*, Harlow: Longman Group.

Pennycook, Alastair (1998) *English and the Discourses of Colonialism*, London: Routledge.

Phillipson, Robert (1992) *Linguistic Imperialism*, Oxford: Oxford University Press.

Phillipson, Robert (2010) *Linguistic Imperialism Continued*, London: Routledge.

Phipps, Alison (2013) 'Linguistic incompetence: Giving an account of researching multilingually', *International Journal of Applied Linguistics* 23(3): 329–341.

Pickles, E. (2013) 'We'll use millions lost on translations so EVERYONE can learn English Drive to teach English', *The Sun*, 13 January. Available at: www.thesun.co.uk/sol/homepage/news/4741905/Eric-Pickles-on-Government-drive-to-get-everyone-speaking-English.html [last accessed 13 January 2013].

Plummer, Ken (2003) *Intimate Citizenship: Private Decisions and Public Dialogues*, Seattle and London: University of Washington Press.

Povinelli, Elizabeth (2011) *Economies of Abandonment: Social Belonging and Endurance in Late Liberalism*, Durham, NC: Duke University Press.

Prabhat, Devyani (2018) *Britishness, Belonging and Citizenship: Experiencing Nationality Law*, Bristol: Policy Press.

Proctor, Kate (2020) 'EU citizens in UK at risk of becoming illegal as coronavirus response prioritised', *The Guardian*, 29 March. Available at: www.theguardian.com/uk-news/2020/mar/29/eu-citizens-uk-risk-becoming-illegal-coronavirus [last accessed: 8 April 2020].

Pulinx, Reinhilde and Piet Van Avermaet (2015) 'Integration in Flanders (Belgium) – Citizenship as achievement: How intertwined are "citizenship" and "integration" in Flemish language policies?', *Journal of Language and Politics* 14(3): 335–358.

Puwar, Nirmal and Sanjay Sharma (2012) 'Curating sociology', *Sociological Review* 60(S1): 40–63.

Pykett, Jessica (2010) 'Citizenship education and narratives of pedagogy', *Citizenship Studies* 14(6), 621–635.

Quinn, Ben (2011) 'David Starkey claims "the whites have become black"', *The Guardian*, 13 August. Available at: www.theguardian.com/uk/2011/aug/13/david-starkey-claims-whites-black [last accessed 5 December 2019].

Raghuram, Parvati (2008) 'Governing the mobility of skills'. In: C. Gabriel and H. Pellerin (eds) *Governing International Labour Migration: Current Issues, Challenges and Dilemmas*, London: Routledge, pp. 81–94.

Razack, Sherene H. (2004) 'Imperilled Muslim women, dangerous Muslim men and civilised Europeans: Legal and social responses to forced marriages', *Feminist Legal Studies* 12(2): 129–174.

Right to Remain (2018) 'Legal updates: Highly skilled migrants facing removal due to minor alleged tax discrepancies', 24 May. Available at: https://righttoremain.org.uk/highly-skilled-migrants-facing-removal-due-to-minor-alleged-tax-discrepancies/ [last accessed 7 November 2019].

Riles, Annelise (2006) 'Introduction: in response'. In: A. Riles (ed.) *Documents: Artifacts of Modern Knowledge*, Ann Arbor, MI: University of Michigan Press, pp. 1–38.

Rimmer, Mark (2008) *The Future of Citizenship Ceremonies*, Report commissioned by the Lord Goldsmith for the Goldsmith Review on Citizenship, London: Justice Department.

Robertson, Craig (2010) *The Passport in America: The History of a Document*, Oxford: Oxford University Press.

Robertson, Shanthi (2014) 'Time and temporary migration: The case of temporary graduate workers and working holiday makers in Australia', *Journal of Ethnic and Migration Studies* 40(2): 1915–1933.

Robertson, Shanthi (2015) 'The temporalities of international migration: Implications for ethnographic research'. In: S. Castles, D. Ozkul and M. Cubas (eds) *Social Transformation and Migration: National and Local Experiences in South Korea, Turkey, Mexico and Australia*, Basingstoke: Palgrave Macmillan, pp. 45–60.

Rojo, Luisa Martín and Alfonso del Percio (ed.) (2019) *Language and Neoliberal Govermentality*, London: Routledge.

Rosa, Jonathan and Nelson Flores (2017) 'Unsettling race and language: Toward a raciolinguistic perspective', *Language in Society* 46(5): 621–647.

Rose, Jacqueline (1996) *States of Fantasy*, Oxford: Clarendon Press.

Rose, Nikolas (1996) *Inventing Our Selves: Psychology, Power and Personhood*, New York: Cambridge University Press.

Rose, Nikolas (1999) *Governing the Soul: The Shaping of the Private Self* (2nd edn), London: Free Association Books.

Roth-Gordon, Jennifer (2016) 'From upstanding citizen to North American rapper and back again: The racial malleability of poor male Brazilian youth'. In: H. S. Alim, J. R. Rickford and A. F. Ball (eds) *Raciolinguistics: How Language Shapes Our Ideas About Race*, Oxford: Oxford University Press, pp. 51–64.

Royal Commission on the Laws of Naturalization and Allegiance (1869) *Report of the Royal Commissioners for Inquiring into the Laws of Naturalization and Allegiance*, London: Printed by G.E. Eyre and W. Spottiswoode for H.M. Stationery office. Available at: https://catalog.hathitrust.org/Record/008559703 [last accessed 12 October 2020].

Ruhs, Martin and Bridget Anderson (2013) 'Responding to employers: Skills, shortages, and sensible immigration policy', In: E. Jurado and G. Brochmann (eds) *Europe's Immigration Challenge: Reconciling Work, Welfare and Mobility*, London: I.B. Taurus, pp. 95–104.

Rygiel, K. (2006) 'Protecting and proving identity: The biopolitics of waging war through citizenship in the post 9/11 era'. In: K. Hunt and K. Rygiel (eds) *(En)gendering the War on Terror: War Stories and Camouflaged Politics*, Aldershot: Ashgate, pp. 145–168.

Rygiel, Kim (2010) *Globalizing Citizenship*, Vancouver: University of British Columbia Press.

Sadiq, Kamal (2017) 'Postcolonial citizenship'. In: A. Shachar, R. Bauböck, I. Bloemraad and M. Vink (eds) *The Oxford Handbook of Citizenship*, Oxford: Oxford University Press, pp. 178–199.

Salter, Mark (2003) *Rights of Passage: The Passport in International Relations*, Boulder, CO and London: Lynne Rienner Publishers.

Salter, Mark (2008) 'When the exception becomes the rule: Borders, sovereignty, and citizenship', *Citizenship Studies* 12(4): 365–380.

Schinkel, Willem (2010) 'The virtualization of citizenship', *Critical Sociology* 36(2): 265–283.

Schweizer, Harold (2005) 'On waiting', *University of Toronto Quarterly* 74(3): 777–792.

Scott, James C. (1998) *Seeing Like a State: How Certain Schemes to Improve the Human Condition Have Failed*, New Haven, CT: Yale University Press.

Shachar, Ayelet (2009) *The Birthright Lottery. Citizenship and Global Inequality*, Cambridge, MA and London: Harvard University Press.

Shachar, Ayelet, Rainer Bauböck, Irene Bloemraad and Maarten Vink (2017) 'Introduction: Citizenship – Quo Vadis?'. In: A. Shachar, R. Bauböck, I. Bloemraad and M. Vink (eds) *The Oxford Handbook of Citizenship*, Oxford: Oxford University Press, pp. 3–11.

Shachar, Ayelet and Ran Hirschl (2007) 'Citizenship as inherited property', *Political Theory* 35(3): 253–287.

Sharma, Aradhana and Akhil Gupta (ed.) (2006) *The Anthropology of the State*, Oxford: Blackwell.

Shore, Cris and Susan Wright (ed.) (1997) *Anthropology of Policy: Critical Perspectives on Governance and Power*, London and New York: Routledge.

Shore, Cris, Susan Wright and Davide Però (eds) (2011) *Policy Worlds: Anthropology and the Analysis of Contemporary Power*, New York and Oxford: Berghahn Books.

Skutnabb-Kangas, Tove (1988) 'Multilingualism and the education of minority children'. In: T. Skutnabb-Kangas and J. Cummins (eds) *Minority Education: From Shame to Struggle*, Clevedon: Multilingual Matters, pp. 9–44.

Skutnabb-Kangas, Tove (2000) *Linguistic Genocide in Education – or Worldwide Diversity and Human Rights?*, London: Routledge.

Slade, Christina and Martina Möllering (eds) (2010) *From Migrant to Citizen: Testing Language, Testing Culture*, Basingstoke: Palgrave Macmillan.

Smith, Rogers M. (1997) *Civic Ideals: Conflicting Visions of Citizenship in US History*, New Haven, CT: Yale University Press.

Somers, Margaret R. (2008) *Genealogies of Citizenship: Markets, Statelessness, and the Right to Have Rights*, Cambridge: Cambridge University Press.

Somerville, Siobhan (2005) 'Notes toward a queer history of naturalization', *American Quarterly* 7(3): 659–675.

Soysal, Yasmine (1995) *Limits of Citizenship: Migrants and Post-national Membership in Europe*, Chicago, IL: University of Chicago Press.

Staeheli, Lynn A., Patricia Ehrkamp, Helga Leitnera and Caroline R. Nagel (2012) 'Dreaming the ordinary: Daily life and the complex geographies of citizenship', *Progress in Human Geography* 36(5): 628–644.

Stendahl, Sara (2016) 'To reside: to live, be present, belong', *European Journal of Social Security* 18(2): 232–245.

Stepan, Nancy Leys (1998) 'Race, gender, science, and citizenship', *Gender & History* 10(1): 26–52.

Stoler, Ann Laura (1995) *Race and the Education of Desire*, Durham, NC: Duke University Press.

Stoler, Ann Laura (2002) *Carnal Knowledge and Imperial Power: Race and the Intimate in Colonial Rule*, Berkeley, CA: University of California Press.

Taylor, Diane (2019) 'Home Office cites Iraq in "copy and paste" refusal letter to Jamaican man', *The Guardian*, 31 October. Available at: www.theguardian.com/uk-news/2019/oct/31/home-office-cites-iraq-in-copy-and-paste-refusal-letter-to-jamaican-man [last accessed 16 April 2020].

Taylor, Matthew (2014) 'Growing majority of public think it is necessary to speak English to be British', *The Guardian*, 17 June. Available at: www.theguardian.com/uk-news/2014/jun/17/british-values-speak-english [last accessed 18 September 2019].

Thompson, Charis (2005) *Making Parents: The Ontological Choreography of Reproductive Technologies*, Cambridge, MA: MIT press.

Tonkiss, Katherine and Tendayi Bloom (2015) 'Theorising noncitizenship: Concepts, debates and challenges', *Citizenship Studies* 19(8): 837–852.

Torpey, John (2000) *The Invention of the Passport: Surveillance, Citizenship and the State*, Cambridge: Cambridge University Press.

Tudor, Alyosxa (2018) 'Cross-fadings of racialisation and migratisation: The postcolonial turn in Western European gender and migration studies', *Gender, Place and Culture* 25(7): 1057–1072.

Tyler, Imogen (2013) *Revolting Subjects: Social Abjection and Resistance in Neoliberal Britain*, London: Zed.

United Nations (2020) 'COVID-19 and Indigenous peoples', Department of Economic and Social Affairs. Available at: www.un.org/development/desa/indigenouspeoples/covid-19.html [last accessed 30 June 2020].

Van Avermaet, Piet and Sara Gysen (2009) 'One nation, two policies: Language requirements for citizenship and integration in Belgium'. In: G. Extra, M. Spotti and P. Van Avermaet (eds) *Language Testing, Migration and Citizenship: Cross-National Perspectives on Integration Regimes*, London: Continuum, pp. 125–147.

Vandevoordt, Robin and Gert Verschraegen (2019) 'Citizenship as a gift: How Syrian refugees in Belgium make sense of their social rights', *Citizenship Studies* 23(1): 43–60.

Van Houdt, Friso, Semin Suvarierol and Willem Schinkel (2011) 'Neoliberal communitarian citizenship: Current trends towards "earned citizenship" in the United Kingdom, France and the Netherlands', *International Sociology* 26(3): 408–432.

van Oers, Ricky (2008) 'From liberal to restrictive citizenship policies: The case of the Netherlands', *International Journal of Multicultural Societies* 8(1): 40–59.

Vargas-Silva, Madeleine Sumption Carlos (2016) *The Minimum Income Requirement for Non-EEA Family Members in the UK*, Oxford: Migration Observatory.

Vink, Maarten P. and Gerard-René de Groot (2010) 'Citizenship attribution in Western Europe: International framework and domestic trends', *Journal of Ethnic and Migration Studies* 36(5): 713–734.

Vora, Neha (2013) *Impossible Citizens: Dubai's Indian Diaspora*, Durham, NC: Duke University Press.

Wacquant, Loic (2010) 'Crafting the neoliberal state: Workfare, prisonfare, and social insecurity', *Sociological Forum* 25(2): 197–220.

Waever, Ole (1995) 'Identity, integration and security: Solving the sovereignty puzzle in E.U. studies', *Journal of International Affairs* 48(2): 389–431.

Waever, Ole (1996) 'European security identities', *Journal of Common Market Studies* 34(1): 103–132.

Walters, William (2004) 'Secure borders, safe haven, domopolitics', *Citizenship Studies* 8(3): 237–260.

Weaver, Matthew and Amelia Gentleman (2019) 'EU nationals lacking settled status could be deported, minister says', *The Guardian*, 10 October. Available at: www.theguardian.com/politics/2019/oct/10/eu-nationals-lacking-settled-status-could-be-deported-minister-says [last accessed 8 November 2019].

Weber, Cynthia (1998) 'Performative states', *Millennium: Journal of International Studies* 27(1): 77–95.

Weber, Cynthia (2008) 'Designing safe citizens', *Citizenship Studies* 12(2): 125–142.

Weber, Cynthia (2015) 'Good citizenship is …'. In: E. Isin (ed.) *The Future Citizen Guide*, London: Tate, pp. 28–36.

Weber, Cynthia (2016) *Queer International Relations: Sovereignty, Sexuality and the Will to Knowledge*, Oxford: Oxford University Press.

Weil, Patrick (2001) 'Access to citizenship'. In: T. Aleinikoff and D. Klusmeyer (eds) *Citizenship Today*, Washington, DC: Carnegie Endowment for International Peace, pp. 17–35.

White, Patricia (2008) 'Immigrants into citizens', *The Political Quarterly* 79(2): 221–231.

Williams, Raymond (1977) *Marxism and Literature*, Oxford: Oxford University Press.

Williams, Wendy (2020) *Windrush Lessons Learned Review: An Independent Review by Wendy Williams*, London: Stationary Office.

Williamson, Judith (1978) *Decoding Advertisements: Ideology and Meaning in Advertising*, London: Marion Boyars Publishers.

Winter, Elke (2014) 'Traditions of nationhood or political conjuncture? Debating citizenship in Canada and Germany', *Comparative Migration Studies* 2(1): 29–56.

Winter, Elke (2016) 'Toward an actor-centered political sociology of citizenship', *Canadian Sociological Association/La Société canadienne de sociologie* 53(3): 361–364.

Wodak, Ruth and Kristof Savski (2018) 'Critical discourse–ethnographic approaches to language policy'. In: J. Tollefson and M. Pérez-Milans (eds) *The Oxford Handbook of Language Policy and Planning*, Oxford: Oxford University Press, pp. 93–112.

Wright, Katie (2012) *International Migration, Development and Human Wellbeing*, Basingstoke: Palgrave Macmillan.

Wright, Sue (2008) (ed.) 'Citizenship tests in a post-national era', *International Journal of Multicultural Societies* 8(1): 1–75.

Wright, Susan and Sue Reinhold (2011) '"Studying through": A strategy for studying political transformation. Or sex, lies and British politics'. In: C. Shore, S. Wright and D. Però (eds) *Policy Worlds: Anthropology and the Analysis of Contemporary Power*, Oxford: Berghahn Books, pp. 86–104.

Yeo, Colin (2018) 'Citizenship, loyalty and treason in British nationality law', paper presented at the workshop, *Resurgences of National Citizenship in Europe? Brexit and Other Restrictions*, Manchester University, 11 December.

Yuval-Davis, Nira (2011) *The Politics of Belonging: Intersectional Contestations*, London: Sage.

Yuval-Davis, Nira, Georgie Wemyss and Kathryn Cassidy (2019) *Bordering*, Cambridge: Polity.

Index

EU authorised representative for GPSR:
Easy Access System Europe, Mustamäe tee 50,
10621 Tallinn, Estonia
gpsr.requests@easproject.com